RIDE THE WAVE

HOW 12 TECHNOLOGIES WILL CHANGE the WORLD AND MAKE YOU RICH

Fred A. Rogers
Richard Lalich

Crucial Trends Press

For Edgar & Jenny Honeycutt and James & Bessie Rogers

--FR

For Marion, Megan, and Emily

--RL

Acknowledgements

We would like to thank a subset of the people who have contributed to the development of *Ride the Wave* and the overall worldview reflected on every page.

For over 45 years, Steven L. Deal, Charles D. Helm, and Neil C. Talley have provided friendship, guidance, and valuable feedback to Fred. His "study group mates" from Harvard Business School, class of 1983—J. Thomas Elbling, Laura A. Martin, Lisa M. Novacek, Carlos L. Obando, and Sushil Verughese-Chacko—have provided these elements plus specific insights and resources that have helped clarify and solidify his vision. And, at crucial moments, other friends and mentors have provided just the right assistance to make all the difference; these include: Samuel F. Gulledge, Joseph T. Piemont, Professor Frank Barnes, Michael Lonier, Scott Oldach, Herschell Gordon Lewis, Professor Julian Simon, Malcolm Decker, Prescott Kelly, and Ginni Rometty.

Rich is grateful to the writers, editors, and colleagues whose work has provided inspiration, including Bill Savage, Bill Zehme, Laurence Gonzales, Dennis Rodkin, Richard Hefter, Marion Lalich, Dennis Tablizo, Clay Cerny, Jan Parr, Gretchen Reynolds, Kate Nolan, Jonathan Black, John Rezek, and Lee Froehlich. Thanks also to Laurence Gonzales and Dan Anderson for their outstanding work as contributors to *Trends Magazine*.

The specific ideas in *Ride the Wave* built on the work of many others. We'd particularly like to acknowledge the importance of work by Matthew Ridley, George Gilder, Daniel Burrus, Wallace Kaufman, Alvin Toffler, Indur Goklany, Professor Clayton M. Christensen, and Professor Carlota Perez.

We'd like to thank Dolly Pratt for working with us for over 25 years, and to especially acknowledge her editorial assistance in helping us to turn a vast body of research into a coherent and concise volume.

We also sincerely thank Sue Carman and Carlos Chacon, Jr. for making *Ride the Wave* truly user-friendly. Similarly, we recognize the enormous contribution of our graphic design director Ann Rintz (of Cyan Design), without whom our creations would be "visually barren." We also recognize the day-to-day work of Iris Chinchilla, Gina Meador, and Carlos Chacon, Sr., without whom our editorial work would never see the light of day, as well as Justin Spafford for his tireless efforts and innovative ideas. And we also want to thank Allen Mitchell, Mark MacLean, Scott Baartman, Geoff Cook, and Gary Cobb, who make the audio and video editions of *Ride the Wave, Trends Magazine, Innovation @ Work, Business Briefings,* and *AudioTech Business Book Summaries* come to life.

Last, but not least, we want to thank Carolyn Thur Rogers for her indispensable advice and moral support, without which none of this would have been possible.

CONTENTS

Preface

Whether we like it or not, we're engulfed in an unstoppable, ever-accelerating tidal wave of technological progress. You can either choose to ride that wave to greater affluence and personal wellbeing, or we can become collateral damage, drowned or crushed by the onslaught. It's your choice.

The current wave is actually the fifth and biggest wave of transformational technology that we've witnessed over the past 250 years.

Since the late 18th century, the technologically advanced world has entered a new economic "Golden Age" roughly every 55 years. During each of these Golden Age periods, the standard of living has risen to new, unprecedented heights, and per capita GDP has more than doubled in roughly 20 years.

Each Golden Age resulted from the full-scale *deployment* of a new, "transformational technology." The "transformational technology" of the current Golden Age, which is *now* at hand, is digitalization; it's built on the foundational technologies of integrated circuits, software, and high-speed communications.

Furthermore, it's the first "Golden Age" era since the wave of globalization that began in the 1980s. For that reason, its impact will be unparalleled. It will fundamentally redefine realities in medicine, computing, materials, energy production, transportation, defense, and geopolitics, not just for advanced economies, but for every human being on the planet. For this reason, it's *not* an exaggeration to claim that "the world will change more in the next 20 years than in the past 2,000 years."

When will this Golden Age dawn? What are the implications? And why do so few people see it coming? You'll find the answers in this book.

1

For our work at *Trends* Magazine, as well as our consulting engagements and special research projects, we've been tracking the changes and researching their implications for the past three decades. And we've been waiting for this moment; the moment when all of the necessary factors were ready to converge to usher in an entirely new paradigm. That time is now!

As you're about to discover, a powerful combination of technological breakthroughs and economic trends will soon sweep away the malaise of the past dozen years and set in motion a new era of prosperity. In forthcoming books in this series, we'll delve more deeply into the demographic, psychosocial, and geopolitical trends that will shape this revolution.

In *Ride the Wave,* our focus is on how breakthrough technologies will transform your life, your career, and your investments.

Buckle up. It's going to be a thrilling ride.

Introduction: How do we blow up the dam and unleash the wave?

If you believe the gloomy news that is reported every day, we live in the worst of times. Today, 23 million Americans are unemployed or underemployed, and Gallup reports that the comparable figure worldwide is near 1.6 billion. The poverty rate in the United States is essentially where it was 40 years ago, despite the $12 trillion spent to fight it. According to the U.S. Department of Agriculture, more than 47 million Americans are now on food stamps—the most in history—while globally more than three billion people live on less than $2 per day. The media routinely cite stories about shortages of food, water, medicine, and energy, as well as overpopulation and pandemics.

Ironically, the solutions to *every one of these problems* as well as longer, healthier lives and myriad other challenges are already working their way through laboratories and start-up companies worldwide. We're now at a crucial moment that historians will look back on as the beginning of a new era. In fact, a global technological revolution has been building for decades, but it is only now reaching the stage where a quantum leap in human affluence is possible. And, every breakthrough in technology brings us closer to a new "Golden Age" of prosperity and freedom.

As we approach that Golden Age, we've been going through a period of rapid, disturbing and turbulent change rocking nations, industries and companies. And, even in the coming boom there will be plenty of losers among the many winners. The objective of **Ride the Wave** is to ensure that *you* end up among the winners.

3

What wave?

So, how are we suddenly going to move from the "stagnant waters" of a moribund economy to riding a wave of unprecedented growth and affluence? To answer that question, we have to consider the last time we faced this kind of existential crisis.

On the morning of December 7, 1941, things looked much the same as they had the day before. Yet, by the end of that day, the world had changed. The Japanese Navy attacked the United States at Pearl Harbor. Almost overnight, the U.S. military was expanded, civilian factories were converted to military use, and domestic consumption of goods was rationed. Unemployment quickly went from double digits to zero, and the labor participation rate skyrocketed. Full employment and rationing combined to fill depleted bank accounts with cash. The nation made huge investments in training and capital goods, which restored an economy that had languished since the stock market crash of 1929. A generation of basic research breakthroughs in areas ranging from telecommunications, to medicine, to nuclear fission was suddenly thrust into high-speed development. Within four years, the global geo-political landscape was reshaped, and the entire international economic infrastructure was transformed.

Today, we find ourselves once again in a state of despair resembling the mood in 1941. Then, as now, we had just gone through 12+ years of weak economic growth following a market bubble. In 1941, experts lamented the slow incrementalism of advances in automobiles, radio, railroads, airplanes, and the electrical grid; many of the pundits of 2013 are similarly warning of the "death of innovation." And, just as the economy of the 1930s was hollowed out by the deterioration of the capital base (i. e., machines wearing out and empty factories sold for scrap), the economy we see in 2013 has been hollowed out by short-sighted off-shoring and a failed education system creating an enormous "skills gap."

Yet the important message in this story is that the greatest wave of prosperity that humanity has ever known was unleashed as World War II ushered in a new "conventional wisdom," which enabled Mass Production to change every aspect of our lives. The rebuilding of both physical and human capital, which began in that moment, paved the way for a Golden Age that ended with the oil crisis of the early 1970s.

And to put it succinctly, "our Pearl Harbor" has already materialized – quietly and largely under the radar – and it's called the North American Energy Revolution. At *Trends,* we forecast this unprecedented opportunity and its powerful transformational implications more than a decade ago, when most experts were obsessed with the "myth of peak oil." And, as we'll explain, it has been slow to evolve largely because of two diminishing counter-trends: "the politics of climate change" and "the culture of scarcity."

But suddenly, both of those barriers have begun to crumble. Rather than a sudden bombing raid blowing up a dam and unleashing a wave of technology-driven progress as we experienced in 1941, we might view the past few years as slowly chipping away at a massive, slowly-melting ice-dam, finally unleashing a torrent of innovation and pent-up capital that will transform human civilization in unprecedented ways. The next few years are going to be much like the period we experienced as World War II superseded the Great Depression and paved the way for the unprecedented expansion we saw from 1948 to 1966. And, just as the pessimistic mood heading toward World War II was wrong, the current economic pessimism is also totally wrong.

Today, as in the early '40s, the "fog of war" makes it difficult to see clearly. So, it's crucially important to understand how the trends driving the development, adoption and interaction of these technologies will impact your life, career, and investments.

As Mark Mills, the CEO of the Digital Power Group, recently wrote in *The American,* "naysayers. . . have been wrong in every one of the 19 economic downturns we have experienced since 1912."

Back in 1975, for example, technology historian, professor, and author Jean Gimpel lamented:

> "No more fundamental innovations are likely to be introduced to change the structure of [today's] society . . . . Like every previous civilization, we have reached a technological plateau."

That, of course, preceded the mobile phone, the personal computer, the World Wide Web, the iPod, the iPad, and a host of other dazzling technologies that have changed the structure of society, the

5

quality of our lives, and the fortunes of entrepreneurs and investors.

Today, similarly pessimistic predictions are widespread:

For instance, consider Tyler Cowen, a professor of economics at George Mason University and author of the book *The Great Stagnation*. Writing in the *New York Times* piece called "Innovation Is Doing Little for Incomes," in January 2011, Professor Cowen asserted:

> "My grandmother, who was born in 1905, spoke often about the immense changes she had seen, including the widespread adoption of electricity, the automobile, flush toilets, antibiotics and convenient household appliances. Since my birth in 1962, it seems to me, there have not been comparable improvements.

> "Of course, the personal computer and its cousin, the smartphone, have brought about some big changes. And many goods and services are now more plentiful and of better quality. But compared with what my grandmother witnessed, the basic accouterments of life have remained broadly the same.

> "The income numbers for Americans reflect this slowdown in growth. From 1947 to 1973—a period of just 26 years—inflation-adjusted median income in the United States more than doubled. But in the 31 years from 1973 to 2004, it rose only 22 percent. And, over the last decade, it actually declined.

> "Most well-off countries have experienced income growth slowdowns since the early 1970s, so it would seem that a single cause is transcending national borders: the reaching of a technological plateau. The numbers suggest that for almost 40 years, we've had near-universal dissemination of the major innovations stemming from the Industrial Revolution, many of which combined efficient machines with potent fossil fuels. Today, no huge improvement for the automobile or airplane is in sight, and the major struggle is to limit their pollution, not to vastly improve their capabilities.

> "Although America produces plenty of

innovations, most are not geared toward significantly raising the average standard of living."

This view is shared by Harvard University history professor Niall Ferguson, who is the author of *Civilization: The West and the Rest*. Ferguson is a senior research fellow at Oxford University and a senior fellow at the Hoover Institution at Stanford University. In a July 30, 2012 *Newsweek* article called "Don't Believe the Techno-Utopian Hype," Ferguson wrote:

"The harsh reality, as far as I can see, is that the next 25 years (2013-2038) are highly unlikely to see more dramatic changes than science and technology produced in the last 25 (1987-2012). . . . The IT revolution that began in the 1980s was important in terms of its productivity impact inside the U.S.—though this shouldn't be exaggerated—but we are surely now in the realm of diminishing returns (the symptoms of which are deflation plus underemployment due partly to automation of unskilled work)."

For the pessimists, the coming Golden Age will appear as if it came from nowhere. But, in reality, it is long overdue. When the dot-com bubble burst in 2000, policymakers tried to compensate for the inevitable collapse of the first wave of the information revolution, known as its Investment Phase (more on this in a moment), by propping up old-fashioned businesses like construction, household appliances and furniture with loose monetary policies.

When that inevitably led to a bursting housing bubble, we faced a second crisis that exceeded the first. Over the past five years, government-led missteps, mistakes, miscalculations, misjudgments, misappropriations, misinterpretations, and misspending have produced no answers because they have all impeded the free market process of cleaning up the mess and redeploying the resources more productively. In effect, the cure became worse than the disease.

But despite these headwinds, within the next few years, the economy will be ready to reach its potential. And, the result will be an unprecedented global economic boom that promises huge rewards for those who see it coming and know how to position themselves to profit.

As you'll learn, this economic revolution rests on the synergistic development of 12 game-changing technologies that we'll explore in detail.

What are the 12 transformational technologies?

Specifically, we can expect to see enormous advances in the following 12 areas as existing research is transformed rapidly into cost-effective solutions for business and consumers:

- Chapter 2: *What lies beyond Moore's Law and why does it make so much difference?* analyzes digital infrastructure ranging from CPUs and memory to mass data storage to communications bandwidth to systems software. These technologies dominated the Investment Phase of the revolution. They will continue to advance as specified by Moore's Law, overcoming fundamental barriers and provide support for truly new technologies and revolutionary technologies. We lay out the road map which will determine the path for so many threats and opportunities in the coming decades.

- Chapter 3: *How will trillions of networked computers improve every life on the planet?* examines the implications of having networked computers (sometimes called "The Internet of Everything") in everything, everywhere, all the time. Today's six billion cell phones represent the tip of the iceberg. Combined with each other, as well as practically free RIFD tags and embedded processors, they will open up endless opportunities.

- Chapter 4: *How will 'Smart Machines' impact your career, life, and investments?* explains what it means when Artificial Intelligence (AI) multiplies human capabilities via applications ranging from language translation to business decision-making to medical diagnosis. We explore not only the economic and social potential of these machines, but assess their realistic limitations.

- Chapter 5: *What are service robots and how will they change our lives, our cities, and our businesses?* explores the wide range of potential robotic applications that exist beyond the factory-floor; these include driver-less automobiles and automated homes optimized for elder-care. The U. S. military and the Japanese healthcare industry are just two well-funded sources of expected breakthroughs, finally making this branch of technology viable. Combining the power of the cloud with enormous progress in sensor technology, service robotics is likely far closer to commercialization than you think.

- Chapter 6: *Why do we care about quantum computing?* examines the world of exotic computers designed to solve problems that are literally "impossible" to solve using conventional computing technology. Both the hardware and software are mind-bogglingly difficult to build; but the potential implications for scientific research, pharmaceuticals, and cyber-security are well worth the effort

- Chapter 7: *What will the amazing potential of bioinformatics mean for you?* explains the technology that lets us quickly and cheaply read, interpret, and even rewrite a genome. No area of research is likely to bear more fruit for more industries than this one.

- Chapter 8: *Why will 'personalized medicine' become the dominant 21st century healthcare paradigm?* evaluates the challenges and implications of a new medical paradigm which improves outcomes and dramatically reduces costs, while eliminating side-effects.

- Chapter 9: *How will bio-reengineering save our world?* explores the application and implications of so-called "molecular biology." This includes conventional gene-splicing, as well as stem cell technology. The focus is on how our exponentially expanding understanding of cellular programming will enable us to prevent disease, extend absolute life-spans, and even grow or repair human organs. Beyond healthcare it will also enable us to eliminate hunger, thirst, and poverty in ways never before imaginable.

- Chapter 10: *How will synthetic life forms impact our economy and our lives?* focuses on how entirely *new* living organisms can safely and cheaply produce food, fuels and drugs, as well as clean up the environment. While useful, naturally occurring organisms are designed to function in nature, not to serve mankind. However, totally synthetic life forms can now be tailored to do our bidding. And the opportunities are almost unlimited.

- Chapter 11: *What Happens When We Begin to Understand How the Brain Works?* explores the commercial implications of "brain-science." Within the next two decades what we've learned about the brain will not only enable us to become more effective marketers and mangers, it will also enable us to treat Alzheimer's, Parkinson's, chronic depression, and stroke far more effectively. It will also open the door to direct brain-machine interfaces and total-immersion virtual-reality entertainment.

- Chapter 12: *How Will Nanomaterials, Microelectromechanical Systems, and Digital Fabrication End the 'Age of Scarcity'?* The Medieval alchemists dreamed of turning lead into gold. Chip builders and bio-tech firms have already done a better job at creating enormous value from the most common elements. However, by integrating nanotech with biotech and infotech, we're about to unlock the secrets of economic growth largely freed from material constraints. As a result, GDP per unit of matter or energy will continue to soar on a global basis, enabling even the world's poorest to have a decent material life.

- Chapter 13: *How will the American energy revolution unleash the wave that changes the world?* explains how cheap fossil fuel will provide the surge needed to unleash the new Golden Age. In the process, it will enable the world's crucial transition from today's economy to a clean, highly-affluent world fueled almost entirely by new nuclear fission and fusion technologies. More importantly, it debunks the challenges to this scenario raised by environmentalist and "neo-Luddites" who say it can't or shouldn't be done.

In Chapter 14, we spell out a proven process that enables any company to consistently answer key questions about the future and integrate the answers into its planning process. In doing so, you'll learn how to close the infamous "knowing-doing gap" and ensure that you are among the winners of the Digital Revolution.

Learning to ride the wave

We wrote *Ride the Wave* in an effort to "jump-start" that process in your business. In Chapters 2-13, we tee-up the 12 most significant technologies of our era. We explain how they are related to one another and we show how they are likely to evolve. And, in many cases, we've provided specific examples of how they are likely to be applied in specific industries. In essence, we act as tour guides to the world of digital revolution spanning the crucial spectrum from infotech to biotech to nanotech.

If the world was evolving at the pace of the 1960s, that would probably be enough. But, as Harvard's Clayton Christensen has shown, every industry increasingly faces "disruption." The products, business models and customer segments that were once so stable are subject to overnight change. That's why success depends on *harnessing* industry disruption rather than becoming a victim of it. So, when it comes to technology, every investor and executive needs to ask himself the right questions, like:

- Could this technology be relevant to my business?
- How could it impact my customers, my suppliers, or my employees?
- Does it create a "new job to be done" for my customers?
- Could it make one of my core competencies, like personal service or a proprietary manufacturing process, more or less valuable?
- Could a competitor use it to launch a different business model that would have a genuine performance or cost advantage, especially with a market category we're not now serving?
- How could a competitor, substitute, or new entrant use it to disrupt my business?

Ironically, most companies don't even ask these questions until it's too late. Here's your chance. Good luck!

1

What's the truth about technology revolutions and economic booms?

> "It was the best of times, it was the worst of times, it was the age of wisdom, it was the age of foolishness, it was the epoch of belief, it was the epoch of incredulity, it was the season of Light, it was the season of Darkness, it was the spring of hope, it was the winter of despair, we had everything before us, we had nothing before us. . . ."
>
> --Charles Dickens

Every five or six decades, a revolutionary new technology emerges that unleashes an economic boom. The renowned economist Carlota Perez has thoroughly documented this in numerous academic papers, countless lectures, and several books, most notably *Technological Revolutions and Financial Capital: The Dynamics of Bubbles and Golden Ages.*[1]

Perez demonstrates that over the past two centuries, the world has experienced five great "Technology Revolutions":

- The first Technology Revolution was the **Industrial Revolution**, beginning with Watt's steam engine in 1771; in

13

that revolution, machinery enabled quantum leaps in the productivity of manufacturing, especially textiles.

- The second was the **Railway Revolution**, starting in 1829, in which railroads and steam power dramatically cut transportation time and costs.
- The third was the **Steel Revolution**, starting in 1875, in which large-scale mills made the bulk production and processing of steel and other industrial materials affordable for the first time.
- The fourth Technology Revolution was the **Mass-Production Revolution**, beginning in 1908, which created mass-produced cars and other goods on assembly lines.
- The fifth Technology Revolution, originating in 1971 and still in force today, is the **Digital Revolution** (also known as the **Information Revolution**), which has brought the wonders of computing power to nearly every product and service.

Technological Revolution	Popular name for the period	Core country or countries	Big-bang initiating the revolution	Year
FIRST	The 'Industrial Revolution'	Britain	Arkwright's mill opens in Cromford	1771
SECOND	Age of Steam and Railways	Britain (spreading to Continent and USA)	Test of the 'Rocket' steam engine for the Liverpool-Manchester railway	1829
THIRD	Age of Steel, Electricity and Heavy Engineering	USA and Germany forging ahead and overtaking Britain	The Carnegie Bessemer steel plant opens in Pittsburgh, PA	1875
FOURTH	Age of Oil, the Automobile and Mass Production	USA (with Germany at first vying for world leadership), later spreading to Europe	First Model-T comes out of the Ford plant in Detroit, MI	1908
FIFTH	Age of Information and Telecommunications	USA (spreading to Europe and Asia)	The Intel microprocessor is announced in Santa Clara, CA	1971

Each of these Tech Booms (or Techno-Economic Revolutions) has followed a very predictable pattern. Specifically, each *technological revolution,* involves five phases: an initial **introductory phase,** a speculative **financial bubble,** a financial **collapse & transition,** a **golden age of rising affluence,** and finally, a **terminal "maturity" phase.** This last phase, dominated by economic plateauing and *political unrest,* ultimately sets the stage for the next revolution.

The life and times of a technology revolution
Recurring phases of each revolution

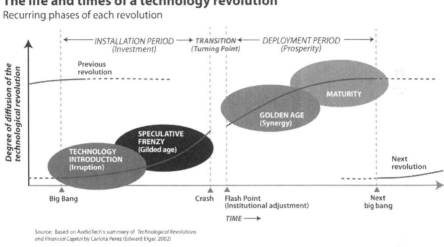

Source: Based on AudioTech's summary of *Technological Revolutions and Financial Capital* by Carlota Perez (Edward Elgar, 2002)

If we look closer at how every revolution unfolds, it's clear that they exhibit two major *growth* periods, each lasting about three decades, with a transitional phase between them during which business and government institutions reconfigure themselves.

The first part, called the Installation Period, is all about "investment." It begins with a so-called "big bang," when the revolutionary technology first appears in commercial form; for example, Henry Ford's assembly line in 1908 or Intel's first microprocessor in 1971. This investment period is when: 1) the new technology is introduced to the marketplace; 2) entrepreneurs experiment with new business models; 3) investors place bets on the winners; and 4) the changes that the technology can bring, gradually emerge. During this part of the revolution, financial speculation and financial assets dominate.

15

The second half is called the Deployment Period, or Prosperity phase. This is when:

- The new transformational technologies almost totally displace the old.
- The surviving business models consolidate their strength.
- The new institutions and approaches optimized for the new transformational technology become the accepted, mainstream "conventional wisdom."

Between these two periods is the critical "transition" from Investment to Prosperity. During the mania at the end of the Investment era, a bubble inevitably forms. It's also inevitable that the bubble bursts, which typically leads to a deep recession. This creates the conditions for a restructuring of the whole system, especially the regulations that must be changed to allow growth to resume and the technology revolution to explode during the first part of the Deployment Period, called the Golden Age. Significantly, whereas the Installation Period starts with lots of great ideas and a shortage of capital, the Deployment Period begins with a surplus of capital and a shortage of great ideas. Today, the world is awash in capital, but it is not flowing aggressively to start-ups because of a fear-induced "liquidity-trap."

During the Investment and Transition stages of a Technology Revolution, the technologies and business models of the new paradigm allow upstart businesses to replace the companies that had powered the growth of the economy under the previous paradigm. However, after decades of financial speculation, massive creative destruction, and enormous returns focused in a narrow set of industries, income inequality has soared, and public mistrust of business tends to peak as the Transition phase ends.

Then, in the Golden Age, the new technologies become deeply embedded in society, transforming people's lifestyles and making businesses of all kinds dramatically more efficient. For example, as Perez reminds us, railroads didn't just change the transportation industry and disrupt the stagecoach business, when they appeared in the early 19th century. Railroads also opened opportunities for hotels that were located far from cities, but reachable by train; for textile manufacturers, who could more easily acquire new raw materials and ship their finished goods; for livestock producers, who could load their cattle safely on boxcars rather than herd them for hundreds of miles; and for countless other businesses.

Similarly, today's Internet, digitization, and social networking, as well as truly new technologies and applications we will see during the Golden Age of the Digital Revolution, will create opportunities not just for companies like Microsoft, Google, and Facebook, but for *every* company and entrepreneur that uses these tools creatively to cut costs, innovate new offerings, and potentially, reach billions of new customers. In short, the firmly embedded technologies of information technology and telecommunications will increase productivity throughout the entire economy.

The flash point

We call the point at which the **Transitional Phase** ends and the **Golden Age** begins, the "Flash Point." That's the point at which money flows to a critical mass of new-technology firms and unleashes the full transformational potential of the new technology. In chemistry, the flash point is the lowest temperature at which a chemical will burn. It provides an apt metaphor for the transition period before the boom because, like a combustible material, the economy will not ignite until the right steps are taken to change the climate and raise the temperature around it.

For the Mass Production revolution, that flash point was America's entry into World War II. Suddenly, demand surged, triggering capital investment and the hiring and training of employees. With the labor participation rate rising to unprecedented levels and the wartime rationing of consumer goods, savings soared and were reinvested in new and existing companies. The capital base and personal savings that were depleted by the depression were replenished. R&D projects for the war effort quickly commercialized the accumulated laboratory science of the 1930s and '40s.

Our "Pearl Harbor" has already occurred quietly, largely under the radar: it's called the North American Energy Revolution. Rather than a sudden bombing raid blowing up a dam and unleashing a wave of technology-driven progress, we've been systematically chipping away at a massive, slowly melting ice-dam, unleashing a torrent of innovation and pent-up capital that will transform human civilization in unprecedented ways.

The nascent energy revolution will deliver a powerful wind to the sails of both America's domestic economy and to international trade on which so much of the developing world still relies as the engine of growth. But, the United States isn't the only big winner of the energy revolution: Canada, Israel, and China are among the nations that will reap huge *direct* benefits.

Furthermore, the consequences of the energy revolution for America's global agenda are so large, that the chief effect of the revolution is likely to be its role in shoring up the foundations of "the American-led world order." In other words, forget "the post-American world."

As we've explained previously in *Trends*, the new energy bonanza changes the American outlook far more dramatically than most executives, politicians, and investors yet realize. In fact, it will become the catalyst that triggers the Golden Age of the Digital Revolution. As analyst Walter Russell Mead wrote in a 2012 landmark essay series for *The American Interest,* "This is a Big One, a game changer, and it will likely be a major factor in propelling the United States to the next (and still unknown) stage of development—towards the next incarnation of the American Dream."

The transformation won't take place instantly, but it will happen within the next few years. What's important now is to be aware that the change is coming so you can anticipate when and where to invest resources for maximum profits during the Golden Age.

A golden age is not just a "bull market"

The solution to nearly every economic challenge facing our country (ranging from an aging population to an excessive debt-load) lies in returning the U.S. economy to its long-term growth trajectory of 3.5 to 4 percent per year. To do so, further change is needed; education, regulation and finance, which still rely heavily upon the "conventional wisdom" of the Mass Production revolution, are particularly ripe for reinvention.

But, as the misguided policies and practices that have delayed the Golden Age are revised or replaced, U.S. growth will return to its long-term average rate of 3.5 percent-plus between 2016 and 2033. In the first few years, the rate could realistically average well over 5 percent, as business compensates for over 12 years of lackluster growth.

This is an entirely reasonable projection. As explained in our analysis of the trend, RESTORING AMERICA'S ECONOMIC VITALITY (http://www.audiotech.com/trends-magazine/restoring-americas-economic-vitality) in the September 2011 issue of *Trends*, Stanford economist John Taylor calculates that the economy could grow at a 5 percent pace if targets are met in two areas: employment growth and productivity growth.

First, consider *employment growth*. In the year 2000, 64.7 percent of Americans aged 16 and over were actually employed. Today, it's 58.4 percent. Returning to the workforce participation rates we saw in 2000 would require an increase of 10.8 percent in the number of jobs filled. Allowing for the 1 percent expected annual population growth, an average 2 percent per year growth in the number of jobs would get us above 65 percent participation by 2020.

Next, consider *productivity growth*. According to the Bureau of Labor Statistics, productivity growth has averaged 2.7 percent since 1996. This growth has been driven by the technologies of the Digital Revolution. If not stifled, this growth will continue for at least the next two decades, as the truly *new* technologies we discuss in Chapters 4-12 build upon the growing foundation examined in Chapters 2 and 3.

Combining these reasonable targets for employment and productivity growth yields an average of 4.7 percent annual economic growth over the coming decade. This simple calculation suggests that a 5 percent target for U.S. GDP growth is definitely a realistic goal.

In fact, this estimate may even be *too conservative*, because the technologies of the Digital Revolution will bring quantum leaps in productivity and prosperity.

Because of the constant doubling of the price-performance of information technologies, everything from processing speed to memory capacity to network capacity is constantly improving, making a wealth of digital products increasingly faster, more efficient, more useful, more affordable, and more powerful.

As Mark Mills points out, from 1950 to 1980, computer speeds, largely on mainframe computers, increased 1,000 times while computing costs dropped by 10,000-fold. Over the same three-decade period, the speed of communicating, primarily over wired networks, rose by a factor of 10 million.

However, all of that progress is miniscule compared to the exponential growth in computing and communication speeds from 1980 to 2010. Over those three decades, Mills writes, computing speeds became 200,000 times faster, as costs dropped 1 million-fold. At the same time, communication over wireless networks became 1 million times faster, as costs of bandwidth declined by 100-fold.

Back in 1970, a state-of-the-art IBM 370 mainframe processed 1 MIPS, or million instruction sets per second, and it cost up to $1.8 million. Today, an ordinary iPad can process *1,000* MIPS, and it costs about $400. And of course, it is much smaller, it doesn't have to be stored in a refrigerated room, and it is infinitely easier to use.

Technology-Driven Affluence

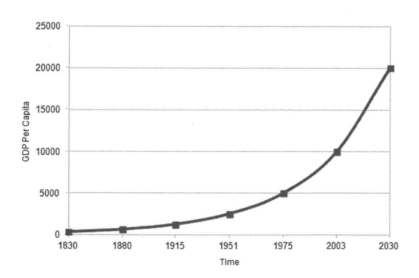

It's almost impossible to imagine what the *next* three decades will bring. Today, processing power, digital storage, and bandwidth are virtually free. This has enabled companies like Google, Amazon, Facebook, and Apple to thrive. But as the Digital Boom unfolds, we'll see unprecedented innovations in information technologies, and breakthroughs in biotech and nanotech that will improve the lifestyles, health, and longevity of people of every generation.

2

What lies <u>beyond</u> Moore's law and why does it make so much difference?

> "If GM had kept up with technology like the computer industry has, we would all be driving $25 cars that got 1,000 mpg."
> --Bill Gates, December 3, 2010

The Digital Revolution began in 1971 with a classic "big bang" event: Intel launched its first microprocessor, the model 4004. Like most disruptive technologies, this innovation was not suitable for any mainstream computer applications and it entered the market as an alternative to standardized industrial controllers, programmed in a very limited machine language. Fortunately, as that tiny "computer-on-a-chip" moved up-market and evolved into the 8086 processor, non-mainstream customers saw the potential of the 8086 and its rival, the Motorola 6502. In fact, two computer hobbyists, named Wozniak and Jobs, were so excited about the 6502 that they built a fully-functional computer around it that became the Apple II.

Mass-production economics associated with microprocessors,

23

solid-state memory, and data storage devices relentlessly drove costs down and performance up. And once IBM, the leading *mainstream* computer vendor, bought into the paradigm, the floodgates of software development opened, and the only major limitation became the rate at which new generations of processors could become denser, faster, and cheaper. This steady improvement in transistor density came to be defined by what we call Moore's Law: the idea that computer chip transistor-density doubles every 18 months, on average, leading to proportionally more powerful and less expensive chips.

Microprocessor Transistor Counts 1971—2011 & Moore's Law

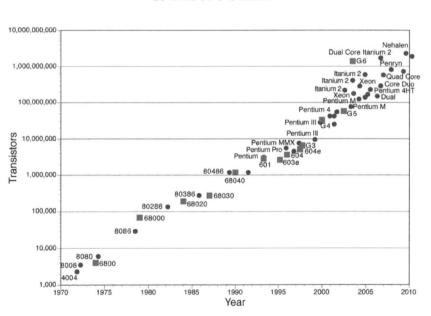

Source: Intel Corp.
Since the "big bang" of the Digital Revolution in 1971, Moore's Law has reliably predicted the advance of semiconductor technology.

In the past 20 years alone, computing performance has seen a dramatic increase of about 10,000 times. This increase has, of course, been due to the advances predicted by Moore's Law.

The impact has been profound: driving increases in

productivity and efficiency for individuals, small businesses, and major corporations, while spawning innovations in medicine, defense, entertainment, and communications. In fact, the only area that has not seen dramatic increases in IT-driven productivity is the public sector.

Experts generally agree that, unfortunately, Moore's Law (as originally formulated) is rapidly approaching the physical limits of the silicon technologies inherent in current computer chips. And, each new hurdle is becoming more difficult.

For example, Extreme UltraViolet (EUV) photolithography is a very challenging manufacturing technology requiring billions of dollars in research and tens of billions in capital equipment. Yet, it is the only short-term way forward. Similarly, quantum effects in nanoscale silicon are playing havoc with chip performance at these ever-shrinking dimensions. Another problem is that traditional on-chip metal connections cease to perform at the new nanoscale, requiring new and exotic replacements.

To ensure that the rapid increase in computing performance doesn't stop anytime soon, scientists are working to extend the limits of silicon computing, optimizing parallel-processing technology, and creating whole new hardware paradigms based on graphene and even newer emerging semiconductor technologies.

This challenge has not caught the industry by surprise. It has been known all along that there are serious technical issues associated with packing more transistors and connections onto silicon chips. These limitations may be roadblocks for continued improvement of silicon chips made in traditional ways, but other innovative technologies and processing approaches are being developed that have the potential to keep processor power advancing in line with the trajectory we've associated with Moore's Law. We will examine four of them:

1. New strides in silicon chip fabrication technology.
2. Extending the applicability of massively-parallel computing architectures.
3. Circuits made from the nanotech "wonder material" graphene.
4. Circuits based on a new substance called molybdenite.

New strides

Several promising developments in silicon technology have been discovered as it moves to the nanoscale. One of them is a new technique in photolithography invented by researchers at MIT and the University of Utah. It enables the production of complex shapes and finer lines on chips, delivering additional leaps in computational power from conventional slivers of silicon.[1]

Photolithography is the process of transferring the circuit paths and electronic elements of a chip onto a wafer's surface using light sources. With traditional photolithography, features on chips are limited to being larger than the wavelength of the light used. This new technique has produced features that are one-eighth that size.

Although this feat has been achieved previously, this is the first time it's been done using equipment that is suitable for quick, inexpensive manufacturing processes. The technique relies on less-expensive light sources and conventional chip-manufacturing equipment, putting the cost on par with that found in current chip-making plants.

In the short run, Intel and certain industry partners have placed their bets on a crash program to commercialize a more expensive approach called *extreme ultraviolet (EUV) photolithography* as soon as year-end 2013.[2] This should eliminate traffic jams on the information superhighway for a couple of more years.

Parallel paths

Fortunately, even if our progress in speeding up individual processors is slowed, massively parallel computing architectures should provide another *interim* path for pushing the limits of silicon-based processors in order to continue the persistent pace of doubling performance.

This type of hardware and software configuration has been around for a while. It increases performance by breaking up a problem into pieces and allowing simultaneous processing by multiple computing cores. In fact, such hardware and software is already common in video cards and supercomputers with hundreds or thousands of processors; it is becoming even more commonplace as consumer PCs acquire a dozen or more of processor cores.

However, most computer applications aren't ideally suited to parallel processing: they can only be broken into a few parallel streams and they can't afford the delays of one processor communicating with others. For that reason, parallel computing is currently being *fully* exploited only for narrow sets of image processing, scientific, and engineering applications. To make the most of this, some state-of-the-art supercomputers are actually built from thousands of traditional microprocessors working with thousands of high-end graphics cards. With each graphics card using over a thousand processor cores, the machine can focus the power of millions of processors on addressing optimally designed applications.

Expanding this technology to a broader set of applications will require new algorithms, programming models, operating systems, and computer architectures. Many industry experts argue that these challenges must be addressed so massively-parallel computing can become a viable option for improving computer performance, longer term, without abandoning silicon.

However, the promise of today's parallel computing model is dimmed by energy management challenges that arise when many processor cores are placed on a single chip, and by the bottlenecks involved in communications among chips.

The latter problem is already being extensively researched by engineers addressing the bottlenecks in communication between individual super-chips in today's supercomputers. Light can be faster than electrons moving though conductors when it comes to inter-processor communication. But, speed and bandwidth bottlenecks remain an issue, especially when large quantities of data are transmitted to and from a computer via fiber optics.

Why? The information must be translated from light into electrical signals for computers to use, and then translated back to light for retransmission. This process is relatively slow. It also makes the data susceptible to cyber-attack and requires expensive hardware features.

To resolve this problem, researchers at Purdue University have

27

recently created a passive optical diode that consists of two tiny silicon rings that are about one-tenth the width of a human hair.[3]

Because this diode can be easily integrated into industry-standard CMOS computer chips and requires no external assistance for transmitting signals, it could eliminate the need for translation, paving the way for faster, more powerful, and more secure super-computers containing thousands of connected processors. And, over the longer term, this could filter down to massively parallel mainstream servers.

However, the communication challenge goes beyond processor-to-processor exchange; it also involves connecting components within a chip. That means that, as the size of each silicon-based processor shrinks, so must the copper pathways (called interconnects) that carry electricity and, therefore, the information between the transistors and other components within a processor.

This size reduction of the interconnects causes several problems, including running less efficiently, using more power, generating more heat, and being more prone to permanent failure. These failings are significant impediments to continued performance gains for silicon computer chips.

To meet this challenge, researchers are trying to replace the copper. One material that holds promise is graphene.

In reality, it is a single layer of the graphite found in a pencil. This substance is made up of carbon atoms, arranged in a sheet, one atom thick, appearing much like a nanoscale chicken-wire fence.

To address the interconnect challenge, a team of researchers at Rensselaer Polytechnic Institute has discovered that stacking several thin graphene ribbons on top of each other enhances their ability to transmit electricity, enabling the structure to act as an interconnect.[4]

Significantly, graphene does not exhibit the same negative characteristics that copper does when the interconnects shrink. As copper nanowires shrink, electrons travel sluggishly, which creates a lot of heat, causing atoms of copper to be dragged along with the electrons.

Consequently, as electrical resistance increases, the movement of electrons is decreased, and computer speed and performance is degraded.

While single-layer graphene ribbons exhibit their own problems as interconnects, researchers recently discovered that these problems can be eliminated by stacking the graphene interconnects four to six layers thick. As a result, the researchers are highly optimistic about the use of graphene to replace copper interconnects. And it appears that stacking graphene will be compatible with mass production.

The graphene alternative

Similarly, scientists are overcoming barriers that have, so far, prevented graphene from being used as a viable alternative to silicon itself. One such issue is a characteristic called *band gap,* which is an energy gap that prevents electrons from flowing freely. It's that band gap that permits silicon transistors to switch off and on. Graphene sheets have no "natural" band gap.

On the other hand, semiconductors like silicon and germanium function *because* they exhibit narrow band gaps. That is, the band gap is large enough for the semiconductor to act as an insulator until an increase in electric field causes electrons to jump the gap, switching the semiconductor's state from off to on. Without band gap, there is no control of the circuitry. So, without a band gap in graphene, it cannot be used to fabricate transistors.

Researchers at Rensselaer Polytechnic Institute believe they have resolved this issue. They were able to create a band gap in graphene by exposing it to humidity. By controlling the amount of water absorbed, they are able to precisely tune the band gap.[5]

This ability to turn graphene into a semiconducting material makes it an extremely viable candidate for use in a new generation of transistors, diodes, and nanophotonics.

Molybdenite

However, graphene is not the only substance getting attention today as an eventual mainstream alternative to silicon chips. Molybdenite is a relatively abundant, naturally occurring substance that can be easily manufactured by reacting sulfur with the metal molybdenum. And it definitely has the potential to overshadow graphene as well as silicon as the basis of the next epoch in information processing.

One of the key advantages molybdenite holds over silicon is that it can allow the size of transistors to shrink even further. Silicon cannot be made into layers any smaller than two nanometers thick. Thinner layers can allow a chemical reaction to take place that oxidizes the surface and redefines the electronic properties.

Conversely, molybdenite can be formed into layers that are only three atoms thick, which is three times smaller than the silicon layers; and yet, even at this size, it is stable, with conductivity that is easy to control.[6]

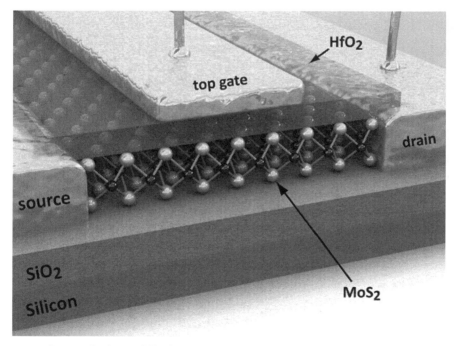

Source: Institute of Physics
Molybdenite can be formed into layers that are only three atoms thick, which is three times smaller than the silicon layers; and yet, even at this size, it is stable, with conductivity that is easy to control.

It's this characteristic that gives it a crucial advantage over graphene. Molybdenite naturally exhibits band gap, making it suitable for use in electronics, whereas graphene must undergo adaptations to gain band gap.

Even though it's still on the "bleeding edge" of technology, integrated circuits have already been produced using molybdenite. This work, at the Laboratory of Nanoscale Electronics and Structures, has shown molybdenite's advantages over silicon in terms of smaller scale, less energy consumption, and greater flexibility.[7]

Even more exciting, researchers at Switzerland's École Polytechnique Federale (EPFL) have succeeded in creating a flash memory chip combining graphene and molybdenite. This demonstrates the practical synergy between the two new technologies.

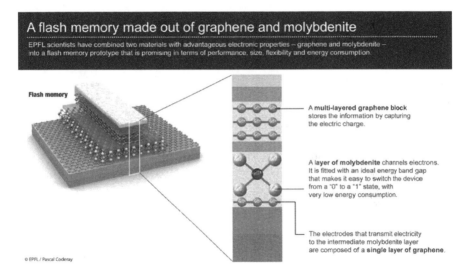

A flash memory made out of graphene and molybdenite

EPFL scientists have combined two materials with advantageous electronic properties – graphene and molybdenite – into a flash memory prototype that is promising in terms of performance, size, flexibility and energy consumption.

Flash memory

A multi-layered graphene block stores the information by capturing the electric charge.

A layer of molybdenite channels electrons. It is fitted with an ideal energy band gap that makes it easy to switch the device from a "0" to a "1" state, with very low energy consumption.

The electrodes that transmit electricity to the intermediate molybdenite layer are composed of a single layer of graphene.

© EPFL / Pascal Coderay

Source: Institute of Physics
Graphene is a sheet of carbon resembling "chicken wire" just one atom thick. It was discovered in 2004 and has a number of unique electronic and mechanical properties that mean it could be used in electronic devices. Physicists in the UK have found a way to prevent current from leaking through a device when it is switched off. They did this by making a new type of transistor from graphene that contains layers of boron nitride or molybdenum disulphide sandwiched between graphene sheets.

However, there are many questions that still must be answered before molybdenite or graphene circuits can be produced on a large scale. Yet, both now appear to have a promising future in helping to keep the price-performance curve of Moore's Law intact for the next decade and beyond.

Storage and bandwidth keep pace with processing

Evan as processor power continues to grow, networking technologies are becoming dramatically faster. For instance, Taiwanese scientists have developed a new short-range, high-speed wireless technology that's 1,000 times faster than Bluetooth. Called VIRTUS, the new chipset is more than a re-design of existing devices—it's an entirely new technology that sends data in large packets in the mm-wave band. These extremely high frequency (EHF) waves operate at 30-300 GHz and can transmit information with very low power consumption.[8]

The chipset, which runs at a clock speed of 60GHz, includes an antenna, a full radio-frequency transceiver and an integrated processor, allowing transfer rates up to 2 gigabits per second. At those speeds, an 8 GB DVD could be downloaded in about 30 seconds. The revolutionary technology is aimed at low power devices such as phones and tablets, but allows data to be transferred between multiple platforms, including computers, televisions, and projectors. This would enable a whole new range of applications, including mobile-distributed computing and high-definition video streaming.

And the latest leaps in computing hardware aren't simply limited to processing power and networks. New research just published in the journal *Nature Materials* paves the way for a one-inch *memory* chip that will be able to store multiple *terabytes* of data. This discovery was enabled by a team of researchers led by scientists at the Lawrence Berkeley National Laboratory. It provides the first atomic-scale insights into the ferroelectric properties of nano-crystals.[9]

Working with the world's most powerful transmission electron microscope, these researchers mapped the ferroelectric structural distortions in nano-crystals of germanium telluride (a semiconductor) and barium titanate (an insulator). This data was combined with data from electron holographic polarization imaging to yield detailed information on the polarization structures and scaling limits of ferroelectricity on the nanoscale.

Ferroelectricity is the property by which materials can be electrically polarized, meaning they will be oriented in favor of either a positive or negative electrical charge. The polarization can be flipped with the application of an external electrical field. This property can be exploited for non-volatile data storage, much as we use ferromagnetic materials today, but using much smaller, far more densely packed devices.

The researchers also demonstrated room-temperature polarization flipping down to dimensions of about five nanometers where ferroelectric behavior disappears. This indicates that five nanometers is likely a size limit for data storage applications. Once commercialized, these ferroelectric memory chips will increase data storage density by orders of magnitude.

Economic implications

Those parts of the economy that are driven primarily by information handling have improved at an average annual rate of 59 percent. However, early in the Digital Revolution, Moore's Law and its related paradigms for memory, storage, and bandwidth applied only to that small fraction of the economy where value creation activities depended on processing, storing, and communicating data. The big change has been the steady progress of such technologies in moving from the periphery of our lives and businesses to the center. And that advance of digital technology into wider spheres of the economy is largely responsible for the fact that real economic growth continued at a long-term average annual rate of 3.5 percent until the financial panic of 2008.

This implies that the U.S. and global economy will grow at an accelerating rate going forward as industries previously trapped in the value creation dynamics of the Mass Production Revolution, or even earlier epochs, fully embrace the Digital Revolution. Those who look at the digital revolution as just a process of getting more and cheaper digital devices into the hands of more and more people will inevitably miss the truly disruptive and transformative power of this technology. However, it's easy to fall into that trap because most of the big technology-oriented money made over the *past* 40 years has been made by these communication devices, computers, computer applications software, and services directly exploiting digitization.

Going forward, every sector of the economy, from agriculture, to energy, to healthcare, will be driven by digital technology. Penetration will be determined by the cost and performance of digital technologies compared to more analog-mechanical alternatives. And, as the price of a given amount of hardware performance falls 59 percent each year and is accompanied by software suited to solving customer problems using that hardware, these technologies will be adopted.

In the next chapter, we'll take a closer look at how "virtually free" computing, memory, and storage connected by ubiquitous networks have already started to transform our lives. Like all the trends we'll discuss here, mobile and embedded computing rests firmly on the foundation of Moore's Law. But, unlike some of the trends we'll address later, this one is already growing explosively and laying the foundation for many of the other technologies.

What's ahead?

First, by early 2014, the semiconductor equipment industry will be ready to deliver extreme ultraviolet (EUV) lithography fabrication technology to Intel and others, but the many delays in mainstreaming this technology will make the search for the "next big thing" more urgent. The limitations of CMOS silicon are becoming painfully obvious and expensive. Intel just provided $4 billion to fab technology leader ASML to give them the resources they need to get this new technology out the door.[10] Spin logic circuits and other technologies that promise to bypass these **roadblocks** are increasingly worth pursuing.

Second, processor price-performance advances will keep on track, in accordance with Moore's Law, for at least the next decade. An explosion of information technology in virtually every aspect of business and personal life, and our increasing dependence on it, will demand the continued improvement. No scientific "show-stoppers" are expected. Ultimately, the marketplace will decide whether advanced forms of silicon, graphene, molybdenite, or some other

34

material emerges as the mainstream technology of the 2020s. Without development of these alternatives, advances in information technology will stall; and with it the economic potential of the 21st century.

Third, between 2020 and 2025, Moore's law, which depends on transistor-density on silicon, will reach a fundamental roadblock imposed by quantum mechanics and human ingenuity. But there's no reason to panic. Parallel computing architectures coupled with new materials like Graphene and Molybdenite will push any genuine "show-stoppers" out to beyond 2050. Consequently, by 2030, computer price-performance will have improved by a factor of over 1,000 times versus 2013 levels. Furthermore, physical flexibility is an attractive characteristic of molybdenite, which means it could readily lead to computers that roll up, or electronic devices that could be applied directly to the skin.

Fourth, graphene and molybdenite are both made from abundant natural resources, so we don't have worry about materials shortages. And ironically, these manufacturing processes are expected to be more environmentally-friendly than those associated with silicon.

Fifth, the commercial potential of extending Moore's Law will depend on parallel performance improvements in related technologies. Extraordinary advances will also take place in data storage density, random access memory performance, and network bandwidth—all critical for seamless, "anytime, anywhere" information access. In the not-too-distant future, many kinds of problems that remain unsolvable by conventional computers will be off-loaded to cloud-based quantum computers, a topic we will examine in Chapter 6.

Sixth, new computing technologies will be dramatically more energy-efficient, causing a major improvement in MIPS/KwH. This will translate into a major leap in GDP per unit of energy input, as well as embedded processors powered by ambient energy. For those in advanced economies like the United States, this means our quality of life will improve substantially, despite using less energy. Meanwhile, the standard of living for those in the developing world can rise explosively without a corresponding increase in energy demands.

3

How will trillions of networked computers improve every life on the planet?

"I do not fear computers. I fear the lack of them."
--Isaac Asimov

As we discussed in Chapter 2, Moore's law and the new, innovative alternatives to silicon chips imply that networks, computers, and sensors will literally become so cheap, fast, and tiny that they'll soon be in everything, everywhere, all the time.

This is in line with the long-term trajectory for all of the devices of the digital age. In 1949, *Popular Mechanics* predicted, "Computers in the future may weigh no more than 1.5 tons." This forecast, of course, was *technically* accurate—it just missed the mark by being far too conservative. Considering that the iPhone 5 weighs less than four ounces, the experts at *Popular Mechanics* failed to foresee that computers would weigh *12,000 times less* than their best estimate.

Over the ensuing decades, computers have increasingly become smaller and lighter—as well as faster, cheaper, and easier-to-use. From mainframes to minicomputers to desktop PCs to laptops to smartphones, the evolution of computing technology has marched forward at a relentless pace, and there is no chance that it will come to a screeching halt any time soon.

Just as computers moved from data centers to desktops to laps to pockets, the next frontier in computing will bring them increasingly closer to our everyday lives; in fact, they will become embedded in all the devices we use and nearly every object that surrounds us.

This is the vision of the "Internet of Things"—a vision in which we won't just plug into technology once in a while, but instead will be completely and constantly immersed in a digital universe of seamless connections to everyone and everything.

In their book *Trillions: Thriving in the Emerging Information Ecology,* Peter Lucas, Joe Ballay, and Mickey McManus point out that the world now produces *10 billion* microprocessors per year, and that number is continually increasing.[1] Only a small fraction of those processors are used to make desktops, laptops, tablets, and cell phones. The vast majority are embedded in everyday products like washing machines, microwave ovens, vacuum cleaners, toasters, and wristwatches.

Global Semiconductor Value
Expect a 59 Percent Annual Price-Performance Jump Plus 5 Percent Spending Growth

	2011	2012	%	2013	%	2014	%
Discretes	21.39	19.30	-9.7%	20.35	5.4%	21.54	5.8%
Optoelectronics	23.09	25.99	12.5%	27.78	6.9%	29.48	6.1%
Sensors	7.97	7.93	-0.5%	8.52	7.4%	9.13	7.2%
ICs	247.07	236.71	-4.2%	246.41	4.1%	258.62	5.0%
Analog	42.34	39.68	-6.3%	41.12	3.6%	43.52	5.8%
Micro	65.20	60.32	-7.5%	62.08	2.9%	64.96	4.6%
Logic	78.78	80.54	2.2%	85.46	6.1%	90.38	5.7%
Memory	60.75	56.17	-7.5%	57.75	2.8%	59.76	3.5%
TOTAL	299.52	289.94	-3.2%	303.05	4.5%	318.77	5.2%
Americas	55.20	52.77	-4.4%	54.73	3.7%	57.35	4.8%
Europe	37.39	33.40	-10.7%	33.70	0.9%	35.20	4.5%
Japan	42.90	42.02	-2.1%	43.42	3.3%	45.35	4.4%
Asia Pacific	164.03	161.75	-1.4%	171.21	5.8%	180.87	5.6%

Source: World Semiconductor Trade Statistics, Autumn 2012 forecast, in US $B and percent growth.

The reason is that it is far cheaper to manufacture an appliance in which all of the information is in software, which is easy to duplicate and basically free once the first unit is created. Compare that to a mechanical knob on a washing machine, which is costly and complicated to make and install.

While economics drove the redesign of countless products, there is a benefit that has not yet been exploited. The processors in these products allow users to communicate with them more easily. However, the real potential for changing the world will materialize when all of these products can also *communicate with each other.*

Until now, according to Lucas and his co-authors, we've been at a stage of the "connectivity revolution" that is equivalent to the time when people began to use PCs to replace typewriters and calculators, but lacked an efficient way to connect them. It wasn't until modems and the Internet allowed computers to communicate with each other that they realized their potential. Similarly, we now are surrounded by billions of processors that, in most cases, still can't exchange information with each other. But all that will soon change.

According to Research Professor Heikki Ailisto of the Technical Research Centre of Finland, known as VTT, "Three big waves can be identified in telecommunications in the past century or so. First, the telephone connected 500 million places. The mobile phone then connected 5 billion people. The Internet of Things will connect 50 billion devices, machines, and objects."[2]

And, Lucas believes that 50 billion is just the beginning, hence the name of his book. He declares that "a near-future world containing trillions of computers is simply a done-deal."

VTT is one of the many firms developing one of the basic components of this new reality. With researchers from the University of Tokyo, the organization has been working on universal identification (uID) technology. This will enable everyday products, as well as parts and materials, to be tagged with sensors that will identify and track them throughout their entire life-cycle. Ailisto explains, "A timber plank, for instance, can be tagged with information on which forest the timber was cut from, where it was sawn, how many times it has been painted, and with what paints."

Another initiative is a program called OPENS, for Open Smart Spaces. So far, it has resulted in the creation of an interoperability platform named Smart M3, which is designed to allow all of the digital appliances and objects in the home or office to communicate and share information with each other, even if they were made by different companies.

What will this mean in practical terms? Here are a few everyday examples cited by various sources:

- If you can't find your car keys, you'll simply send them a text message, and they'll reply with a message that tells you their location.
- If the eggs in your refrigerator are about to expire, the refrigerator will send you a message.
- If you are eating too much unhealthy food—based on data that your smartphone will collect from the number of times you call for pizza delivery and the inventory system your refrigerator will keep—you will get a text alert reminding you to eat more fruits and vegetables.
- Sensors will be able to constantly monitor your health when you are well, and if you have a medical condition you can have updates automatically sent in real time to doctors or other caregivers.
- Cars will drive themselves, and will be able to identify their location, avoid objects in the road, and communicate with other vehicles, as we will discuss in Chapter 14.
- You'll be able to monitor how much you're spending on electricity from the smart grid with new metering technology that will allow you to identify when it would be cheapest to turn on an appliance. You'll also be able to sell unused electricity from your electric car back to the grid.
- Information collected from all of the devices and things around you could theoretically be captured and used for companies to tailor marketing messages to you based on your specific location, interests, and activities. (Clearly, not everyone will welcome this threat to their privacy; we'll come back to this topic later in this chapter.)

The unstoppable momentum of network effects

It's hard to remember what the world was like, less than a quarter-century ago (in 1989), when Tim Berners-Lee conceived the World Wide Web, HTML, and the first primitive browser. Fast-forward to 2013, and we see that the convergence of network effects, Moore's Law, and wireless technology is paving the way for a world in which everything is literally networked with everything else.

One underlying factor that has been widely misunderstood is the impact of "network effects." The phenomenon of network effects refers to the fact that the theoretically possible number of connections in a network increases proportional to the square of the number of nodes in the network.

Mobile Phones

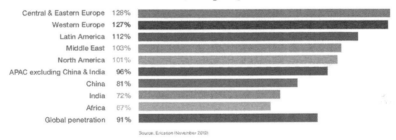

Source: Ericsson Mobility Report

Network effects tend to magnify the impact of technologies that are linked to each other. The classic example is the fax machine: The first machine was essentially worthless because it could not be used to send a fax since there was no machine to receive it. As each new machine was put into use, however, the potential value of the network and each machine that could access it increased exponentially. We will see an even greater impact from the "Internet of Things." When trillions of devices and objects are able to communicate with each other, the effect will surpass anything we can imagine today.

In a world filled with mobile devices, embedded processors,

sensor networks, and a vast array of servers and re-definable networks, it is inevitable that homes, hospitals, streets, offices, stores, factories, and airports will all become suffused with potentially useful resources.

Unlike every previous revolution fueled by technology, this one isn't limited to England, the U.S., and perhaps a handful of Westernized economies. Instead, it is the first truly *global* technology revolution.

Part of this is driven by the trend of globalization, but an essential difference lies in the very nature of the technology itself. Economic value in the digital age is based not on vast swaths of infrastructure that can't easily be transported from one country to another, as in the past—think railroads and mass-manufacturing plants—but instead it resides today in the form of chip designs, software code, digitized content, and brand identities. Each of these new types of economic value is quick, easy, and virtually free to duplicate in endless quantities and to transport instantly anywhere in the world.

Furthermore, the economic equations of the Digital Revolution are based on "economies of scope" rather than economies of scale. *Scale* economies focus on creating large batch sizes of identical products. *Scope* economies involve using the same resources over and over again to create value in as many markets as possible.

This has given rise to the "disaggregated supply chain": Those functions that are subject to "economies of scope" are retained by the innovator, while those that are most subject to "economies of scale" are outsourced to "focused contractors" who maintain a clear competitive advantage in those areas via low wage rates, specialized equipment, and cumulative experience.

There exists no clearer example of this than Apple's relationship with Foxconn. The unique and proprietary characteristics of the iPhone or iPad reside in Apple's hardware and software designers in Cupertino, CA. However, Apple's core organization represents only a tiny fraction of the people involved in producing an iPhone for the consumer, even when its retail network is considered.

The globalization of production has pushed purchasing power, consumer demand, and manufacturing capabilities out to the rest of the world at unprecedented rates. The McKinsey Global Institute summarized it this way: "The original Industrial Revolution, hatched in the mid-1700s, took two centuries to gain full force. Britain, the revolution's birthplace, required 150 years to double its economic output per person; in the United States, locus of the revolution's second stage, doubling GDP per capita took more than 50 years. A century later, when China and India industrialized, the two nations doubled their GDP per capita in 12 and 16 years, respectively. Moreover, Britain and the United States began industrialization with populations of about 10 million, whereas China and India began their economic takeoffs with populations of roughly one billion. Thus the two leading *emerging* economies are experiencing roughly ten times the economic acceleration of the Industrial Revolution, on 100 times the scale—resulting in an economic force that is over 1,000 times as big."[3]

Social media like Facebook, Twitter, and Tumblr are just in their infancy. Yet, they are already playing a role in geopolitical affairs. For better or worse, consider the "Arab Spring" of 2011 or the recent opening up of Myanmar. Both were facilitated by social media. And even as specific social media sites, like Facebook, plateau, the total number of platforms will proliferate, and their cumulative impact will increase as worldwide Internet users grow to more than 3.5 billion by 2015.

Why is this impact so great? Because it involves the simultaneous acceleration of multiple technologies. For example, the exponential improvement in the price-performance of processors, memory, storage and bandwidth is complemented by aggressive improvements in applications software and content on the Internet. The combination makes the transformational impact far greater and more rapid than if each technology was emerging independently.

Consider this: 3 billion people still live on less than $2 per day. Yet, thanks to $50 Android-based tablets available in 2013, such people living in rural Indian villages can now have access to educational content, news, communications, entertainment, and computational capability unavailable even to the top 1 percent of Americans in 1993. And as a result of this and the other technologies documented in this book, within a generation, they will no longer be living in abject poverty. The resulting rise in human capital and international trade will transform them into consumers and producers with their own comparative advantage.

The smart home in the smart city

In 2007, for the first time in human history, more people lived in urban areas than rural. And, while geographic dispersion is likely to dominate the most affluent countries in the longer-term, urbanization will be a key driving force for the bulk of humanity throughout the 21st century. Technologically, this is driven by several factors:

1. 21st century global agriculture is following the trajectory of 20th century North American agriculture, which went from employing 80 percent of the population to just 2 percent, while total output surged.
2. Access to technology is raising expectations for affluence and imparting vocational skills to a wider audience.
3. Labor-intensive manufacturing jobs supplying the developed world have attracted underemployed rural populations to urban centers looking for a better life.
4. The new wage-based employment has created a new consumer economy in these exploding urban centers.

In turn, this wave of technology-driven urbanization is creating enormous profit opportunities, as well as problems to be solved. Consider just a few:

1. Affordable production and distribution of safe food, drink, and other consumer products for millions of relatively poor people in crowded urban centers.
2. Targeted entertainment, communications, and education for those people.
3. Adequate public safety services like fire and police.
4. Adequate healthcare services recognizing the increased vulnerability of these new cities to pandemics.
5. Transportation and employment opportunities that make the city an economically self-sustaining entity.

Many of the mechanisms that will let companies tap the

44

opportunities and resolve the problems of urban life are increasingly embodied in the form of ubiquitous mobile and embedded computing technologies.

Later chapters will highlight the enabling role of super-cheap networked computing in transformational sectors like nanotech and biotech that will play a big role in transforming squalid mega-cities into viable places for people to live. However, in this chapter we focus on the roles this technology will play directly in addressing not only the needs of the affluent developed world, but in transforming the lives of those in the poor, crowded urban centers of the developing world.

The incredible speed of global penetration that has typified the Digital Revolution has introduced the concept of "trickle-up innovation," to complement the historically-proven paradigm of "trickle-down innovation." Trickle-down innovation was seen most clearly in the industrial revolution, when almost every important innovation began in the UK and then spread to continental Europe and North America.

The unique economics of the Digital Revolution imply that its Golden Age will not be defined solely by trickle-down innovation starting in the OECD. Because economies of scope matter more than economies of scale, expect to see disruptive innovations emerge from the developing world and well as less prominent OECD members. That's because these centers are the places that have a critical mass of consumers for whom disruptive solutions are "good enough."

The incredibly large installed base of smartphones in the developing world provides an obvious starting point. The openness of the Android platform is particularly conducive to adding functionality via apps and peripherals. A few years ago, the idea of street vendors accepting debit and credit cards, or handling their inventory and replenishment electronically was absurd. The same is true for nurses and doctors in tiny clinics running EKGs and blood tests with phone peripherals. And we're just beginning to see the possibilities.

Yet despite this new paradigm (which every multinational should learn to harness), the coming Golden Age will still be dominated by "trickle-down innovation." However, the difference between this and the prior revolutions will be the rate of diffusion across the globe.

For example, German computer scientists, electrical engineers, and mathematicians at the Technical University Darmstadt and the University of Kassel are working together to implement their vision of a so-called "smart city." In such a metropolis, all devices would be intelligently linked to one another through a backbone of wireless sensors that receive, analyze, and transmit streams of data. Users of each device would benefit from the added-value gained as data is analyzed and retransmitted.[4]

On a smaller scale, a smart home could be built on this model. Systems throughout the home, such as heating, air conditioning, refrigeration, media centers, and lighting, could communicate and automatically adjust to meet our specific demands.

Already, it's relatively easy to imagine major appliances being connected and controlled by a smart network. But soon, even individual light bulbs will have IP addresses and they'll be connected via Wi-Fi. This has become possible with the advent of compact fluorescent and LED bulbs, which already contain tiny circuit boards that control their function.

NXP, a Netherlands-based semiconductor company, has suggested that adding a tiny Wi-Fi system to these boards is relatively easy and cheap. Using a laptop or iPad, users will be able to schedule light patterns that make it appear someone is at home, or set up motion sensors that turn lights on as people enter a room. By downloading a simple app, homeowners will be able to track their energy expenses and configure a lighting plan that cuts costs.

The key to connecting all these domestic devices, as well as equipment in factories, and ultimately, all the devices within a city, will be a network of interconnected, low-cost wireless sensors. These sensors, along with the ubiquity of the Internet, will usher in the "Internet of Things."

An effort called the "Cluster ESNA project" is helping move us closer to that vision with the development of a flexible framework for "wireless-sensor network applications." This framework will make communication possible between the various types of smart devices. These wireless networks leverage small, matchbox-sized devices that are exceptionally inexpensive and can be built into almost any device. These devices can be equipped with the capability to detect a specified combination of temperature, humidity, movement, radiation, chemicals, and light. More importantly, they can form a "dynamic network" which automatically rearranges itself if one or more nodes fail.[5]

The characteristics that allow these wireless networks to adapt to changing circumstances will also enable them to rebuild the network in response to changing needs, thereby increasing the way all things will be connected.

Called "ad-hoc mobile networks," they assemble themselves from any devices that happen to be in the area. Considering the fact that nearly everything around us, from traffic lights to mobile phones, is actually a small computer, there is no shortage of such devices. As these devices move in and out of wireless range, the network will continue to adapt.

So instead of powerful routers linking a relatively few, relatively powerful computers that make up the networks found in today's offices, these ad-hoc mobile networks will leverage low-power devices that perform wireless routing, connecting devices that would otherwise be out of radio range.

These ad-hoc network connections have great potential to positively affect areas such as emergency management, healthcare, and traffic control.

For example, consider a scenario in which a fire occurs in a highway tunnel: Fixed communication resources are quickly destroyed, and the tunnel fills with smoke. Today, under such circumstances, emergency crews would find it difficult to locate the fire and to rescue the people who are trapped.

But, in the near future, wireless sensors could take over, providing information on visibility, temperatures, and the locations of vehicles and people. Maps and instructions could then be forwarded to firefighters inside the tunnel via hand-held terminals or helmet-mounted displays.

And, it's not just the handling of large-scale events where the "Internet of Things" will pay off. More commonly, we'll see small improvements in our everyday routines, from improved traffic patterns, to quicker and easier shopping experiences, to alerts from our refrigerators that particular foods are about to expire.

Ultimately, the "Internet of Things" will lead to "smart" everything. Earlier, we mentioned the smart home, where connectedness will deliver energy savings plus other benefits. Soon we'll hear of the smart hospital, the smart industry, and even the smart farm. The common element will be the way that components within each system communicate with each other.

For example, patients will have mobile sensors that will report their status continually as they are moved about within a healthcare system. Farms will use wireless sensors to better gauge the need for irrigation, thus saving water and therefore reducing costs. These smart institutions will all leverage a network of real-time data to improve efficiencies.

Over the coming decade, Radio Frequency Identification technology will integrate seamlessly into the "Internet of Things" to streamline our lives. Imagine never again waiting in line in a store. This will become the norm thanks to RFID technology. These small tags are read wirelessly, providing information in real time, such as which products are on a pallet moving through a distribution chain.

The big news is that the cost to make these tags continues to drop, making it cost-effective to place them on nearly every piece of merchandise. This will allow retailers to track these products from the factory to the point of purchase. At checkout, these tags will replace the ubiquitous bar codes that get scanned one by one. Since RFID tags are read wirelessly and instantly, a whole shopping cart of products can be processed in mere seconds without unloading and reloading the cart.

Eventually, there won't even be checkout lines. We'll merely walk our carts out the door, where products and payment devices will be read wirelessly. Buying 100 items will be a fast, streamlined process. Just as important, these tags will stay with the merchandise all the way through disposal; this will make it easy to know that your jacket is at the cleaners or when the milk in the fridge has expired.

Tiny vibration and strain sensors on bridges and highways will identify maintenance problems before disasters occur. Thousands of tiny moisture sensors spread around farms will direct smart irrigation systems to dramatically improve irrigation efficiency. Telematics, embedded not just in automobiles but appliances and industrial machines, will trigger service warnings, preventing accidents and eliminating downtime.

Inexpensive, high-speed chemical sensors will spot contaminated food during processing, eliminating illnesses and huge recall costs for manufacturers. Embedding copy-protected codes unobtrusively into genuine products, including pharmaceuticals, will foil counterfeiters and save companies hundreds of billions of dollars per year in lost revenues and potentially damaged credibility.

Applied to the developed world with traditional appliances, communication networks, and media, this technology promises to be transformational. But for those in the developing world, access to these capabilities promises to be revolutionary. Police will be able to cost-effectively monitor every street all the time with wireless solar-powered cameras. Tiny stores and street vendors will stay replenished via supply chain networks. Literacy and skills will soar as people tap into "edutainment" via mobile devices. Epidemics will be averted as networked health services share information about diseases. And local firms will realize synergy with multinationals when they are inexpensively equipped to access the global supply chain.

Managing the risks

There are, however, at least three obstacles:

- First, privacy issues will be one of the biggest factors limiting universal deployment of the "Internet of Things." When people are truly immersed in it, all of their movements, purchases, and activities will be tracked, and this will create a threat to individuals' privacy and security. It is already possible to track people by their cell phone usage, their credit-card purchases, their Internet history, and the GPS devices in their cars, but this is nothing compared to the data that will be collected when all of the appliances, objects, and devices in homes, office buildings, and public places are constantly monitoring where you are and what you are doing. But we expect solutions to these issues to be fairly simple. For example, clothing will come with RFID tags intended to let you keep track of your wardrobe and update it by having your closet read the tags and send information to stores where you shop. But if you don't want that service enabled, equipment installed at the point of purchase will be able to zap the RFID tag so that it no longer works, eliminating a significant privacy threat to some people. An entire industry will spring up to do nothing but deactivate or reprogram intelligent sensors for those who don't want to share certain data with others. Ultimately, the companies that do the best job of protecting data will perform the best in the marketplace.

- Second, technical issues will also need to be addressed before the "Internet of Things" can become a reality. For example, bandwidth will quickly become a problem as everything begins to connect wirelessly to everything else. Right now, only around 15 to 20 percent of the capacity of the most frequently used bands has been allocated. This is destined to change and to change quickly. One answer to this problem will be "reconfigurable devices" that are capable of "beam forming," a technology that uses antennae that behave more like spotlights than the current antennae that radiate in all directions. The result would be a much more efficient use of scarce frequency bands. Until recently, the biggest barrier was the looming shortage of Internet addresses because the original Internet address system, called IPv4, allows for roughly 4.3 billion unique addresses. Logically, in a world of 7 billion people, with requests for addresses doubling every year, 4 billion will certainly not be enough. The transition to IPv6, now underway, will solve this problem. Implementing this new addressing scheme involves transition costs, but it will allow more than enough addresses: 340 undecillion. To put that figure in simpler terms, it is equivalent to the number 34, followed by 37 zeroes.

- Third, our growing dependency on networked technology will make us increasingly vulnerable to disruption. Here are the three greatest risks:

1. Cyber-attacks represent a particularly significant threat because they can often be executed anonymously. Of all the arguments put forth against an envisioned *smart grid,* its vulnerability to cyber-attack is perhaps the most damning. As we discussed in the *Trends* article **WHERE'S THE SMART GRID?** (http://audiotech.com/trends-magazine/wheres-the-smart-grid) any time that data begins to flow, there is the risk of that data being compromised. In the electrical grid, it could mean more than the *misuse* of that data; it could mean the crippling of the power grid by bringing down the network and reducing service quality. The launch of the "Stuxnet" worm revealed that utility companies are already vulnerable. As the grid becomes more dependent on the flow of data, clever hackers will have even more opportunities to exploit critical infrastructure vulnerabilities.

2. Electromagnetic pulse weapons present another threat that could theoretically disable networks and permanently destroy devices. Fortunately, these weapons must be delivered physically and all nation-states are susceptible to retaliation. Therefore the key strategies involve isolating and shielding strategic resources in multiple locations, deploying preemptive defenses such as anti-ballistic-missile systems, and making sure retaliatory capabilities are credible.

3. Natural disasters are another potential source of disruption. Extremely powerful solar flares and other natural events that could particularly threaten a society reliant upon digital technology generally fall into the category of "black swan" events. The key is to consider them in our decision-making processes in the same way we consider disease pandemics, terrorist attacks, and tidal waves.

What's ahead?

First, the number of Internet users will reach 3 billion by year-end

2013. A team of researchers in China recently published evidence that a function analogous to Moore's Law accurately describes the actual growth pattern of the Internet. This led them to conclude that the Internet is doubling in size every 5.32 years. The Internet reached 1.5 billion users around September 2008, so the Chinese study implies it will reach 3 billion users around the end of 2013. As of June 30, 2012, there were an estimated 2.4 billion Internet users worldwide, which suggests that this projection remains on target.[6]

Second, ubiquitous connectivity pioneered by mobile technologies will raise billions of people out of poverty. Already, mobile phones are having this influence in Africa, where they allow the free flow of market information to otherwise isolated peoples. Entrepreneurs are using them to create their own markets, where goods and services can be exchanged seamlessly across previously uncrossable distances. People in rural China, India, and Africa also use cell phones to transfer money and pay bills in areas where no banks exist for such transactions. A study at Harvard University tracked fishermen off the coast of India and discovered that when they started using cell phones to find out where they could get the best price for their catch even before they reached the shore, their profits rose by eight percent, on average. Similarly, the London Business School found that a nation's GDP rose half a percentage point for every 10 mobile phones that were introduced per 100 citizens. These phenomena are accelerating the rise of the middle class. Savvy investors and business leaders need to recognize that the ad-hoc economies that are now emerging in the world's poorest regions can rapidly develop into robust middle-class economies as people thrive and bootstrap themselves out of poverty on the back of this new technology.

Third, pervasive connectivity will make it possible to benefit from embedding knowledge in every aspect of our environment. Nearly everything around us is already starting to plug into channels of communication. Soon, RFID tags and smart networks will permit virtually every item in the home, office, store, or factory to communicate in some way with the other items and the people who own them. You can already buy electrical outlets that send their power usage statistics to a Web site so that you can track where you're wasting electricity. With the advent of service robots, the technology will take another huge leap forward, creating new markets in everything from elder care and health care to warfare and resource exploration.

Fourth, smartphones and tablets promise to become the platform of choice for much of the developing world. The lack of land-line infrastructure, coupled with the rapid development of mobile apps and peripherals, makes the tablet or smartphone a natural default for consumers and small businesses in the developing world. And inevitably, as these "good enough" mobile solutions improve, they will "trickle up" to the developed economies. As a result, traditional PCs and laptops will simultaneously be replaced by enhanced mobile solutions and absorbed into ever-friendlier home entertainment centers. Those entertainment systems will transition into the hub of the smart home, with much of the intelligence and storage in "the cloud." Laptops and traditional desktops will not totally disappear; they'll simply become niche-oriented work-stations mostly for vocational tasks at home or in the office.

Fifth, toiling in the "virtual workplace" will become the standard practice for many more jobs as companies transform their business processes, social norms, and policies to fully realize the technological potential. Slowly over the past 20 years, companies have implemented this model with the goals of reducing overhead and increasing employee morale. As one would expect, these efforts have met with mixed results. But fortunately, a set of "best practices" is beginning to emerge and companies are now increasingly ready to fully embrace the virtual workplace model. Much of the productivity surge we'll see over the next decade in North America and the EU will come from reducing occupancy costs and commuting time, while raising employee enthusiasm. The optimized use of real-time communications and on-line meetings to involve remote personnel in decision-making will play a big role.

Sixth, through at least 2020, the "app-ification" of computing will continue to accelerate the delivery of more diverse and feature-rich functionality to everyone, everywhere. Consumer mobile technology has been evolving at an unprecedented rate since the debut of smartphones. One reason for the accelerating evolution is the dawning of the "era of apps," the tiny free bundles of code optimized for addressing specific "jobs-to-be-done." A big advantage of apps is their nearly-instantaneous availability worldwide. Apps leverage many of the key trends in business and society that go beyond pure technology like "crowdsourcing," "mash-ability," "open innovation," "social networks," and "trickle-up innovation" (which are examined more closely in our next book). App-ification is quickly growing beyond the world of dedicated mobile platforms. For instance, GM and Ford recently announced that coming generations of automobiles will be open to apps.

4

How will "smart machines" impact your career, life, and investments?

> "Computers are magnificent tools for the realization of our dreams, but no machine can replace the human spark of spirit, compassion, love, and understanding."
> --Louis Gerstner, CEO IBM Corp.

In the 1950 and '60s, the Mass-Production Revolution was in its Golden Age. And mainframe digital computers were exploiting the power of newly invented transistors to perform two primary tasks: processing enormous batches of routine transactions, and solving in minutes enormously complex computational problems that required years to solve by hand. It was in this context that theoretical pioneers like John von Neumann, Alan Turing, and Norbert Wiener explored the possibilities of so-called "artificial intelligence."

They and their colleagues dreamed of making machines that were intellectually indistinguishable from human beings. Applications like real-time universal speech translators seemed only a few years away, and creating computers that were functionally equivalent to the human mind appeared quite feasible. If fact, they came to believe that with a few orders of magnitude improvement in performance, dramatic

55

breakthroughs could be achieved.

Now, 60 years later, with price-performance improvements on the order of one million times behind us, we've only begun to scratch the surface. Admittedly, voice recognition systems like Apple's Siri and Microsoft's as yet unnamed "real-time language translation software" are impressive within defined contexts. IBM's Watson certainly shows the promise of AI in addressing free-form queries. And Google has "image recognition software" that is actually becoming useful in many applications. However, this all falls well short of what the pioneers expected to see by the 1970s or '80s.

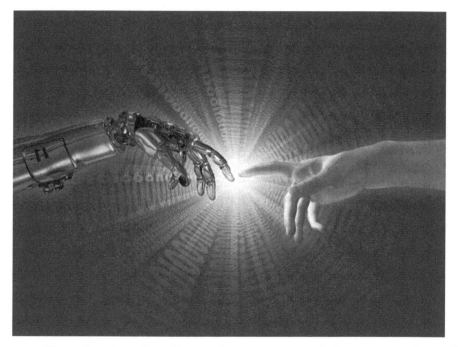

But despite the disappointments, a whole community of enthusiasts, most prominently led by inventor Ray Kurzweil, believes computers will not only reach parity with humans sometime between 2040 and 2050, they will then go on to far surpass us. As a result, human intelligence and creativity will ultimately become irrelevant.

While this vision sounds pretty frightening to most of us, Kurzweil sees it as a vehicle by which humans can attain "virtual immortality." For humans alive today, this immortality would begin by integrating technology into the biological body. The mind would become increasingly connected to steadily evolving technology until the human brain was eventually replaced by an electronic one running the mind of that person. In effect, we would become computers and computers would become us.

Even though the enthusiasts don't expect this vision to reach its "tipping point" before 2040 at the earliest, interest in this concept among the cyber-elite ensures that it will gain increased visibility in the coming decade. More importantly, its perceived feasibility will determine to a large extent how so-called "smart machines" will evolve, and what roles they will realistically play during the Golden Age of the Digital Revolution.

The Singularity: "artificial intelligence" meets hard reality

This brings us to two crucial questions:

1. Is there solid empirical evidence for believing that computing devices mimicking the functionality of the human brain can actually ever achieve a genuine state of "consciousness" (i.e., the ability to "think" in a way that is indistinguishable from a

57

human being)?

2. What capabilities can we expect commercial artificial intelligence to actually deliver, especially in the "Golden Age" immediately before us?

Obviously, these are the kind of questions that all of us should revisit periodically as human knowledge advances. However, we'll address them objectively from the perspective of 2013 to provide an initial starting point.

To answer the first question, let's start with consciousness itself. Consciousness has been defined as "an awareness of one's awareness." As humans, we take consciousness for granted. But imagine designing a *machine* that has the same capability. Such a machine would have the ability to actually "think and invent," not just "calculate, store and retrieve." As such, it would be able to design and build faster, more capable machines that, in turn, would build even faster, even more capable machines. At that point, technological progress enabled by smart machines would be so rapid that humans would be relegated to a peripheral role.

Beyond that point, which many call "the Singularity," machine consciousness and human consciousness could *theoretically* merge. Those who accept this vision believe that eventually, we will abandon our flesh-and-blood bodies entirely and upload our digitized psyches, including whatever gives us individual identity and consciousness, into computers. There, we will dwell happily forever in cyberspace.

Answering our first question will determine whether any of this is even realistic. Before we examine the facts and offer our assessment, let's review some relevant history:

John von Neumann, one of the pioneers of computer architecture, originally coined the term "Singularity" to describe the point beyond which progress is so rapid that for all practical purposes, it is infinite. The rate of technological innovation has been speeding up throughout history, and currently it is doubling about every 10 years. This broader rate of advance is eclipsed by the dizzying pace of improvements in IT. By every measure—including speed, capacity, bandwidth, and price-performance—the power of IT is now doubling about every 12 months.

By extrapolating this phenomenon into the future and imagining where it might lead, a small group within the world's technological elite is embracing an all-encompassing new vision of "the Singularity" and the world that lies beyond it. This vision (variously termed Singularitarian or "transhumanist") is being most articulately popularized by Kurzweil

As Kurzweil sees it, the Singularity will launch an era in which our intelligence will become trillions of times more powerful than it is today. He asserts that in this new world, there will be no distinction between human and machine, or between physical reality and virtual reality.

To understand Kurzweil's vision, you need to know about three of its fundamental elements:

- First, technological progress will continue to advance at an increasing rate. Already the accomplishments of the entire 20th century are equivalent to just 20 years of progress at today's rate of change. We'll make another stride equal to the progress of the whole 20th century in the next 14 years, and then we'll do it again in just 7 years. Kurzweil argues that because of the explosive power of exponential growth, the 21st century will be equivalent to 20,000 years of progress at today's rate of change.
- Second, within 40 years (give or take a decade) artificial intelligence will so dwarf human intelligence as to make our abilities nearly irrelevant.
- Third, at some point, around 2045 to 2050, Kurzweil believes the human consciousness will actually be uploaded to machines running our personalities, just as today's computers run software.

A small, but growing, number of computer scientists and futurists agree with these predictions, believing machines will successfully become the functional equivalents of the human mind in a matter of a few decades.

However, we respectfully disagree with these predictions.

To understand our skepticism, it's helpful to consider what we know about the brain.

A healthy adult brain contains about 100 billion nerve cells, or *neurons*. A single neuron can be linked to as many as 100,000 other neurons via output links called axons and input links called *dendrites,* via *synapses,* which are gaps between axons and dendrites.

Crunch the numbers and you find that a typical human brain has quadrillions of connections among its neurons. A quadrillion is a one followed by 15 zeroes.

These synaptic connections are constantly forming, strengthening, weakening, and dissolving. The latest research shows that old neurons constantly die and new ones are constantly born.

But that's simply the "physical structure" that we're finally beginning to superficially see and test. As we learn in Chapter 11, the practical implications of this work are enormous. However, it has not even scratched the surface when it comes to answering the question, "What creates consciousness itself?"

In a 2008 article titled, "Can Machines be Conscious?" authors Christof Koch and Giulio Tononi offer the following observation: "At the moment, nobody really knows exactly what consciousness is. Some of the most brilliant minds in human history have pondered consciousness, and after a few thousand years we still can't say for sure if it is an intangible phenomenon or maybe even a kind of substance different from matter."[1]

Nobel Prize-winning neuroscientist Eric Kandel of Columbia University Medical Center echoes that thought: "Neuroscientists still do not understand at all how a brain makes a conscious mind: the intangible entity that enables you to fall in love, find irony in a novel, and appreciate the elegance of a circuit design. No one has the foggiest notion."[2]

Without this understanding, it's hard to imagine how anyone could build an artificial brain sophisticated enough to sustain and nurture human consciousness.

Nevertheless, Singularitarians insist the brain *is* a computer. It just has an extremely messy wiring diagram. Looked at from this perspective, neurons resemble transistors, absorbing, processing, and re-emitting the electrochemical pulses.

According to Singularitarians, within a decade or so, computers will surpass the computational power of brains. And, they will leave us in their "cognitive dust" unless we embrace them through bionic convergence or uploading.

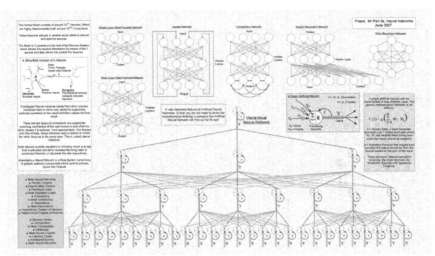

Source: Neural Networks by James Childs

Singularitarians are quite right that, if current trends continue, supercomputers will exceed 10 quadrillion operations per second within a decade.

And even now, attempts are being made to pit the fastest computers against humans to see if they can think like humans. One interesting match-up had IBM's supercomputer called "Watson" squaring off against Jeopardy game-show champions Ken Jennings and Brad Rutter. Watson is designed to show how computer systems can analyze and process natural language, and deliver predictions or answers based on context, like humans do.

To answer a question, Watson must churn through the 200 million pages of text that IBM loaded onto it, and with 10 refrigerator-sized racks of IBM Power7 systems, this task is done quite quickly. As it sifts through the information, it must determine the likelihood of an answer being correct.

In a 15-question practice round, Watson won. The question is: Did it *know* it won? Will computers ever have this kind of awareness?

61

Most experts are saying, "no."

Gerald Edelman, a Nobel laureate and director of the Neurosciences Institute, says Singularitarians do not comprehend just how complicated the human brain is. Each brain is different from other brains, and each of them is in a state of continuous change as it learns from new experiences.

In addition, Steven Rose, a neurobiologist at England's Open University, rejects the basic premise of uploading—that our psyches consist of nothing more than algorithms that can be transferred from our bodies to entirely different substrates, whether silicon or glass fibers or quantum computers. No evidence exists that the information processing that constitutes our selves can operate in any medium other than a social, emotional, flesh-and-blood primate.

However, it's understandable why people want to believe in such a vision of the future. In an article titled "The Consciousness Conundrum," in *IEEE Spectrum,* John Horgan sums up why there is popular belief in the Singularity. "Such yearning for transcendence, whether spiritual or technological, is all too understandable. Both as individuals and as a species, we face deadly serious problems."[3]

In other words, the prima facie evidence indicates that the Singularity is really a religious vision rather than a scientific one.

In the end, IBM's Watson may have appeared to be human-like to those observing the game, but no one could argue with the fact that internally, it was doing nothing more than processing logical instructions created by people. The only one in the room unaware of this was Watson.

Looking ahead, it is likely that by 2025, computers and the robot technologies we'll discuss in Chapter 5 will have improved exponentially, even as all but the most die-hard disciples begin to see the futility of the more controversial aspects of the Singularitarian vision. In many cases, computers will realistically mimic humans. However, we argue that the quest to unravel the ultimate mechanics of human thought will "hit a brick wall."

Kurzweil's models rest upon the naturalistic presumption that the mind and the personality are simply the product of patterns of chemical interactions within the brain, and if we simply dig deeply enough, we'll be able to completely understand it. That's a view held almost universally by secularists, because it eliminates the need for supernatural solutions. However, this inference isn't supported by a body of empirical data; at this point it's merely one of many unproven hypotheses.

We believe that between 2025 and 2030, it will become apparent to most that the quest for the "spiritual machine" is in vain. For example, while computers using genetic algorithms are likely to come up with innovations involving unexpected combinations of existing components, the "main line of technological progress" will continue to be constrained by human capabilities.

From that point forward, instead of continuing to progress at an ever-faster rate, the rate of acceleration will plateau at the level at which man, assisted by smart machines, is able to manage the process. Change will then continue to advance at a *roughly* constant rate, but likely much faster than we see today.

The impact on the economy

That brings us to our second, and far more important, question: "What capabilities can we expect commercial artificial intelligence to deliver?"

The rise of smart machines will happen quite naturally, requiring no grand plan or Congressional act or mandate. In fact, the less the government intercedes, the quicker and smoother the transition. The ability for companies and individuals to become more efficient, boost their productivity, and save money will drive the adoption of more and more smart devices that leverage our growing information infrastructure.

At the heart of this change is Moore's Law, which we examined in Chapter 2. As processing power escalates, what used to be science fiction is now common, everyday fact. Great strides in computers and devices are being made not in lifetimes, but in mere years.

The advance of processing power is following an exponential path; however, the first part of the curve, the part we have experienced so far, has been relatively flat and linear. But, we are now entering the part of the curve that begins to race upward at a tremendous rate. The implication is that we will begin to see jaw-dropping applications as the result of incredible processing power in small objects. Virtually every task, job, and industry will be affected.

Countries that learn to harness this coming wave will be the ones that will see tremendous economic growth and job creation. For an idea of how smart machines will be used to advance our economy, we turn to the world of chess.

In 1997, a $10 million specialized supercomputer called Deep Blue played the world's most brilliant human chess master, Garry Kasparov. The machine won—a first for the machines of the world. As machines grew more powerful and their wins became routine, a new category in the arena of chess competition was formed, which allowed any combination of people and machines to compete. Suddenly, the world's best chess player was a team of humans paired with computers.

The instructive lesson comes from one of these recent freestyle matches, where it wasn't the best human players, nor the most powerful computers, that won. Rather, two *amateur* American chess players using three computers were able to use their skill at manipulating and "coaching" their computers to counteract the superior chess understanding of their grandmaster opponents who had greater computational power, as well. In the end, their better process was superior to an inferior process.

Applying this insight to the business world, smart machines won't simply replace people; instead, effective strategies will be designed to unleash the combined capabilities of people and machines working together. Rather than racing against machines, people will race with them. This pattern will be true throughout the economy, in medicine, law, finance, retailing, manufacturing, and even scientific discovery.

This coupling of humans and machines will be so powerful because each possesses key strengths the other is lacking. Humans are the strongest where computers are the weakest, and vice versa. Computers are, of course, exceedingly fast at raw number crunching and providing virtually instant answers within predefined domains. Outside those domains, they are lost, and if a task requires intuition and creativity, they fail. In contrast, these are the very realms where humans excel. These differences create a powerful partnership.

The key is tapping into the potential of these partnerships to create jobs. This means going beyond simply having the technology available. As we've seen with every innovation in history, the new technologies will migrate across the globe. The sustainable differentiation will be in how they are used. It's likely that, as in the past, American ingenuity will devise the best new organizational structures, processes, and business models that will unleash the partnership between ever-advancing technology and human skills to create real value.

Already, we see examples of this pairing of abilities paying off.

In the medical field, healthcare workers are partnering with a system called Quick Medical Reference to diagnose diseases. Relying on artificial intelligence, which operates on a type of neural network called a Bayesian network, this system models 600 significant diseases and 4,000 related symptoms.

Other forms of artificial intelligence have greatly improved speech recognition, taking this technology from error-prone to impressively precise. For example, arduous transcribing of doctors' dictated notes is being replaced by efficient, direct-to-document models. Apple's Siri personal assistant is another example of speech recognition that is powerful enough to improve efficiencies.

IBM's Watson computer, which beat *Jeopardy!* champions at their own game, is being refined and augmented to work in healthcare, financial services, and customer relations. The vision is to have these systems partner with human agents, prompting them with appropriate questions and answers for particular situations.

In some industries, information technology is quickly making fixed hours, fixed locations, and fixed jobs obsolete. The payoff is in the way people can become more efficient and productive. For example, Best Buy has implemented a program called the "Results Only Work Environment," where workers have the freedom to do their work anytime and anywhere, based solely on their individual needs and preferences. The company has seen an average productivity increase of 35 percent, and a 90 percent decrease in voluntary turnover rates.[4]

Companies will succeed at leveraging the human/machine partnership by implementing a set of key principles. Specifically:

- Processes will be created that combine the speed of computers with human insight.
- Creativity of employees will be encouraged, with technology being used to test their creative ideas.
- New forms of human collaboration and commerce will be enabled by the leveraging of information technology.
- Human insight will be applied to IT-generated data to further improve effective processes.
- IT will be used to propagate the improved processes that people develop.

Because these worker-technology partnerships will evolve most rapidly in a free-market competitive environment, progress will depend on maximizing the number of creative entrepreneurs. That means entrepreneurial thinking needs to be encouraged early and often. This can be done through education, starting in the younger grades, and by creating clearinghouses and databases that provide templates for new "smart-machine" businesses. Another key step will be the elimination of the many governmental taxes and regulations that create barriers to business creation. The idea is to maximize the flow of ideas, encourage people to combine insights from different areas into new innovations, and eliminate bottlenecks to collaboration.

Chematica: the industry-transforming power of smart machines

Perhaps the clearest example of the smart machines on a trajectory to transform an entire economic sector is a system called Chematica. This software application developed by Bartosz Grzybowski and his team at Northwestern University is best described as a "collective chemical brain."[5]

Over a 10-year period, the team programmed over 250 years'

worth of chemistry knowledge into the package, including all the details associated with synthesizing over 17 million substances. But Chematica is more than just a big database. It can also be described as a massive search engine that enables chemists to search and analyze chemicals and reactions, as well as to synthesize new compounds.

Most importantly, it's a "knowledge base" that maps the optimal path from one reaction to another, in an efficient and environmentally-friendly manner. Helping drive this capability are the more than 86,000 rules about chemistry embedded in the software.

Early on, the Northwestern team realized they could do more than simply create a repository of chemical methods. So, they set out to create an entirely new knowledge platform by linking all the known chemical compounds and reactions between them into one giant network. The components that make this network truly useful are the algorithms that are used to search and analyze reactions, predicting what compounds can be made.

Grzybowski describes this process as "learning from the past and current structure of chemistry to project into its future." As he explains, "With appropriate network algorithms, we can traverse the network of reactions to explore all possible chemical syntheses, not only the few that chemists typically consider."

In contrast to the subjective criteria chemists have been taught, the Chematica algorithms rank the syntheses according to objective rules based on all cumulative chemical knowledge in the knowledge base.

As a result, this new technology offers at least five important benefits:

1. Speed
2. Innovation
3. Cost savings
4. Productivity
5. Safety

The first benefit is speed. Humans could never achieve the search speeds of this knowledge platform, which can explore billions of possible syntheses in a fraction of a second. From the results of these searches, the program can then select the synthesis route that is the most economical, or the most environmentally friendly, or the one that uses only easy-to-obtain chemicals.

Because Chematica is programmed to find synthetic shortcuts, it can identify ways to combine multiple reactions into one step. This can deliver what experts refer to as "the holy grail of organic chemistry": the one-pot synthesis. This involves the production of the desired "end results" in just one step.

Making the one-pot synthesis the norm wherever possible would provide a tremendous advantage over current multi-step pathways, where the purification of mid-step intermediary substances can account for up to 80 percent of the total cost of synthesizing the final product.

In a two-step reaction, for example, chemical A is converted into chemical B, which is converted into chemical C. But before the conversion from B to C can be made, in most cases chemical B needs to be purified, using techniques such as chromatographic columns, or environmentally dangerous solvents.

One-pot wonder

A key molecule with the potential to treat asthma normally takes four steps to produce. Chematica software shows how it can be done in one, and also shows one-step ways to produce other potential drugs in the same family

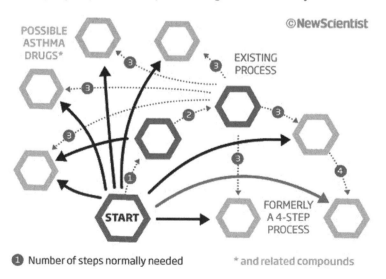

POSSIBLE ASTHMA DRUGS*

©NewScientist

EXISTING PROCESS

START

FORMERLY A 4-STEP PROCESS

❶ Number of steps normally needed   * and related compounds

It's not uncommon for there to be as many as 15 steps to get to the end result. Each step, with its needed purification, adds extra chemicals, waste products, and of course, extra time. All of that translates into added cost.

Using Chematica, chemists can now search for and evaluate one-pot sequences in mere seconds. In fact, even in its infancy, Chematica has already determined over 1 million previously unknown one-pot reactions. Over 30 of these predicted reactions have been tested in the lab and have proceeded very cleanly, with excellent yields.

Another enormous benefit of this tool is its ability to mimic the serendipity that often leads to innovation. Researchers are using it to discover multiple new pathways to a particular result that can require many fewer steps or permit the use of alternative chemical compounds as inputs. One of the reasons Chematica is proving to be so useful is that it arrives at alternative syntheses in unintuitive ways. In other words, it is delivering beneficial alternatives that no human chemist would have ever discovered except by sheer accident.

The Chematica software is being marketed by Grzybowski's company ProChimia. Not surprisingly, one of the first companies to adopt Chematica was an industrial chemical company. As a producer of 51 products, the company leveraged the software to refine its processes, resulting in a 45 percent reduction in production costs. These optimized processes also reduced the production of environmentally harmful substances and overall waste.

Grzybowski reports that one of the most exciting examples to date was the simplification of an anti-asthma drug synthesis. Upon analysis, the computer predicted the four steps of this synthesis could be combined into one. An actual test of the reaction confirmed this conclusion, resulting in a doubling of the yield and eliminating the cost of purification at the middle steps. There are similar success stories taking place at other pharmaceutical companies.

This reveals another of the key benefits that Chematica has to offer: cost savings through efficiency. These savings could be enormous due to:

- Reduction in input chemical costs

- Reduction in time spent
- Reduction in the cost of dealing with waste

Just as significant are increases in productivity due to higher yields. ProChimia has identified new syntheses in which yields are significantly higher than traditional multi-step syntheses.

Increased safety is yet another benefit. Using Chematica, researchers can determine if a proposed mixture is dangerous before they actually combine the chemicals.

Just as there is a potential negative side to most things, there is a possible dark side to this knowledge platform. Those with evil intent could use this tool to more easily make dangerous substances. Sarin gas, for example, currently requires about 17 different chemical processes to be synthesized. The big question is, "What if this software reveals a pathway to the same endpoint using only three processes?" Even worse, "What if all the needed inputs were available at a local discount store?"

This scenario brings us to another benefit of Chematica that could potentially turn this negative on its head. As Grzybowski explains: "Since we now have this unique ability to scrutinize all possible synthetic strategies, we also can identify the ones that a potential terrorist might use to make a nerve gas, an explosive, or another toxic agent." This observation by Grzybowski suggests that knowing the pathways that might be taken for lethal substances will make it easier to track and recognize dangerous behavior.

The arrival of the Chematica knowledge base is a solid example that the Golden Age of the Digital Revolution is at hand. Why? Because information technology has achieved the critical mass necessary to fundamentally transform established industry sectors such as chemicals.

It was the maturing of IT that enabled Grzybowski to act on an observation that he, like many before, had made. He lamented the fact that so much of the knowledge amassed during the careers of trained chemists disappears when they retire. He also noticed that although we were in the midst of a technological revolution where everything was being networked, this was not happening in the field of chemistry. It was remaining fragmented. Pairing the modern-day power of IT

70

with the entirety of chemistry, Grzybowski has now created what he calls the "immortal scientist."

Super-turing computers: another approach

In this chapter, we've discussed why we believe the Singularitarian vision is flawed, and we've presented an alternate view, in which smart machines and smart humans will work together to achieve more than either could alone. Now let's consider another possibility: an innovative computing architecture that mimics the brain's own structure.

As we've discussed in the article, MACHINE LEARNING AND THE FUTURE OF ARTIFICIAL INTELLIGENCE, published in *Trends* Magazine, researchers have recently begun to explore the possibility that analog computers, based on so-called "neural networks," will be able to exhibit certain abilities of the human brain that are beyond the capabilities of current digital computers.

Consider the facts. We humans learn, for example, that an object in the foreground that creates a large retinal image in the eye can actually be smaller than an object in the distance that projects a smaller image on the retina.

It's also easy for a human to recognize a tiger running behind some bushes in a nature video even when very few visual clues are provided; for today's best digital image processors, this is a daunting task. Similarly, humans have the capability to distinguish between male and female faces, a task that proves very difficult for artificial vision systems.

That's because our minds, unlike digital computers, are also able to perform data mining very efficiently. This enables us to pick out the relevant data in an image and filter out the irrelevant. No classical algorithm can perform this complicated task.

In a related manner, our brains can work in different modes of operation, automatically switching between them. We can, for example, focus on crossing a busy street while ignoring the birds singing—even though our ears detect the sound wave—and while also ignoring the advertising message on a passing bus—even though the

71

image appears on our retinas.

Amazingly, we accomplish this without any energy or conscious effort; we select the desired sensitivity and level of attention based on the task that needs to be done. This type of adaptation and mode change has proven to be very difficult to design into an artificial system.

However, humans don't achieve better performance in this kind of complicated computing because our brains work faster than conventional computers. In fact, our neurons are five to six orders of magnitude slower than a silicon logic gate. The big difference lies in the structure of our brains, which are made up of a highly parallel architecture of neurons.

Information is continuously being transferred, creating a dynamic system that lacks static memory, yet it remembers. Unlike the static architecture of today's digital computers, the architecture of the human brain adapts and changes as part of the learning experience.

It is the replication of this adaptive structure in computers built around a neural network architecture that offers the promise of new levels of computing. This requires a departure from the established concepts of computing based on the theoretical work of mathematician Alan Turing during the 1930s.

Since the early '90s, Professor Hava Siegelmann of the University of Massachusetts Amherst has been working on moving Turing's ideas to the next logical level by using neural networks. The end product of this new paradigm is referred to as a Super-Turing machine.

Using an analogy to describe the difference between the concepts, Siegelmann states, "If a Turing machine is like a train on a fixed track, a Super-Turing machine is like an airplane. It can haul a heavy load, but also move in endless directions and can vary its destination as needed."[6]

Siegelmann also explains that much like the adapting human brain, a neural computer can change at each computational step in response to a stimulus.

The computational model that Siegelmann envisions includes a conventional collection of neurons plus loops. What's lacking is the familiar distinction of a memory region and a processing unit found in a conventional computer. Instead, memory and processing are strongly coupled.

The whole structure acts as a complex dynamical system, where the connections and influences between neurons are represented by real numbers. As a result, the processing of information has more in common with physics than conventional computing. And this is why learning can occur.

Digital computers operate within a so-called "discrete-space model." As the computer functions, the conventional computing paradigms don't change; they are static.

On the other hand, a neural network can evolve dynamically because it is in a "continuous-phase space." Such a computer, with the ability to change its internal constants, can evolve and react to incoming stimuli. So, when a Super-Turing computer of this type gets input, it literally becomes a different machine.

In reporting on her research, Siegelmann shows that when immersed in an environment that offers constant sensory stimuli, such as the real world, a neural network Super-Turing machine will exhibit a greater set of behaviors than would a conventional computer.

What's ahead?

In the near future, smart machines will create an unprecedented level of creative destruction, which will open up a new world of niches for prepared entrepreneurs to populate. These entrepreneurs will, in fact, play a central role in the cycle of disruption. They will capitalize on the stagnation of median wages and slow job growth to create new business models that will create value by combining mid-skilled workers and cheap, powerful technologies. The possibilities for combinations will be endless and the opportunities will be great. And, even if technological advances ended today, there would be no shortage of combinations to try.

Even now, the possibilities are excellent for creating new business processes, business models, and products by reconfiguring

73

the many different applications, machines, tasks, and distribution channels. And, far greater potential still lies ahead.

First, by 2025, computerized diagnostic systems will be working in tandem with para-physicians to address the looming physician shortage. In 2012 the Association of American Medical Colleges predicted that as soon as 2020, the physician shortage will amount to more than 90,000 doctors, including 45,000 patient care physicians; many experts believe this forecast is optimistic.[7] Throughout history, industry after industry has been transformed by division of labor and automation. By 2025, almost all *routine* diagnoses will be performed by medical technicians and "physician's assistants" using lab equipment tied to computers millions of times as powerful as IBM's Watson. The result will be greatly reduced health care costs and much better outcomes.

Second, within as little as five years, Chematica will transform the science of chemistry and pave the way for similar systems in other industries. It's already clear that this software will have a positive effect in the pharmaceutical industry for creating new drugs. In the energy sector, this tool will likely be used to create better and more environmentally friendly fuels. Since the plastics industry is so solidly based on chemical reactions, the effect of creating less-harmful plastics with fewer steps and lower costs will be profound. This will ultimately lead to new, cost-effective materials that will change the economics of entire industries ranging from aerospace, to automobiles, to food, to retailing. More important for working chemists, the automation of synthetic organic chemistry will shift the emphasis from how to synthesize chemicals to what needs to be synthesized. There will initially be some skepticism that a computer program will be able to match human creativity. However, the same thing was said about computerizing other activities such as math and chess, and in both of those arenas computers are now frequently surpassing human ability. Computers are even making great strides against human creativity in music and the visual arts. Since chemical synthesis is highly rule-bound, as is music, it is a good candidate for algorithmic derivation. Naturally, human design of synthetic schemes will not become obsolete, but it will become greatly overshadowed.

Third, by 2020, Super-Turing computers based on neural

networks will prove themselves in many applications requiring learning and adaptation. This technology is likely to pay big dividends in the service robotics applications that we'll discuss in Chapter 4.

Fourth, by the time the new Golden Age ends, real-time voice-to-voice language translation will be a commonplace commercial reality. The real game-changer for spoken language translation won't come until a system can translate in real time, as two speakers speak at a natural pace. This will only be possible when the required computing power becomes cost-effective. That may happen in the next 10 years, but could take as long as 20 years.

Fifth, accurate real-time machine translation of spoken conversation will revolutionize business and education. Coupled with social networking and mobile technology, real-time translation will suddenly demolish long-standing cultural barriers and trigger an unprecedented exchange of information worldwide. That exchange will, in turn, release waves of innovation.

Sixth, AI-based business "decision-support systems" will be necessary to compete in most B2C and B2B markets by 2025. These systems will include merchandise planning and pricing systems for retailers, recommendation engines for on-line retailers, supply chain optimization systems for manufacturers, and business intelligence systems that explore the Internet, collecting and interpreting customer sentiments from social networks. Fortunately, cloud-based technology will provide small and mid-sized firms cost-effective access to these smart applications.

Seventh, applying smart machines to terabyte data-sets will generate new waves of productivity growth and consumer surplus. The increase in actionable information will improve efficiency and effectiveness. This represents a move past the benefits of the first stage of the Internet, where computing and low-cost communications were combined to facilitate commercial transactions. In this next stage, Internet-scale data-sets will be leveraged to establish whole new businesses, as well as to predict consumer behavior and market shifts that are crucial for established businesses. In the process, companies will discover ways to do more with less, producing higher-quality products and services. This productivity growth will lead to savings that will accrue to both firms and their customers. For example:

- According to McKinsey & Company, retailers that fully leverage big data could potentially increase their operating margins by more than 60 percent.[8]
- Similarly, the U.S. healthcare system could easily create $300 billion a year in additional value, mostly by improving treatment decisions through more complete information.
- Consumers could realize savings of more than $600 billion a year worldwide just from services enabled by "personal location data," alone.

Eighth, within the next five years, smart machines will enable public and private organizations to quickly and reliably determine the veracity of the statements people make. For instance, a system developed by the University at Buffalo is already showing promising results. The system, which analyzes eye movements, correctly identified whether interview subjects were lying or telling the truth 82.5 percent of the time. That's about the same accuracy rate as a polygraph. Over time, as the system is refined, it is likely to provide even more reliable results.

5

What are service robots and how will they change our lives, our cities, and our businesses?

"The Three Laws of Robotics:

1. A robot may not injure a human being or, through inaction, allow a human being to come to harm.

2. A robot must obey the orders given it by human beings except where such orders would conflict with the First Law.

3. A robot must protect its own existence as long as such protection does not conflict with the First or Second Law.

"The Zeroth Law: A robot may not harm humanity, or, by inaction, allow humanity to come to harm."

--Isaac Asimov, *I, Robot*

In science-fiction novels, robots are routinely depicted as anthropomorphic automatons that are a just a random software glitch away from going on a destructive rampage. But the service robots that will become increasingly common in our everyday lives as this century progresses will be manufactured in a variety of shapes for a multitude of uses, and they are about as likely to cause mayhem as an ordinary household toaster or vacuum cleaner.

We have been tracking the evolution of "service robots" for many years. As we define them, service robots include self-driving cars, self-piloting airplanes, and autonomous wheelchairs, as well as C3PO-like anthropomorphic robots and simple cleaning robots such as the iRobot Roomba.

The International Federation of Robotics (IFR) defines a service robot is "a robot which operates semi- or fully autonomously to perform services useful to the well-being of humans and equipment, excluding manufacturing operations."

Robots have been commonplace in factories for decades, and their numbers are growing every year. According to the Robotic Industries Association, during the first nine months of 2012, North American businesses spent $1.1 billion on 16,363 factory robots, an increase of 29 percent in price and 20 percent in units.[1]

But now, a new generation of robots is also beginning to show up in homes, offices, and hospitals, as well as on the battlefield. The more sophisticated robots are looking for snipers, minding children, caring for the elderly, acting as tour guides, and giving people baths or doses of medicine. Less advanced units are performing basic tasks like cleaning floors and mowing lawns. As with all digital technologies, the prices of robots are falling, while at the same time, their capabilities are growing rapidly.

According to IFR, 16,408 professional *service* robots were sold in 2011, the most recent year for which figures are available; that's a 9 percent increase from 2010.[2] Total sales reached $3.6 billion, up 6 percent. The three most common uses for professional service robots are:

- Military and defense applications, such as unmanned aerial vehicles, which surged to 40 percent of the units sold.
- Field applications, such as milking robots, which accounted for 25 percent.
- Medical applications, including robot-assisted surgery, which totaled 6 percent of units sold.

Other uses of professional service robots include:

- Construction and demolition
- Professional cleaning, inspection, and maintenance
- Rescue and security
- Underwater systems

Meanwhile, the market for personal and domestic service robots is growing rapidly. In 2011, roughly 2.5 million mass-market service robots were sold for personal and home use, an increase of 15 percent over the previous year. Total sales of personal and domestic services robots rose 19 percent to $636 million.[3]

The most common uses for these service robots include:

- Vacuuming and floor cleaning
- Lawn maintenance
- Entertainment and leisure, such as toy robots

We've explored many of the advances that are making robots more powerful and more useful in *Trends*. For in-depth discussions, please refer to:

- **ROBOTS ADOPT HUMAN-LIKE ANATOMY**
  (http://www.audiotech.com/trends-magazine/robots-adopt-humanlike-anatomy)
- **ROBOTS THAT FEEL OUR PAIN**
  (http://www.audiotech.com/trends-magazine/robots-that-feel-our-pain)
- **THE SERVICE ROBOT ECOSYSTEM EVOLVES**
  (http://www.audiotech.com/trends-magazine/service-robot-ecosystem-evolves)
- **ADVANCED MANUFACTURING: THE KEY TO AMERICA'S INNOVATION ADVANTAGE**
  (http://www.audiotech.com/trends-magazine/advanced-manufacturing-the-key-to-americas-innovation-advantage)
- **AUTOMATION AND THE FUTURE OF AMERICAN AGRICULTURE**
  (http://www.audiotech.com/trends-magazine/automation-and-the-future-of-american-agriculture)
- **ROBOTS ARE SET TO OVERHAUL SERVICE INDUSTRIES**
  (http://www.audiotech.com/trends-magazine/robots-are-set-to-overhaul-service-industries)
- **MACHINES THAT CAN SEE**

(http://www.audiotech.com/trends-magazine/machines-that-can-see)

Who is winning the robot wars?

Currently, the world leaders in robotic research are Japan and the United States, though some important development work is also coming out of European institutions. There are, however, dramatic differences in the focus of what American and Japanese robots are being targeted to do.

Source: www.globalsecurity.org
The Gladiator robot, developed for the Marine Corps by Carnegie Mellon University, is directly controlled via an interface system worn on a soldier's vest.

In the U.S., the primary emphasis is on military applications, where robots will be used in place of humans for dangerous battlefield situations. Human soldiers will not be replaced entirely; but the parts of their jobs having the greatest potential for harm will be carried out by expendable robots. As long as we are engaging in a fight against terrorism, this will be a well-placed priority.

For example, *The Economist* recently reported on several military robots:[4]

Source: Foster-Miller, Inc.
This TALON robot from Foster-Miller is configured with a 50-caliber machine gun. It is one of many military robots that contractors have developed for the U.S. armed forces.

- The SUGV is the size of a briefcase. Made by iRobot, the manufacturer of the Roomba vacuum cleaner based in Bedford, Massachusetts, the SUGV can scan faces to identify a suspect from a mugshot, and then follow him through a crowd.
- Another iRobot innovation, the FirstLook, can be thrown over a wall or into an open window; once inside a target area, it uses four cameras to transmit images of its surroundings so soldiers know what to expect before they attack.
- The Scout XT Throwbot can be hurled through closed windows. It is has a spiked wheel on each end that allows it to crawl on uneven surfaces. Recon Robotics of Edina, Minnesota, has already received a $14 million order from the U.S. Army for 1,100 Throwbots.

On the other hand, Japan is looking to place robots in a very different role—one that will ultimately become quite common worldwide: that of "caregivers to the aged."

Japan is ahead of the curve in this regard because the country's aging population will increasingly need long-term nursing care. Consider these numbers:

- Nearly 20 percent of the Japanese population is already over 65—the highest percentage in the world. In rural Japan, it's 25 percent.
- It's projected that the number of Japanese who will need nursing care by 2015 will number 5.7 million.
- Meanwhile, there was a record low of only 16.9 million Japanese children under the age of 15 in 2010.

These factors are combining to create a shortage of healthcare workers and the revenues to support the elderly—right when they will be most needed. So, it's hoped that armies of robotic caregivers will be ready to march in to fill the void.

But there is another very important reason Japan will likely lead the way in care-giving robotic technology: Japanese culture highly values precision in every aspect of life. MIT-trained robotics engineer Dylan Glas, who has lived and worked in Japan for over eight years, offers some useful insights about Japan's adoption of service robots.

In a past issue of *The Futurist,* Glas observes, "At work, there is no deviation from the established best practice. When I go to the supermarket, they always say exactly the same thing and deliver customer service exactly the same way. So I think the idea of robots doing that sort of work is very natural."[5] This mindset helps explain why Japan has consistently led the world in the adoption of industrial robots.

Adding to this willingness to accept robotic caregivers and other service robots is the Japanese population's aversion to immigrants. This leaves the country without a source of cheap human labor to handle care-giving chores.

When these factors are added up—an aging and decreasing population, an acceptance of automation, and an aversion to immigrant

82

labor—it's clear why Japan will be the leader in humanoid robotic research and development.

Because its needs are so desperate, the Japanese are more likely to accept robot caregivers that are merely "good enough"—that is, at a lower level of sophistication than would be accepted by people in most other affluent nations where there is easy access to immigrant labor.

This dynamic is significant because, as Harvard's Clayton Christensen explains, most disruptive technologies enter the market at the low end, serving those for whom the technology is barely "good enough." In the case of service robots, the lack of acceptable human alternatives in Japan has hospitals, nursing homes, and private residences waiting eagerly for robotic caregivers—even the models that are still in the early stages of development.

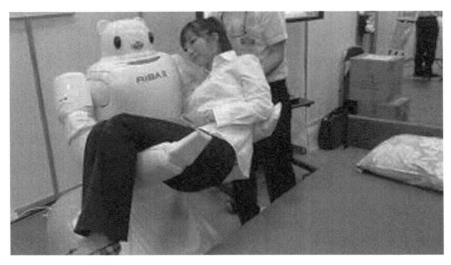

Source: RIKEN
The RIBA II, developed by researchers at Japan's RIKEN Institute, can lift a patient weighing up to 80kg off floor-level bedding and into a wheelchair, freeing care facility personnel of one of their most challenging tasks. With its sophisticated tactile sensors and precision movements, it represents another step toward addressing Japan's enormous elder-care challenge.

In all likelihood, robotic caregivers will follow the usual path of disruptive technologies. Over time, the technology becomes so good that it takes over everything except the highest end of the market. Those companies that aren't in the market early run the risk of being left behind, since the early entrants with the "good enough" solutions will get the opportunity to learn and build brand equity.

Service robots still fall short of the characteristics needed for large-scale adoption. However, researchers are converging on that point more quickly than generally realized. Just consider six R&D achievements:

1. Ashutosh Saxena, an assistant professor of computer science at Cornell, along with graduate student Yun Jiang, developed a fast and efficient algorithm that uses images from a camera to identify the best places on objects for a robotic arm to grasp.[6] This may sound mundane, yet to do practical, helpful tasks, it will be necessary for service robots to master the ability to pick up objects they have never seen before.

2. Possibly as important will be a robot's ability to "feel" through its "skin" as humans do. Scientists at the Institute of Cognitive Systems at the Technical University of Munich are now developing an artificial skin that will enable a robot to gain tactile information that will enhance its perception of its surroundings and nearby objects when that information is combined with input from other sources, such as cameras and infrared scanners.[7]

3. Researchers at the Georgia Institute of Technology recently focused on how people react to being touched by a robotic nurse—an important issue for the future of healthcare service robots. In their study, people had a generally positive response toward being touched, as long as the intent was to perform a task, such as cleaning, but not to comfort.[8] Interestingly, these results mirror those from similar studies done with human caregivers.

4. Not only will robots need to touch us, their usefulness and effectiveness will be enhanced if they can get "in touch" with us by reading our emotions. Researchers at the Polytechnic University in Madrid have developed an automated voice analysis program that analyzes the sound measurements of a conversation to deduce human emotion.[9] Another approach is envisioned by European researchers who are using artificial

neural networks that are adept at reading varied and changing inputs in order to learn if a person is sad, happy, or angry. Emotion-reading robots are desirable because they will be more-readily accepted by the people they serve.

5. To enable placement of robots in unsupervised environments where they will operate independently, engineers at NUI Galway and the University of Ulster are mimicking the neuron structure and operation of the human brain with bio-inspired, integrated circuit technology. Training is similar to the human brain where links between neurons are made and strengthened. Dr. Fearghal Morgan, one of the directors at NUI Galway, explains the researchers' goal: "Our aim is to develop a robust, intelligent hardware neural network robotics controller which can autonomously maintain robot behavior, even when its environment changes or a fault occurs within the robotics system."[10]

6. European researchers, led by scientists and engineers at Eindhoven University of Technology in the Netherlands, are designing an end-to-end system that includes robots within a smart home. The goal is to make it possible for elderly people to live independently, at home and without full-time human caregivers, for far longer than otherwise would be possible. Two of the robots for the smart home have already been delivered for testing. Those robots communicate with each other and with alarms, reporting hardware, and software that contacts live operators if a problem arises. The system also integrates with special clothing for the home's human occupants which monitors each wearer's vital signs. The system also reminds people in the smart house when to eat or when to take medication. The robots assist the elderly people to make phone calls, create shopping lists, and do other everyday tasks, such as retrieving items from high shelves or opening the curtains.[11]

The smart home of the future will soon be a reality

Smart homes won't just be for the elderly. Increasingly, as more and more of our digital devices and appliances are networked, our homes will evolve into residences that meet our needs in unprecedented ways. Looking ahead 15 years, we can say with some certainty that Americans will be older, richer, and more security-conscious. We'll need:

- Better monitoring of our health condition.
- Ways to reduce the amount of work we have to put into maintaining our homes.
- Even more entertainment options.
- A high degree of safety and security.

Technologically, it's fair to say that the price performance of CPUs, bandwidth, and data storage will be at least 10,000 times better than it is today. That means that low-cost networked computing will be buried within almost every appliance, toy, and tool. And, because of networking, every appliance could take advantage of the home's computing power, sensors, or media connection. As we'll discuss, three of the biggest areas of technological progress will be as follows:

- **Smart appliances** will eliminate the drudgery of kitchen chores, including ordering groceries, preparing meals, and cleaning dishes.
- **Robots** will perform many housekeeping duties, from vacuuming floors to folding laundry.
- **Digital wallpapers, paints, and fabrics** will enable us to redecorate our homes in real time.

First, let's talk about smart appliances and the digital home. The home of the future will include systems that control all of the home's computing, media, lighting, heating and cooling, and security. More than 20 years ago, the early PCs could work with X-10 controllers or similar technologies to control the lighting and appliances in a home. It never really caught on because of the effort required to integrate and coordinate all of the "dumb" appliances.

However, the appliances of 2028 are going to be "intelligent." And they'll be able to carry on a continuous dialogue with other appliances in the home. Standards will be developed to ensure that the communication is seamless and unambiguous.

Obviously, a crucial component of such a network would be the HVAC and plumbing systems. To give us an idea of how that might work, General Electric has developed its own vision of the home of the future. On its Web site, GE describes a Total Environment Control Unit, which would be a single device that would heat and cool the home, plus use reverse osmosis water purification to filter the home's drinking water.

Because computers are getting so small, inexpensive, and ubiquitous, the PC as we've known it will essentially disappear from the home of 2028. To illustrate this, Microsoft's concept home of the future does not include desktop PCs or laptops. The operating assumption is that computing power, mesh networking, and thin LCD screens will become so cheap that people will be able to interact with computers no matter where they are in their homes.

For example, touch-sensitive organic LED screens under the paint on every wall gives the owners an easy way to access the home's computer system. When e-mail arrives, a light display shaped like a sculpture in the corner of the living room flashes red.

When a visitor rings the doorbell, his picture is taken with a digital camera and transmitted to the homeowner's cell-phone. The homeowner then has the option of talking to the visitor or pushing a button on his cell-phone to unlock the door.

According to Eric Lai of PCAdvisor, even the bulletin board in the kitchen of the Microsoft concept home is digital. When a party invitation is pinned to it, the question "Accept invitation, yes or no?" appears on the display below it. The bulletin board is also able to read the RFID tags on coupons. For example, when a pizza coupon is pinned to the board, the restaurant's menu and phone number is displayed.

We can glimpse the potential of tomorrow's smart appliances by looking at some products that are just starting to emerge from the pipeline. Here are six examples:

The smart coffee maker. We already have fully-automated espresso machines that grind the beans, brew the coffee, froth the milk, combine the ingredients in the cup, and dispose of the grounds. As long as water and electricity are connected, all you have to do is add roasted beans to a hopper. As these machines become more reliable and cheaper, they will typify a new set of smart appliances. With the inclusion of a network interface, it will be able to check to make sure you have plenty of coffee beans and milk by reading the perpetual inventory of the refrigerator and kitchen cabinets. If authorized, it would simply add any items in short supply to your electronic shopping list.

The intelligent oven. Retailing at $7,495, the Intelligent Oven allows users to program it remotely by phone or Internet so that meals are ready when they come home. Sold online by TMIO, the oven also includes built-in refrigeration to keep foods fresh before and after cooking. Twenty years from now, the need for refrigeration and planning ahead for the evening meal may be a thing of the past. A specialized robotic appliance will be able to remove packaged meals from the refrigerator and place them in the oven. Robots are unlikely to be well suited to preparing gourmet meals from scratch in 20 years, but they will be dexterous enough to retrieve trays long before that time. Identification will be simplified by RFID tags—or ordinary barcodes.

The digital refrigerator. Manufacturers of refrigerators are starting to include computers in the units. As you put your groceries away, the computer scans the bar code on each item and creates a shopping list for your next trip to the supermarket. As RFID tags become ubiquitous, this will become simpler and inventory will be updated in real time.

The networked washer and dryer. Among the new appliances integrated into the NextGen concept home on display at the 2013 CES were a combined washer and dryer appliance by LG. Just add dirty clothes, detergent, and fabric softener. The appliance cleans and dries the clothes automatically. It then alerts the rest of the network when the drying cycle is finished with a pop-up message on the digital home's television and computer screens. You just need to fold the clothes and put them away. As we'll discuss shortly, in Bill Gates' latest vision, that task could be handled by a specialized robot.

In addition to the smart appliances in the digital home, the second major transformation will be the mainstream use of robots in the home. However, most of them won't be anthropomorphic, general-purpose robots like Honda's Asimo or C3PO from Start Wars. Instead, they will be mobile units with artificial intelligence, designed to perform very specific tasks.

Precursors of these robots are already on the market. Robotic lawnmowers, such as the RoboMower from Friendly Robotics, automatically trim lawns. The robotic mowers use sensors to identify trees, rocks, and other obstacles. After a one-time set-up that involves placing a guide wire around the outer edges of the lawn to mark the boundaries for the mower, the robot can be programmed to automatically start cutting the grass at a specified day and time, and to return to the charging station by itself.

The Robomower by Friendly Robots is shown in its re-charging station.

Then there's the Roomba robotic vacuum cleaner, which cleans carpets. Its manufacturer, iRobot, has sold more than 6 million units. The Roomba zooms around a house, vacuuming and using sensors to avoid walls and furniture. It relies on algorithms such as wall-following and spiral-cleaning to cover all of the space in each room.

iRobot also launched the Scooba, which is a robotic floor washer. Similar to the RoboMower and the Roomba, the Scooba scoots around hardwood and tile floors. It squirts cleaning solution on the floor, scrubs it in, and then absorbs the dirty water.

These models are just the early versions of the robots that will one day make our lives easier. Bill Gates compares today's robotics industry with the personal computing industry of 30 years ago. Robotics lacks a standard operating software system to allow programs to run on different robots, so designers usually have to start from scratch when they design new robots.

Gates suggests that networks of wireless robots could be linked to desktop PCs so they could tap into the processing power of computers to navigate around a house, identify people and objects, and recognize speech. By taking advantage of voice recognition software, distributed computing, and sensors such as laser range finders, robots will achieve a quantum leap in usefulness.

As Gates points out, the barriers to broad market penetration of robots in everyday life are falling rapidly. For example, hardware costs are plummeting. The cost of laser range finders, which robots use to measure distance, is dropping from $10,000 a few years ago to under $2,000 today.

Also, the amazing progress we've made in computing power is helping scientists to solve many of the remaining challenges, such as giving robots the capability to orient themselves in a room and to understand not just words, but what the words mean in context. A megahertz of processing power cost $7,000 in the 1970s; now it costs just pennies. As computing power continues to expand, Gates believes that robot designers will build better and cheaper machines that will ultimately reach critical mass.

Gates envisions a home in which robots clean the floors, dispense food and medicine, fold laundry, mow the lawn, and provide security. He cites predictions by the Japan Robot Association that robotics will become a $50 billion industry in 2025, compared to $5 billion today.

Once again "demography is destiny." Japanese companies are already developing robots to care for its aging population. Some robots can help patients get in and out of bed. Another machine operates like a washing machine for humans, by giving them a bath.

Finally, the third major transformation that will revolutionize the home of the future is advances in materials that will allow us to redecorate our surroundings in real time.

For example, the NextGen home of the future at the CES used new materials technology—which is being developed at such companies as Philips Electronics—that will display huge photos or video from the Internet.

Meanwhile, Northwestern University researchers, led by chemistry and materials science professor Tobin Marks, have developed transparent transistors that can be manufactured at low cost, yet perform to high standards. In fact, they provide a sharper picture than the transistors used in today's LCD television screens.

What this means, according to a report in *Technology Review*, is that clear, crisp displays could be laminated on to surfaces to serve as televisions and computer monitors, and then become invisible when they were not being used. Also, as the journal *Nature Materials* reports, the process could be used to embed displays on windows or on a plastic substrate, which would mean consumers could have flexible transparent displays anywhere throughout the house.

In a related development, a team of Cornell University researchers has created a new type of organic semiconductor that acts as a photovoltaic cell. Like the Northwestern breakthrough, this technology, which uses an "ionic junction," could lead to semiconductors that could be produced on flexible sheets and used to create displays on cloth or paper. However, the journal *Science* reports that another use of the research could be to create cheap solar cells. Ultimately, the home of 2028 could store enough energy from hundreds or thousands of solar cells in the roof and walls to power all of the devices inside of it.

Driverless cars will soon accelerate into the mainstream

It won't be just our homes that will get smarter; our cars will, too. Recall the definition of service robots as "a robot that operates semi- or fully-autonomously to perform services useful to the well-being of humans and equipment." If we broaden that definition to encompass *any machine* that performs such services, it's clear that vehicles will soon qualify.

In just one generation of drivers, the experience of driving a car has evolved dramatically. A typical economy-class car now includes such standard features as automatic transmission, power windows, and cruise control. Higher-end models offer intelligent transportation systems, such as enhanced cruise control and self-parking technology. According to *Businessweek,* the demand for such intelligent transportation systems has grown into a $48 billion industry in the U.S.[12]

But while all of those improvements make driving easier than ever, they are designed with human drivers in mind. By the end of this decade, that will begin to change, and we'll witness the biggest change in personal transportation since the Model T replaced the carriage horse. Thanks to the rapid acceleration of technological progress, cars will begin to drive themselves.

We've been following the progress of this technology for more than a decade. We're now pleased to report that all of the necessary trends—in demographics, psychology, and technology—are finally converging to make driverless cars a reality:

- First, demographic trends support the need for autonomous vehicles. The aging of the population is increasing the demand for cars that will enable drivers with weakened eyesight and slower reflexes to remain both mobile and independent. At the other end of the age spectrum, young people are increasingly reluctant to drive. According to a U.S. Public Interest Research Group report, the number of vehicle miles driven by Americans aged 16 to 34 dropped 23 percent during the past decade.[13]
- Second, consumers of all ages are increasingly becoming prepared psychologically to cede control of the steering wheel. Self-parking technology, crash-avoidance systems, and telematics have made consumers comfortable with intelligent transportation systems.
- Third, the key supporting technologies of a driverless-car system are now in place. The "Internet of things" and improved GPS technology have paved the way for vehicles that know exactly where they are and can report their status to other vehicles around them. Enormous geographic databases such as Google Maps and its "StreetView" feature enable vehicles to

recognize landmarks and synchronize them with GPS data. The relentless advance of Moore's law has made the necessary computing power available at very low cost. Wireless communication infrastructure has made instant access to databases and sensor networks shared between multiple vehicles a cost-effective reality.

With all of these forces in favor of the new paradigm, the automobile manufacturers are fast-tracking the development of their autonomous car programs. Among the companies that are known to be working on driverless cars are Ford, Volkswagen, BMW, Mercedes-Benz, Volvo, Cadillac, and Audi.

According to *Businessweek,* while the driverless car systems vary in design, they typically include GPS, cameras, lasers, and radar to identify the car's position on the road, the location of obstacles and pedestrians, and its distance from other vehicles, as well as laser-fast processors to combine all the data and enable the car to react in real time.[14]

The early results are promising: BMW's engineers have programmed a 3 Series vehicle to drive itself safely around a speedway at 75 miles per hour with human passengers, slowing to 40 miles per hour at a treacherous S-curve. Google has modified a Prius with a roof-mounted lidar unit, which slowly revolves to scan its surroundings; the Prius has already driven itself 300,000 miles in normal traffic in California.

Moreover, the new technology has already passed an important legal hurdle. California and Nevada have passed laws that will allow consumers to operate driverless cars on state roads after safety standards are set for their use. Other states will soon follow. Each car would have to be tested to ensure that it met those standards, and owners of such cars would have to apply for a special permit to use them.

Ultimately, an autonomous car will drive itself for every mile of every trip, but when these cars *first* hit the market, humans will drive the car until it reaches designated highway lanes for driverless cars, where the "autopilot" system will take control. Google recently received a patent for a system that will enable a car to make the transition to self-driving when it reaches a so-called "landing strip" on the road.

According to FoxNews.com, the strip will be similar to a QR code that will be located on an overhead sign or painted onto the asphalt to mark the beginning of a "self-driving zone." When sensors mounted on the car identify the code, the system will locate itself with GPS and then use Google Maps data and landmarks to navigate through the zone.[15]

Autonomous cars should deliver at least six benefits, including:

1. *Safety:* According to the World Health Organization, more than 1.2 million people throughout the world are killed in car crashes every year. Another 50 million people are injured in accidents. The National Highway Traffic Safety Administration blames human error for at least 60 percent of traffic fatalities. As Tom Jacobs of the Nevada Department of Motor Vehicles, who took a test drive in Google's Prius, told *BBC News Magazine*, "When the car is on self-driving mode, it doesn't speed, it doesn't cut you off, [and] it doesn't tailgate."[16]

2. *Time savings:* Self-driving cars that can keep track of each other using sensors could maintain the speed limit with a minimum of distance between them. Vehicles would be automatically rerouted to less-traveled roads—and traffic congestion could be eliminated.

3. *Convenience:* A car could be left at the entrance to a parking garage, where it would park itself. Or to avoid the expense of parking at a convention center or airport, it could simply drive itself back to the owner's driveway.

4. *Efficiency:* Since the typical car is idle for 96 percent of the time, allowing cars to drive themselves would maximize their usage. For example, a car could return home after dropping the owner at work, eliminating the need for a second car to take the children to school. Cars could also be shared between groups of users under a wide range of business models.

5. *Cost savings:* According to *Businessweek,* if projections about the world's population growth hold true and if trends in car ownership continue, the number of cars on the road will

multiply from 850 million today to 7.7 billion in 2050. Those cars will burn 375 million barrels of oil per day, quintuple the global production in 2008, according to MIT professor John Sterman.[17] While we believe the projected number of automobiles is exaggerated and that oil will not be fueling most vehicles four decades from now, there is no question that the growing middle class in China and other developing countries will increase the demand for cars, just as there can be no argument that America's highway infrastructure has reached its limits. Rather than building new highways or widening existing ones, our current roads could handle two or three times as many cars if "robotic precision" were used to allow cars to drive closer together, according to engineer Sebastian Thrun, who heads Google's Driverless Cars program.

6. *Productivity:* When autonomous cars become the norm, people will become even more productive. Initially, a licensed driver will still need to sit behind the wheel in case the system fails. But we expect that, by the mid-2020s, traveling in one's own car will become just as passive an experience as taking a train. Automobile interiors will be redesigned so that seats can swivel sideways to face other passengers instead of facing forward, and desk surfaces will be built into the cabin walls or will fold out from the sides of the seats. Millions of drivers who once needed to remain focused on the road will be free to devote their full attention to their work as they commute to their offices or homes. This increase in productivity will make a positive impact on the economy, just as the adoption of personal computing, e-mail, and the Internet led to productivity gains that increased the nation's GDP.

What's ahead?

First, caregiver robots will become "good enough" for the American and EU markets between 2020 and 2025, and that will lead to explosive growth for the industry. To appreciate how this will happen, consider the tablet computer. Back in the early 1990s, there were rudimentary monochrome tablets with touch-screens running MS-DOS. These used a 2400-baud modem coupled to an analog cell phone to run very job-specific applications. By today's standards, they were crude and unappealing. Hardly anybody wanted one. But significantly, they offered a huge competitive advantage for those companies that could use them effectively. They were neither high enough quality, nor robust enough in features, for the mass market; they were simply "good enough" for their limited applications. Decades of consumer experience with laptops and the imagination of Apple eventually paved the way for the mass adoption of the iPad. And that paved the way for innovative Android and Windows-based tablets. Similarly, care-giving service robots are likely to be "good enough" for many Japanese institutions and homes when they become reliable enough for widespread deployment—perhaps as soon as 2015. Once they are deployed in the hundreds of thousands due to Japan's adoption, prices will plunge and capabilities will soar. Nevertheless, it will likely be 2025 before they become "good enough" to replace human caregivers in the West. Yet, when that tipping point arrives, expect the breakthrough entrant to become the care-giving robotic equivalent of the iPad.

Second, by 2025, robots will become commonplace in home and in non-factory workplaces, disruptively transforming employment in the service sector. Jobs, like those of hotel bellmen, receptionists, tour guides, and even bus drivers will ultimately be replaced by robots. We have already embraced robots at airline ticket counters and grocery stores, where automated check-in or checkout is a fact of life. This has allowed airlines to reduce staff. In the short term, this won't have a large impact, except in the low-level end of the service industry. But in the longer term of 15 to 20 years, robots will displace a large number of workers. Fortunately, the robotics industry will also create new jobs and new wealth to keep the economy going. In addition, the shift is likely to take place gradually—the way computers replaced many basic bookkeeping and accounting jobs—so that it won't have a harmful impact on economic stability.

Third, service robots will cost-effectively replace humans in most jobs in which the work is highly monotonous, extremely precise, requires continuously high levels of concentration, physically very demanding, or done in prohibitively dangerous environments. This includes industrial cleaning, equipment maintenance, and data acquisition. These types of robots are already with us:

96

- The da Vinci robotic surgery system is a service robot, along with a whole host of other medical/healthcare robots such as rehabilitation robots, and prosthetic and orthotic devices.
- The robotic rovers Spirit and Opportunity are now exploring Mars.
- The Pyramid Rovers exploring inside the pyramid of Cheops are another type of service robot.

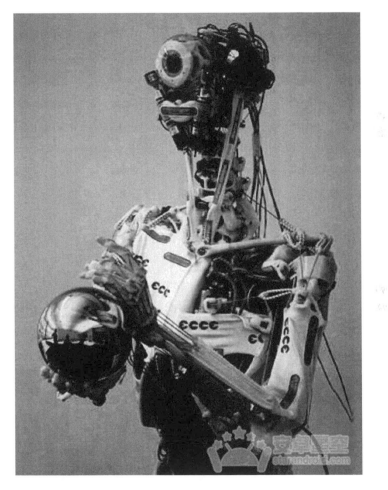

- ECCEROBOT-1 is particularly interesting because its structure and movements are specifically modeled on those of the human body.

- The unmanned vehicles and drones being used by the military are service robots, too.
- The service robots used to clean up Japan's Fukishima nuclear

facility saved many lives.

Robots are now in use doing inspection, security, construction, demolition, edutainment, lawn mowing, mining, harvesting, and delivery. And, the range of these functions will only expand over time.

Fourth, within 15 years, robotic butlers will become available to wealthy customers, and within 25 years they will be as common in middle-class homes as televisions and toasters are today. It may happen even sooner. Robert Hecht-Nielsen, who founded HNC Software, asserts that he could build an electronic butler within five years if he had the right resources. According to the New York Times, at HNC, Hecht-Nielsen successfully used neural network technology to duplicate the processes of the human brain to detect credit card fraud. He sold the company to the Fair Isaac Corporation, where he is now leading research into "confabulation," a theory about how the human brain makes decisions. At IBM, he has demonstrated how software based on confabulation can read two sentences and then create a third sentence that makes sense. Using confabulation, Hecht-Nielsen believes he can build a robot butler that will hold conversations with its owner and handle such chores as ordering groceries.

Fifth, within 30 years, advances in robotics will merge with advances in computing power and breakthroughs in nanotechnology to yield intelligent, life-like machines that will revolutionize every area of human life. Computing power will continue to double every 18 months due to Moore's Law, and computers will shrink to the size of molecules thanks to nanotechnology. Ultimately, nanobots will be swallowed in capsules to prowl our bloodstreams to eradicate diseases and cancerous cells, which will transform healthcare. Robots of various sizes will assume many of the functions that people perform now. They will be put into service as office receptionists and building security guards. They will shop for clothes and prepare meals. They will diagnose medical conditions and perform surgeries. This will lead to a dramatic change in society, as fewer humans are needed in the workforce. However, the gains in productivity as human workers are replaced by low-cost bots—which will never need sick days, lunch hours, or vacations—will create unprecedented wealth, allowing people to pursue a more leisurely and spiritual life.

Sixth, widespread use of service robots will depend on the development of the supporting environment needed to fully utilize them. In the next 15 years, service robots will integrate into a broader web of technology—the "Internet of Everything." Within this tiered network, all devices will be intelligently linked to one another through a backbone of wireless nodes that will receive, analyze, and transmit streams of data. The so-called "smart home" is at the heart of this idea. Within this paradigm, systems throughout the home, such as heating, air conditioning, refrigerators, multimedia centers, and lighting will be automatically regulated to meet specific demands. This will extend all the way down to RFID tags on nearly every item in the closet or refrigerator. The network will even integrate the residents' clothing, which will monitor their health. Service robots will function within that environment, interacting with the people, as well as the house and its contents. Outside the house, GPS and other navigational aids will enable robots to function effectively. The service robots and their ecosystem are likely to show up first in hospitals, nursing homes, and assisted-care facilities; but once proven, they will transition rapidly into private homes. To make this vision cost-effective requires little more than the steady advance of Moore's law and a parallel increase in wireless system performance over the next 15 to 20 years. While breakthroughs are clearly necessary in the software world, much of the fundamental research is already underway in Japan, the U.S., and the EU.

Seventh, it's possible that the growing "skills mismatch" will delay widespread adoption of service robots. In *Trends,* we've discussed the growing skills mismatch in the human labor market: a severe shortage of high-skilled technologists, coupled with a surplus of workers with a high school diploma or less. (This situation is further exacerbated by the surplus of college graduates with degrees in fields that have a low technology content.) To develop service robots and an industry to support them, we'll increasingly need people to design, build, program, and monitor these robots. Meanwhile, widespread adoption of robots will eliminate many jobs that are now filled by relatively unskilled workers, while creating higher paying jobs for highly skilled workers. Because of the skills gap, these new jobs will be slow to fill, potentially delaying the emergence of service robots.

Eighth, in many ways, robots will be the PCs of the 21st century. Since the technology is just now reaching the point where truly practical robots are possible, the situation is similar to that of the early 1970s, when the components of computers became cheap and plentiful, leading to the proliferation of personal computers and the monumental technological revolution that reshaped our lives. Today, a high school student can get started on his own with a Lego Mindstorm robot kit for less than $300. Enthusiasts can work their way up the price scale in $100 or $200 increments all the way to the $1,000 Kondo KHR-2HV Humanoid Robot Kit, with 17 degrees of movement and downloadable software. In the near future—nearer than you might think the first general-purpose robots will be introduced to the market. Developers will quickly begin writing software to make them do practical and cool things, while others will build hardware add-ons and modifications to extend those capabilities. This technological race will be going full-tilt within the next five years.

Ninth, by 2016, we'll see the development of a set of industry protocol standards for the home. This will be the key breakthrough that will unleash the potential of the smart appliances that are reaching the market today. Once we can integrate the whole house around a network and a set of standards, everything—refrigerators, ovens, coffee makers, laundry units, HVAC systems, robots, security systems, TVs, music players, window blinds, wall displays, and so on—will be able to communicate with everything else. By installing facial recognition and voice recognition software to a processor on the network, you would have a tool for giving instructions orally or letting the system monitor your well-being when you're home alone. Next, assume you buy a set of vacuuming, mopping, and mowing robots. Now you combine the sensors on the machines with the sensors on the webcams to help these units navigate effectively and avoid obstacles. The networked refrigerator and kitchen cabinets would inventory the food, cleaning supplies, and other consumables every day based on their RFID tags. According to Bill Gates, robots will perform specific jobs in various rooms of the house, such as folding clothes as they emerge from the dryer, or dispensing food and medicine to sick and elderly people who can't get out of bed.

Tenth, robots and smart appliances in the digital home will free people from household chores, resulting in more leisure time.

Studies show that as Americans' working hours and commuting times have steadily increased, the amount of time they have for recreation has dropped. But when robots and digital devices perform their housework and yard work, people have more time for non-work activities. Currently, according to the Bureau of Labor Statistics, married Americans spend 2.1 hours per day doing household chore such as housework, cooking, or lawn care; even single people spend 1.4 hours a day on these activities. When those chores are off-loaded to machines, a new renaissance will become possible, as people will have the potential to indulge in recreational pursuits and continuing education. Businesses that help customers use their newfound leisure time will flourish.

Eleventh, the future is likely to unfold in ways that even the best minds can't foresee. The biggest obstacle is that most people's perspective is shaped by what is, instead of by what could be. Consider Microsoft's vision of the future as embodied in the concept home on its campus. Bill Gates and his engineers predict that the future home's mailbox will use GPS to reveal the location of the mail carrier and that RFID tags in the envelopes will allow people to know what mail is on the way. But this vision is based on a 20th century mental model, in which the mail consists of envelopes that are delivered by hand; we predict that long before 2028, physical mail and the U.S. Postal Service as we know it today will disappear, all documents and catalogues will be converted to digital form, and they will be delivered electronically and instantaneously.

Twelfth, the emergence of autonomous vehicles poses a critical threat to the profitability of the insurance and advertising industries. Because human error is blamed for 60 percent of traffic fatalities and 99 percent of car accidents, proponents of driverless cars believe that roads will be much safer without human drivers. In fact, preventing fatal traffic accidents is what motivated Google engineer Sebastian Thrun to start developing autonomous cars after a friend died in a car crash. If the cars succeed in eliminating wrecks, will car owners still need collision insurance? And, how much should liability insurance cost? There's a lot riding on the answers to those questions. According to the U.S. Census Bureau's *2012 Statistical Abstract,* auto insurance is a $180 billion business in the U.S. Because the market is highly competitive, auto insurance companies spend a lot on advertising: According to *The Wall Street Journal,* Geico alone spent just under $1 billion on marketing in 2011, while State Farm and Allstate weren't far behind.[18] All of that revenue could be at risk if private automobile insurance becomes largely obsolete.

Thirteenth, expect the car manufacturers to lobby vigorously for laws that absolve them of liability if an autonomous car crashes. A case could be made that if the car is driving itself, the manufacturer should be liable for any mishaps. That issue concerns the car makers; the Alliance of Automobile Manufacturers opposed California's bill to allow driverless cars on the state's roads because it did not address the issue of liability.[19] It's too early to predict how this issue will be resolved, but one possibility in the short term might be a relatively small liability surcharge that would be bundled into the sale of the vehicle so the cost would be passed on to the consumer. However, once the technology becomes virtually foolproof and highway accidents become as rare as plane crashes and train wrecks, this issue should become less relevant.

Fourteenth, despite the overall improvements in safety that autonomous cars will bring to individual passengers, our increased reliance on the kinds of technology needed for driverless automobiles will make us increasingly vulnerable as a nation. Among the potential threats that must be addressed are electromagnetic pulse weapons that could be launched by terrorists or foreign powers, as well as natural disasters such as solar storms.

Fifteenth, another issue that must be resolved is the matter of privacy. Some critics contend that Google's driverless system will track users' every movement and store data on their habits and destinations. The nonprofit privacy organization called Consumer Watchdog sent a letter to California's lawmakers urging them to prohibit Google's cars from collecting data for marketing or other purposes. In a press release, Consumer Watchdog warned, "Now that Google is taking to the freeways, we must prevent inappropriate collection and storage of data about our personal movements and environment before we allow Google's robots to take to the roads and report back to the Googleplex."[20] At issue is whether people will tolerate the trade-off between giving up some privacy in exchange for convenience—and, as the popularity of Google's search engine can attest, it is a bargain that hundreds of millions of people have been willing to make.

6

Why do we care about quantum computing?

"Quantum computation is . . . a distinctively new way
of harnessing nature . . . It will be the first technology
that allows useful tasks to be performed in collaboration
between parallel universes."

--David Deutsch

Roughly 50 years ago, legendary quantum physicist Richard Feynman
formulated the theoretical principles upon which a quantum computer
could be built. However, actually building a computer based on
quantum mechanics has proven overwhelmingly difficult.

Yet, it finally seems that the first primitive quantum computers
are ready to enter the workplace. And, while these machines are suited
for only a narrow subset of applications, their impact promises to be
significant. More importantly, they'll pave the way for even more
powerful and useful machines in the coming decade.

This is critical because, since the invention of the transistor in
the late 1940s, the increasing density of manufacturable circuits has
always led to faster and cheaper machines. This brings us, again, to
Moore's Law, which states that computers double in speed, on

average, every 18 months, while their price-performance ratio is cut in half.

At every point where this trend appeared ready to stall, scientists have found new ways forward. For example, while clock speeds have been stalled at around 4 GHz, microprocessors have added multiple cores running at those speeds. However, as discussed in Chapter 2, somewhere in the next few decades, quantum mechanics will combine with the complexities of parallel processing to create a practical limit to the power of traditional computers based on silicon.

Ironically, though, the same quantum mechanical principles that will eventually block the road toward ever more powerful conventional computers will also offer the opportunity to create specialized computers that transcend such limits. As we've chronicled in *Trends,* quantum computing represents an entirely new way of computing aimed at solving problems that are impractical or impossible for traditional computers.

In conventional electronic computers, a bit of data is represented as either a 0 or a 1. In the weird world of quantum mechanics, a quantum bit, or "qubit," can not only register a 0 or a 1, it can register both *simultaneously*—a phenomenon known as "superposition." Although it is difficult to grasp how this can be, the precise laws of quantum mechanics enable predictions of what quantum computers will do.

A small computer of only a few tens of thousands of qubits would be enormously powerful, since qubits in superposition work together to handle exponentially more data. In fact, for some applications, such a quantum computer would be more powerful than all the computers that have ever been built, combined. But getting to tens of thousands of qubits is still an enormous hurdle.

The first quantum computer

However, a big step in quantum computing has recently been reached: the sale of the first "quantum computer." It was purchased by Lockheed Martin for $10 million.[1]

How does it work? First, magnetic fields are used to input data and instructions by setting the states of the qubits and couplers. After a short time and a series of quantum mechanical changes, the computer provides the final answer using magnetic fields.

Called the D-Wave One, this computer features 128 qubits. As explained in the *Trends* article QUANTUM COMPUTING BEGINS TO EMERGE (http://www.audiotech.com/trends-magazine/quantum-computing-begins-emerge), the qubits are formed by loops of niobium metal, a material that becomes a superconductor at very low temperatures. Niobium is commonly used in MRI scanners. Couplers, also made of niobium, link the qubits and control how the magnetic fields, which represent the qubits, affect each another.[2]

As Geordie Rose, D-Wave's co-founder, describes it, "You stuff the problem into the hardware, and it acts as a physical proxy for what you're trying to solve. All physical systems want to sink to the lowest energy level, with the most entropy, and ours sinks to a state that represents the solution."[3]

This process of sinking to the lowest energy level that Rose refers to is called "annealing." The D-Wave One processor calculates solutions by piggybacking a user's problem onto "quantum annealing" to reveal the solution.

The D-Wave One performs a single type of mathematical operation called "discrete optimization." Through this algorithm, the computer provides approximate answers to problems that can only be solved by trying every possible solution. Allan Snavely at the San Diego Supercomputer Center describes these problems as the type "where you know the right answer when you see it, but finding it among the exponential space of possibilities is difficult."

Reminiscent of the time when a computer filled a whole room, the D-Wave One occupies over 1,000 cubic feet. Its size, and its specialized and possibly dead-end reliance on "quantum annealing," makes this quantum computer roughly analogous to ENIAC, the first *digital* computer. ENIAC was incredibly large, slow, and unreliable, with fewer capabilities than a 1975 HP programmable calculator. However, it is universally acknowledged as the forerunner of every current digital computer ranging from the iPad to the fastest supercomputer. By bringing quantum computing out of the lab for the first time, the D-Wave One may, in a similar way, prepare the way for a whole new industry.

Lockheed Martin certainly views this computer as a usable tool, not a lab curiosity. Operating the D-Wave One in conjunction with a conventional computer, the combined system learns from past data and makes predictions about future events. Lockheed needs this capability to identify unforeseen technical problems in products that are complex combinations of software and hardware. These types of glitches contribute to cost over-runs, such as the one the company is experiencing with the F-35 strike fighter, which is 20 percent over budget.

Other applications are looking equally promising. Google is testing the D-Wave computer to see if it can speed up software for the interpretation of photos. Faster database searches might also be possible with quantum computers.

Search engines like Google could also use quantum computing to assess the relevance of Web pages. As reported in the journal *Physical Review Letters*, a team at USC has developed a quantum computer algorithm for this purpose. In a simulation, they proved that a quantum computer could return the rankings of the most important Internet pages faster than traditional computers.[4]

More importantly, quantum computers could lead to the creation of more powerful computer models for everything from analyzing complex chemical reactions to genetic analysis, and from controlling a robot to predicting the path of a hurricane. Such models can involve solving millions of linear equations with millions of variables. In another article from the journal *Physical Review Letters*, MIT researchers presented a new algorithm that could allow a quantum computer with just 40 qubits to quickly solve a trillion simultaneous linear equations with a trillion variables.[5]

Consider the impact on pharmaceutical research. Conventional computers cannot model the molecular and biological systems involved in the development of a new drug, including such daunting challenges as determining how the 3D structure of proteins will interact with a new chemical compound. Currently, researchers have to use costly and time-consuming trial-and-error experiments to eliminate one possibility at a time, which can take years or even decades. A quantum computer would enable researchers to design a new vaccine or a new drug as easily and quickly as architects can design a house, today.

What's ahead for quantum computing?

First, at the current rate of development, the best guess for the arrival of personal quantum computers is around 2040, but they should to be accessible via the cloud by 2025. Nevertheless, most tasks will be performed better by conventional, von Neumann-type computers. In applications where quantum computers are faster, they will be exponentially faster. But most people will continue to use conventional computers, which will improve dramatically over the next couple of decades, as discussed in previous chapters.

Second, by 2025, quantum computers will take over many complex applications in science and industry using algorithms that are currently hard to imagine. Quantum computing will excel in solving problems that involve millions, and perhaps trillions, of factors. For example, weather forecasting could become more accurate. They might even enable us to predict future natural disasters such as earthquakes.

Third, as soon as 2015, quantum computing could make today's network security technology totally obsolete. Even small quantum computers will possess the kind of computing power needed to break all known codes in use today. This would be a major disruption for the way we interact on the Internet. As a result, we will be forced to rethink security. Not surprisingly, this issue has captured the attention of the Central Intelligence Agency. The CIA is among the investors that recently poured $30 million into D-Wave.[6] Fortunately, so-called quantum encryption techniques are already under development, using quantum entanglement to create security algorithms that even quantum computers themselves can't break. While this will enable law-abiding

110

citizens to maintain their privacy, it will also enable terrorists and organized crime organizations to do the same.

Fourth, the mainstream quantum computers of 2025 to 2030 will be far more reliable and mainstream than today's pioneering technology because they will harness the power of millions rather than hundreds of qubits. Just as ENIAC and its thousands of vacuum tubes was really just a proof-of-concept for today's digital computers, today's D-Wave 128-qubit machine operating at near "absolute zero" and filled with loops of niobium is simply proving that quantum computing can be done. Already, more commercially practical technologies are in the pipeline. For example, the journal *Nature* recently reported that researchers at Princeton University have developed a revolutionary new approach in which the "spin state" of electrons acts as the qubit. The obstacle to such an approach until now has been that attempts to observe the spin state typically disrupts it. The Princeton team trapped a pair of electrons in a cage-like structure called a quantum dot. They pulsed microwaves in one end of the dot and measured how much the spin state of the electrons changed the microwaves as they emerged on the other side. The researchers found that this method works without disturbing the spin, and they believe that it could lead to the creation of a quantum computer with millions of qubits.[7]

7

What will the amazing potential of bioinformatics mean for you?

"DNA is like a computer program but far, far more advanced than any software ever created."
--Bill Gates, *The Road Ahead*

Because humans are living things, the ability to understand and manipulate the processes of life holds a special significance for us. Beyond this, living systems are found in almost every aspect of our economy, from energy to agriculture to healthcare to housing.

Therefore, it's not at all surprising that discovering that life was the product of digital information encoded in the form of amino acid sequences was one of the top ten most significant discoveries in human history. And, once we began to understand the language of life, it became possible to read, write, edit, and execute these instructions just as we would those of a computer program.

In historical terms, this happened virtually overnight, starting with the discovery of the double-helix structure of DNA in 1953. This enabled molecular biologists to investigate life from the bottom up, launching the fields of bioinformatics, genetic engineering, and synthetic life. This, in turn, opened the way for information-intensive personalized medicine, which promises to make our "quality of life" dramatically better, and ultimately bend the health care cost-curve downward, as detailed in the *Trends* article, FAST, LOW-COST HUMAN GENOMES WILL TRANSFORM OUR LIVES (http://www.audiotech.com/trends-magazine/fast-lowcost-human-genomes-transform-lives).

In this chapter, we'll explore Bioinformatics, the foundational technology that brings the power of the Digital Revolution fully to bear on the biological sciences. As we'll see in subsequent chapters, it opens the door to eliminating hunger, curing disease, cleaning up the environment, extending our potential healthy life-spans, thwarting specific varieties of terrorism, and even correcting genetic defects.

Bioinformatics

The digital revolution and molecular biology both grew out of research that began during the Golden Age of the Mass Production Revolution. Just about the time the first mainframes emerged, Francis Crick and James Watson published their seminal research on the structure and role of DNA. It quickly became apparent that DNA's G-C and A-T bonds (guanine-cytosine and adenine-thymine) were a binary code analogous to the zeros and ones in a computer; similarly, three-letter codons were analogous to eight-bit bytes, but specifying amino acids rather than ASCII characters.

Then, just over 20 years later, during the period immediately following the "Microprocessor Big Bang," Stanford University applied for a U.S. patent on recombinant DNA. From that point forward, the economic potential of reading, interpreting, and rewriting the code of life became abundantly clear. The natural synergy between information technology and genetics became crucial to that enterprise.

Fast-forwarding another 25 years brought us another 10,000-fold increase in computing performance, coinciding with the sequencing of the first human genome in the year 2000. In this effort, both the Human Genome Project and Celera Genomics relied heavily on computer-controlled sequencers and associated computational resources. In fact, in 2001, Celera was estimated to have had more computing power at its disposal than any single organization other than the U.S. Government and Walmart. This synergy between IT and genomics effectively "jump-started" the bioinformatics industry.

114

Over the roughly dozen years since then, the price-performance of gene sequencing has improved by three-million-fold and gene fabrication technology has advanced nearly as fast. This is enabling scientists to literally "hijack the mechanisms of life" and harness them to rewrite the economic rules. The resulting elimination of hunger, curing of disease, and provision of shelter will transform the lives of billions and create enormous new market opportunities. Much of that will come from the fields of synthetic life, bio-reengineering, and personalized medicine, which all depend on bioinformatics.

What is bioinformatics? It is a technology that focuses on ways of storing, retrieving, and analyzing biological data. This includes data about the sequence, structure, function, pathways, and genetic interactions of DNA, RNA, and proteins. Applications of bioinformatics generate new knowledge that is useful in such fields as drug design and the development software tools to create that knowledge.

This technology is only reaching critical mass now because of the development of necessary technologies, like microchip-based biological sensors that can quickly collect biological data, feed it to enormous database storage systems, and interpret it using the "big data" tools previously highlighted in Chapter 4. Going forward, artificial intelligence and quantum computing will cost-effectively transform this avalanche of data into useful solutions that were heretofore unimaginable. And, as we'll explain in subsequent chapters, rapidly analyzing biological data will enable us to remake healthcare, agriculture, energy, and the environment in totally new ways.

For example, consider healthcare: One inevitable consequence of the world's aging and shrinking population is that there will be a growing demand for high-quality health care and a shrinking pool of people to provide that care and pay for it. One symptom of this is a potentially catastrophic shortage of primary care physicians that the United States now faces.

A study by University of Missouri School of Medicine professor emeritus Jack Colwill and his colleagues suggests that, within 12 years, the U.S. will need 44,000 more family physicians than it is forecast to have.[1] One reason is that by 2025, there will be a 73 percent increase in the number of Americans over the age of 65, according to the U.S. Census Bureau.

Because people in this age group typically see primary care physicians three times per year, which is twice as often as younger adults, Colwill predicts a 29 percent growth in the number of doctor visits by 2025, while the number of primary care physicians is expected to increase by just 5 percent.

However, stunning advances in biotechnology offer a possible solution to this looming crisis. At the heart of this solution is unprecedented progress in the field of genomics.[2]

The human genome consists of about 3.2 billion DNA nucleotide base pairs, which provide all of the instructions for creating each human being with his or her own unique traits.

Approximately 99.9 percent of these base pairs are the same in all humans. However, scientists have found 1.4 million locations where single-base DNA differences occur in humans, and these differences are believed to explain why some people develop certain diseases, while others are immune.

Thus, the race is on to identify which genetic variations and sequences are associated with which diseases. Ultimately, this should allow doctors to quickly screen patients for the tendency to develop each disease through a blood test. This will allow doctors to prevent people from developing diseases, or to at least detect diseases in the early stages when they are treatable with specially targeted biomedicines.

The key to making this technology really practical is reducing the costs and time involved in mapping each person's genome. Today, these are falling at an incredible pace. In 2003, when the Human Genome Project completed its sequencing of the human genome to great fanfare, the process took 13 years and the cost was an astounding $3 billion.

By 2007, the cost for sequencing the genome of James Watson, the co-discoverer of DNA, had dropped to less than $1 million. Today, a company called Ion Torrent is pioneering a new approach that provides a human genome for less than $1,000. On top of that, it is also much quicker than the conventional sequencing approach, with the entire process taking just one day, according to founder and CEO

116

Dr. Jonathan Rothberg.[3]

The breakthrough that is enabling Ion Torrent's technology to work faster than other technologies is that it uses semiconductors to sequence DNA, rather than relying on conventional wet chemistry.

Other advanced technologies sequence DNA using fluorescently tagged molecules that are scanned by a microscope. Ion Torrent's machine detects DNA sequences electronically with sequencing chips. This offers cost savings since it does not rely on expensive lasers and cameras.

If progress continues at its current pace, by 2020, the cost to sequence a person's genome will fall to $100. Once the era of cheap, quick sequencing arrives, every individual will be able to afford to have his or her genome mapped.[4]

Moreover, when people have their genomes mapped, they will be able to anticipate which diseases they are most likely to develop. Several genes have already been linked to breast cancer, muscle disease, deafness, and blindness. Scientists are also using human variation maps, known as SNPs, to pinpoint the DNA sequences that cause cardiovascular disease, diabetes, arthritis, and various cancers.

Ultimately, pharmaceutical companies will be able to target drugs to specific groups of people who have specific genes and SNPs. They will also be able to determine which drugs will be effective in which people, as well as which medicines will cause harmful side effects in patients with specific genetic markers.

Furthermore, by allowing doctors to both prevent and treat diseases more effectively, biomedicine will reduce the drain on productivity caused by employee illnesses, and allow people to maintain their physical health and mental sharpness so they can continue working well into their 70s, 80s, and even beyond. As we discussed extensively in the *Trends* segment, **BOOMERS MOVE INTO THEIR GOLDEN YEARS** (http://www.audiotech.com/trends-magazine/boomers-move-into-their-golden-years-4), this will largely counter the effect of the shrinking numbers of working-age adults, which will help keep companies fully staffed so that the economy can continue to grow robustly, even as the population ages.

Genes are just part of the story

When the Human Genome Project was completed in 2003, the focus was almost entirely on the 2 percent of the genetic code known as *genes*. Genes are the portions of the DNA sequence that actually code for proteins. At the time, researchers had no idea what functions, if any, were actually performed by the other 98 percent. In fact, until recently, most biologists believed that most of this DNA was simply residual "junk" left over from failed mutations over billions of years of evolution.

However, a massive new effort involving over 80 institutions, funded by the United States National Institutes of Health and called the ENCODE Project, has determined that at least 80 percent of the so-called "junk DNA" functions to turn off and on specific genes, in specific cells, at specific times, in order to accomplish specific tasks.

ENCODE stands for "*ENC*yclopedia *Of* *D*NA *E*lements" and is coordinated by a team at the University of Washington in Seattle. This discovery is, for the first time, giving us an understanding of the actual "programming language," written into the DNA base-pairs, that regulates every aspect of life. Without these switches, called "regulatory DNA," genes are inert.

Using a new technology developed with funding from the ENCODE project, UW researchers created the first detailed maps of where the "regulatory DNA" is located within hundreds of different kinds of living cells. They also compiled a dictionary of the instructions written within the regulatory DNA.

The key findings were reported in two papers in the journal *Nature*.[5, 6] These are the most important of 30+ major research papers initially published based on the early results from the ENCODE project.

The breakthrough studies described in the two *Nature* papers provide the first extensive maps of the DNA switches that control human genes. This information is vital to understanding how the body makes different kinds of cells, and how normal gene circuitry gets rewired in disease.

Significantly, this means that scientists are now, for the first time, able to read the genome of any organism at a high level of detail, and to begin to make sense of the complex instruction set that ultimately influences a wide range of biology.

Here are the three key results of this research:

- First, the instructions within regulatory DNA are inscribed in small DNA "words" that function as the docking sites for special proteins involved in gene control. In many cases, these switches are located far away from the genes that they control.
- Second, of the 2.89 million regulatory DNA regions the researchers mapped, only around 200,000 were active in any given cell-type. This fraction is almost totally unique to each type of cell and becomes a sort of molecular barcode of the cell's identity.
- Third, the researchers developed a method for linking regulatory DNA to the genes it controls. The results of these analyses show that the regulatory "program" of most genes is made up of more than a dozen switches. Together, these findings greatly expand the understanding of how genes are controlled and how that control may differ between normal and diseased cells.

Unfortunately, the existing techniques lack the accuracy to resolve the DNA letters to which the proteins dock. So, to find the actual DNA words recognized by regulatory proteins in living cells, the researchers employed a simple, powerful trick that enabled them to study all the regulatory proteins at once. They looked for their shadows or "footprints" on the DNA.

By using next-generation DNA sequencing technology, the researchers analyzed hundreds of millions of DNA backbone breaks made when cells were treated with the enzyme DNaseI. They then used a powerful computer to resolve millions of protein footprints. In total, they identified 8.4 million such footprints along the genome, some of which were detected in many cell types.

Next, they compiled all of the short DNA sequences to which the proteins were docked and analyzed them using a software algorithm that required hundreds of microprocessors working simultaneously. This revealed that more than 90 percent of the protein-docking sites were actually slight variants of just 683 different DNA words. They are essentially a dictionary of the genome's programming language.

The result is that scientists have gone from a preliminary understanding of the 2 percent of the genome that codes for proteins to the first understanding of the 98 percent of the genome that controls that 2 percent. Coupled with the exponential improvement in gene sequencing price-performance, ENCODE has broken down the biggest barriers to unleashing personalized medicine, which we'll examine in Chapter 7.

What's ahead?

First, demand created by bioinformatics will be a crucial factor driving "big data" IT, and new IT techniques will make it possible to more efficiently handle the mountains of bio-data inherent in bioinformatics. Recently, the *Proceedings of the National Academy of Sciences* highlighted the data logjam associated with genomic data for microbial communities living in soil and oceans. For example, to thoroughly examine one gram of soil, scientists need to generate about 50 terabases of genomic sequence, which equates to roughly 50 terabytes of data. When analyzing this DNA information using traditional computing methods, the data bogs down memory and causes the computers to "choke."[7] However, a new approach developed at Michigan State University employs a filter that compresses the data. This allows computers to nibble at the data and eventually digest the entire sequence. In tests, the MSU team reports a 40-fold decrease in memory requirements, allowing scientists to plow through mountains of data without using a supercomputer. Such advances in methodology will combine with the steady advance of Moore's law to keep bioinformatics on track through at least 2025.[8]

Second, between 2015 and 2020, a standard, dominant DNA sequencing technology will emerge and drive a shake-out of the market, leaving two or three big winners. One leading candidate is Ion Torrent's semiconductor approach profiled earlier. Another exciting candidate works by threading a single strand of DNA through a tiny, molecular-scale eyelet known as a "nanopore." This strategy allows the entire DNA sequence to be read in one pass, rather than cut apart, deciphered in brief fragments and then painstakingly reassembled by computers. A leader in this field, called Oxford Nanopore Technologies, says they'll soon be able to accomplish this feat at the rate of 6 billion nucleotide bases read in six hours at a cost of $900. As explained recently in the journal *Science,* nanopore sequencing "seems poised to leave the lab," and the dream of a $1,000 genome may be close at hand, though challenges remain.[9] A related paper in the journal *Nanotechnology* describes the use of machine learning to train a computer to recognize the signals from the nanopore that correspond to specific DNA bases. In tests, the machine called all four bases with 96 percent accuracy on a single molecular read. Roche Pharmaceuticals has recently licensed the Oxford technology and is likely to bring it to market.[10]

Third, by 2020, your genome will become a part of your standard electronic medical record. At a cost of between $100 and $1,000, everyone will have their genome sequenced as a part of routine medical procedures. This will lay the foundation necessary for the mainstreaming of personalized medicine that we'll discuss in Chapter 8. The business opportunities involved in sequencing, storing, and analyzing a billion human genomes in the decade of the 2020s are enormous.

Fourth, the instant availability of everyone's genetic blueprint will raise serious questions for industries ranging from life and health insurance to healthcare itself. Because genomic data define one's biological destiny, it raises many ethical questions, not just for today's citizens, but for the unborn. For instance, prenatal whole genome sequencing could relieve parents' anxiety. However, the discovery of genes that indicate a tendency toward certain diseases or conditions could lead to an increase in pregnancy terminations. Whole genome prenatal testing could also have other negative consequences. If parents are told that their child's predicted IQ may be low, they might be less likely to expect him to succeed in school, which can cause a self-fulfilling prophesy effect in which the child performs poorly due to low expectations rather than low intelligence.

8

Why will "personalized medicine" become the dominant 21st century healthcare paradigm?

> "The physician should not treat the disease but the patient who is suffering from it."
>
> --Moses Maimonides

In our work at *Trends,* we have been closely following the evolution of "personalized medicine" since it became a realistic possibility about a decade ago. Personalized medicine is the practice of medicine based on the individual patient, rather than a statistical sample. It involves devising "customized therapies" as well as selecting from among "standardized therapies" based on an individual patient's genetic makeup and specific needs.

Personalized medicine represents *the* emerging paradigm of healthcare in the Golden Age of the Digital Revolution. It will leverage the power of bioinformatics to totally change the economics of healthcare, as we've known it.

The problem with so-called "healthcare reform" that we've seen over the past two decades is that it hasn't done much to address the fundamental *economics* of healthcare; that is, delivering better outcomes at lower cost. Instead, it has focused on payment systems and perceived accessibility to a pool of finite and essentially obsolete delivery systems.

Cost-effective healthcare will only become a reality when we reengineer our delivery systems by combining smart-machine technologies (discussed in Chapter 4), mobile/embedded/networked technologies (discussed in Chapter 3), and bioinformatics (discussed in Chapter 7). This interdisciplinary approach will enable the new paradigm of personalized medicine that we'll discuss here.

The necessary trends and policy decisions related to the regulatory, business, and legal climate that will be necessary to implement this new system in a timely manner have been explored in *Trends* Magazine articles like:

- GENOMICS AND THE RISE OF PERSONALIZED MEDICINE 2.0
  (http://www.audiotech.com/trends-magazine/genomics-and-the-rise-of-personalized-medicine-2-0)
- PERSONALIZED MEDICINE MOVES FORWARD
  (http://www.audiotech.com/trends-magazine/personalized-medicine-moves-forward)
- MOVING PERSONALIZED MEDICINE FROM THE LAB TO THE MARKETPLACE
  (http://www.audiotech.com/trends-magazine/moving-personalized-medicine-from-the-lab-to-the-marketplace)
- PERSONALIZED MEDICINE
  (http://www.audiotech.com/trends-magazine/personalized-medicine).

Our focus in this chapter is on understanding the implications and business opportunities growing out of the shift to personalized medicine.

Why personalized medicine makes sense now

Today, 40 years into the Digital Revolution, our healthcare system still rests on the economic assumptions of the Mass Production Revolution. Pharmaceutical companies devote most of their resources to developing and marketing "blockbuster drugs" intended to provide *adequate* treatment for "most of the people" who suffer from "relatively common" ailments. That approach has been enormously successful in reducing cardiovascular disease, treating some cancers, and almost totally eliminating horrific diseases such as smallpox and polio. More recently, integrating the Mass Production model with infotech and gene sequencing has prevented influenza outbreaks from becoming pandemics.

This proven approach has left many relatively obscure ailments "orphaned" and caused tens of millions of patients to needlessly suffer the side-effects of treatments that had little or no likelihood of success given their genetic predispositions. Furthermore, it has not led to lower costs, largely because it has done little to prevent diseases from occurring in the first place.

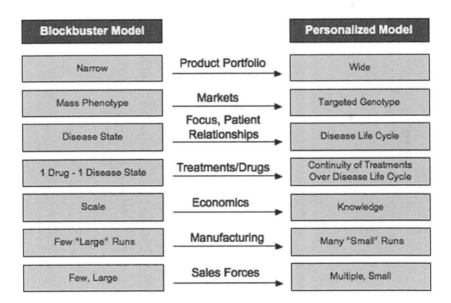

Source: Wikinvest
So far, the impact of personalized medicine on the business models of pharmaceutical companies has been minimal. However, that's all about to change.

Harnessing the data collected, analyzed, and stored via bioinformatics, healthcare providers—including physicians, hospitals, pharmaceutical companies has been minimal, and medical device

125

companies—will soon be able to deliver cost-effective treatments optimized for each individual patient. Furthermore, as we'll see, it will lead to better outcomes in the medium term, as well as lower costs in the long term.

For instance, this shift will enable:

- The reliable targeted destruction of cancer cells.
- The repair of hearts and brains.
- The growth of personalized replacement organs.
- The nearly instantaneous diagnosis of disease, even before conventional symptoms appear.

Tiny sensors and nanoparticles will be able to patrol our blood streams and silently scan our bodies for the first signs of illness. Advances in genetic research will enable us to slow down and even reverse the aging process; this will allow human life spans to increase dramatically. Much of this so-called "molecular medicine" will only work properly when optimized or selected based on the unique characteristics of the specific patient. That's why the 21st century healthcare model will be "personalized."

Contrary to the concerns of many, personalized medicine will not only deliver revolutionary outcomes, it will also sharply bend the healthcare cost-curve downward, making quality healthcare affordable for nearly everyone.

How is this possible? Under the traditional one-size-fits-all approach to medicine, a physician makes an initial diagnosis based on a profile of symptoms. Then the doctor prescribes a treatment, such as the drug or surgical procedure, which has helped the greatest number of other people with that same set of symptoms. If *that* treatment doesn't work, a trial-and-error approach follows. This involves substituting another drug or prescribing more surgery, in an iterative, time-consuming, and costly process.

Except for infectious disease vaccines, very little can now be done to ensure that the patient never gets a disease. Yet, in most cases, the best way to reduce healthcare costs is to prevent ailments before symptoms arise.

One obvious problem with the current model is that different diseases often have the same symptoms. Another problem is that

126

different individuals respond differently to the same treatments; a drug may be much more effective for one patient than it is for another patient with the same condition. As a result, the one-size-fits-all approach can actually end up being obscenely expensive in terms of dollars spent and even more so in terms of lives lost due to ineffective treatments.

By contrast, personalized medicine involves devising customized therapies that take advantage of an individual patient's genetic makeup and unique pathology. These therapies include, but are not limited to, genetic screening and tissue engineering, as well as gene and adult stem cell therapies. Although still in its infancy, personalized medicine is clearly becoming a practical reality, with many ongoing clinical trials and a few commercial applications.

Let's take a look at some of the latest developments in this evolving field and how the evolution of this technology will change our lives.

Implementing personalized medicine

Personalized medicine involves a truly new approach. As the *Harvard Business Review* explains, the doctor using personalized medicine will start with an understanding of the patient's unique physiology down to the molecular level, including his or her ability to metabolize each specific drug.[1]

Research is emerging almost every month that shows the rapid progress personalized medicine is making in the battle against diseases, especially cancers. Consider a few notable examples:

- The European Organization for Research and Treatment of Cancer reported that researchers have been able to detect, in advanced ovarian cancer, mutations in a single letter of genetic code that drive the onset and growth of cancer cells.[2] The finding opens the way for personalized therapy, in which each patient could have her tumor screened, specific mutations identified, and the appropriate drug chosen to target the mutation and halt the growth of the cancer.
- A drug called *gefitinib* was approved as Europe's first

personalized treatment for lung cancer. It is specifically for patients whose tumors carry particular mutations. In materials provided by the European Society for Medical Oncology, Professor Robert Pirker of the Medical University of Vienna states that before a patient receives this drug, the presence of these mutations in tumor cells has to be clearly demonstrated.[3] The steps of this new treatment will become the typical flow in cancer treatment over the next decade.

- The journal *Nature* recently profiled the International Cancer Genome Consortium, which brings together leading cancer researchers from around the world. These researchers are working to catalogue genetic changes associated with the 50 most common cancers, making the results freely available on the Internet. According to Professor Andrew Biankin, a researcher at Sydney's Garvan Institute of Medical Research, this work is already revolutionizing the way cancer research is done. For example, a researcher might find that the aberrations in a subtype of colon cancer are the same as the aberrations in a subtype of melanoma. In that case, the treatment that works in the colon cancer may be appropriate for the melanoma, so the researcher would go ahead and test it. In some cases, testing a drug with 50 other cancers could take 50 years, using old methods and technologies. On the other hand, with these new technologies, the trial phase can be narrowed down to just a few months.[4]

Personalized chemotherapy

Cancer treatment is likely to be the first area in which significant economic benefits are derived from personalized medicine. That's because cancer is inherently tied to the genetic characteristics of the individual, and the implications of poorly chosen therapy are so costly.

New research conducted by The University of Texas MD Anderson Cancer Center shows that customizing therapies based on the molecular characteristics for each tumor may be more effective for many types of cancer than "a one-size-fits-all approach," based on the type of tumor. This suggests that it is important to perform a molecular analysis to ensure that the right drug is used for each

128

patient. This personalized approach would allow doctors to consider several other factors that can lead to more targeted therapies that can improve patient outcomes.[5]

In recent years, using a personalized medicine approach to patients with chronic myeloid leukemia has led to more specific treatments, which in turn has led to higher survival rates. The University of Texas team believes that the same approach can improve outcomes for people with cancers involving *solid* tumors.

According to the journal *Biomaterials*, new therapy being developed at Florida State University also involves personalized chemotherapy treatments. FSU Assistant Professor of Biological Science Steven Lenhert, who led the team, explains, "Right now, cancer patients receive chemotherapy treatments that are based on the accumulated knowledge of what has worked best for people with similar cancers. This is the case because hospitals haven't had the technology to test thousands of different chemotherapy mixtures on the tumor cells of an individual patient. But now, this technology could give them access to that capability, making the treatments truly personalized and much more effective."[6]

Lenhert contends that costs could be reduced and treatments could be more customized if the first phase of the process used by pharmaceutical companies was miniaturized. In that phase, known as "high throughput screening," laboratories test hundreds of thousands of compounds on different cell cultures. While thorough, the process consumes a great deal of time and effort to eliminate the vast majority of the compounds.

The FSU approach streamlines that process. It deposits all of the compounds to be tested onto a single glass surface, and then evaluates how effective each compound is on a specific patient's unique cells. The technology is based on using "liposome microarrays," which are essentially drops of oil containing a multitude of drugs.

Once implemented, this "lab on a chip" technology would slash the cost of this process by a thousand times. The result would be a far cheaper, much more effective treatment for cancer that is tailored to each patient's genetic makeup. The technology could be made commercially available as soon as 2015.

Adult stem cell therapies

Another major frontier of personalized medicine involves stem cell therapy. Amazingly, scientists only began to investigate stem cells 15 years ago. Since then, they have discovered six categories of stem cells, with varying characteristics and issues:

- **Embryonic stem cells** can be coaxed to become any of the more than 200 kinds of cells found in the human body. However, because they are taken from early-stage embryos, their use is controversial, and at this time there are no treatments that are based on embryonic stem cells.
- **Pluripotent adult stem cells** can also turn into any other cell type. While rare, they can be found in many types of tissues, including umbilical cord blood. Researchers have discovered that bone marrow is a prime location for such cells, and they have used them to treat spinal cord injuries, liver cirrhosis, chronic limb ischemia, and end-stage heart failure.
- **Multipotent adult stem cells** offer two advantages compared to the preceding types. They are not controversial because they are not derived from embryos, and they are far less rare than pluripotent adult stem cells. *Multipotent* cells can turn into a variety of other cells, but only those within the same category of cells. Scientists have used them to successfully treat patients with leukemia and other cancers of the blood and bone through bone marrow transplants. In many cases, they can be collected from the patient that is receiving the transplant, so it is highly unlikely that the stem cells will be rejected. Multipotent adult stem cells offer great potential for use in personalized medicine. For example, researchers have found that stem cells can easily be collected when a child's third molar is developing between the ages of 8 and 10. The stem cells taken from the tooth bud can be used to create enamel, blood vessels, dental pulp, nervous tissues, and at least 29 different tissues for various organs. It's likely that these cells will be routinely harvested from children to be used in

personalized treatments later in life.

- **Amniotic stem cells** and **cord blood stem cells** are two other kinds of multipotent cells. Derived from amniotic fluid, amniotic stem cells can turn into bone, muscle, nerve, and liver cells. Cord blood stem cells have been linked to potential treatments for Type 1 diabetes and autoimmune diseases.
- **Induced pluripotent stem cells (iPS cells),** are ordinary adult tissue cells that are transformed into pluripotent stem cells. Cells taken from the skin tissue of adults can be genetically reprogrammed to behave like embryonic stem cells. While much is still unknown, scientists are making steady progress in learning how to control them. One recent success at Harvard was achieved when human iPS cells were programmed to turn into nerve cells that were then implanted into the brains of laboratory rats that were modeling Parkinson's disease. Research has shown that the disease is caused when nerve cells die. By restoring the nerve cells, the treatment cured the rats of Parkinson's.

As promising as iPS cells are to the future of personalized medicine, they are several potential problems with them.

Two of these issues are the cost of the therapy and the time it takes to implement it. According to Dr. Paul Knoepfler of the UC Davis School of Medicine, using current methods it would take six months, at a cost of at least $100,000, to create iPS cells from a patient's skin that could be used for transplants.[7] This simply isn't practical for most patients, especially those with limited funds or life-threatening conditions. However, it is likely that personalized medicine based on iPS cells will follow the same path as the mapping of the genome; as we discussed in Chapter 7, the cost to map a human genome fell from $3 billion in 2003 to less than $1,000 a decade later, and the time the process takes accelerated from 13 years to a single day. We can look forward to similar progress in iPS therapy as new technologies are developed and perfected.

An even greater challenge is the considerable risk that some of the iPS cells used in a transplant may grow into cancerous tumors. Fortunately, researchers may have found a way to achieve the benefits of induced pluripotent stem cells without that risk. A newly discovered class of cells called **conditionally reprogrammed cells,** (CRCs), seem to represent a major breakthrough for regenerative medicine.

This new "stem-like state" of adult epithelial cells was developed at Georgetown Lombardi Comprehensive Cancer Center. As explained in the *Proceedings of the National Academy of Sciences,* these new stem-like cells do not express the same genes as embryonic stem cells or iPS cells. That explains why they don't produce tumors and why they *reliably* produce the kinds of cells researchers want them to produce. It appears likely that CRCs could be used for regenerative medicine to replace organ tissue that is damaged and in other applications where induced pluripotent stems cells have already been proven to work.[8]

One of the reasons that both adult stem cell and iPS cell therapies have stolen much of the thunder from embryonic stem cell therapies is that they usually involve the use of cells derived from the tissues of the patient. This will also be true for CRCs, assuming they are successfully commercialized.

Tissue engineering and replacement organs

No area of personalized medicine is more exciting than organ replacement. But ever since surgeons started saving lives with transplanted hearts and kidneys nearly 50 years ago, the practice has been plagued with rejection problems and a shortage of donors. But fortunately, just as the demand for organs is likely to explode due to our aging population, two breakthrough solutions have emerged:

One solution is called **transgenic xenotransplantation**. This is the use of organs from genetically engineered animals; we'll discuss this solution in the next chapter.

The other solution is called **tissue engineering**. It combines the amazing research scientists have been doing with stem cells with equally amazing advances in the field of 3D printing. The result is a whole new technology that will potentially deliver fully-functional hearts, livers, kidneys, pancreas, lungs, and other organs that are genetically targeted to the recipient.

The leading approach to personalized tissue engineering is called "bioprinting." Using living human cells, bioprinters print human tissue and even entire organs for transplant. Functioning like other forms of 3D printing, these bioprinters build living tissue by putting down layer upon layer of cells.

All bio-printers being developed work essentially the same way. A bioprinthead moves left and right, back and forth, and up and down, placing cells exactly where they are needed to produce the tissue being created. Most of these printers also dispense a dissolvable gel containing growth factors and other components needed to support and protect the cells while printing is taking place.

One of the early successes in bioprinting came from Professor Makoto Nakamura, who in 2002 realized that standard ink-jet droplets are about the same size as human cells. By 2008, he had adapted the technology to create a working bioprinter that successfully printed biotubing similar to blood vessels.

The first commercial organ printer (the NovaGen MMX) was produced in 2009 by Organovo, a San Diego-based company. To date, the company has been successful at creating functional blood vessels and cardiac tissue.

Researchers at Organovo discovered that one of the most complex steps in bioprinting is the positioning of the cell dispensing capillary tip attached to the print head. It needed to be consistently placed within microns of a designated position. Enter Invetech, a partner that provided a computer-controlled, laser-based calibration system that delivered the placement repeatability that was required.

In December 2010, Organovo used this technology to create the first blood vessels made from cells that were cultured from a person. The researchers were also successful at implanting bioprinted nerve grafts into rats.

Although the initial focus of the Organovo bio-printer is to create simple tissues, such as blood vessels and nerve conduit, it holds the potential to build any tissue or organ. The company's goal is to create technology that will provide a wide range of tissue and organs on demand for specific patients. Human trials of these bio-printed tissues are expected to begin by 2015.

The end-game would be to cost-effectively create fully-functional replacement organs ranging from hearts to lungs to livers, starting with cells derived from the patient. This would avoid the scarcity and rejection issues that have limited the potential for organ transplants.

Until now, one of the biggest hurdles in creating fully-functioning, complex organs is growing the various tissues in the same way nature would. This is enabled by the use of *scaffolds*, which are artificial, lattice-like structures capable of supporting tissue formation. In the tissue engineering process, they provide the template to support the growing cells. Then over time, the scaffold is absorbed into the body, leaving behind the natural tissue.

Scaffolds are typically engineered with pores that allow the cells to migrate throughout the material. The pores are often created using salt, sugar, or carbon dioxide gas. However, all of these additives create an imperfect pore structures and, in the case of salt, this require a lengthy process to remove the salt after the pores are created.

However, a new kind of scaffold, just developed at the Feinberg School of Medicine, eliminates these problems. They are created from a combination of ceramic nanoparticles and elastic polymers, formed in a vacuum through a process termed "low-pressure foaming," which requires high heat. The result is a series of pores that are highly interconnected and not dependent on the use of salt.

The resulting tissue scaffolds are not only highly flexible, but they can be tailored to degrade at varying speeds depending on the recovery time expected for the patient. These scaffolds can also incorporate nano-sized fibers, providing a new range of mechanical and biological properties.

What's ahead?

First, personalized medicine will eventually become the standard in care. This change will be driven at first by organizations such as the U.S. Veterans Affairs system, which have low turnover in their membership and can therefore count on recouping their costs. Those

134

organizations will collaborate with diagnostic companies to generate the long-term data needed to determine which tests are worth adopting for which populations.

Second, to encourage the evolution toward personalized medicine, reimbursement systems will be realigned to reward results rather than performing procedures. Today, doctors and technicians are paid each time they perform a procedure, regardless of the outcome for the patient. For example, a genetic test for breast cancer called Oncotype DX can tell a physician whether chemotherapy is likely to work or not. But the test actually decreases the number of patients that the doctor will wind up treating with chemotherapy, therefore reducing his earnings. These incentives will need to be realigned in order to usher in the era of personalized medicine.

Third, expect some applications of personalized medicine to start at the high end of the healthcare market and trickle down. The preventative and screening applications of personalized medicine deliver such clear benefits that sequencing and analysis will become a routine part of healthcare in OECD countries by 2025. However, other personalized therapies, such as manufactured replacement organs, will initially only be available on a limited basis at a high price. However, consumer demand and the IT-driven economics of the underlying technology will deliver even those therapies to the mass market by 2030. From there, most personalized medicine therapies will spread to all but the bottom tier of the developing world by 2050.

Fourth, the new operating realities of personalized medicine will force healthcare processes to change. Over the past 40 years, medicine has come to rely heavily on batteries of tests and that will only become more common as personalized medicine advances. Physicians, laboratories, hospitals, medical device companies, and pharmaceutical companies will all focus on delivering exactly the right solution for each patient. Much of the effort will go into making sure each patient has access to the diet, habits, and preventive therapies needed to stay healthy in the first place.

Fifth, today's FDA procedures will need to be redesigned to accommodate the realities of healthcare based on individualized solutions. Today's regulatory environment is well-suited to the development and regulation of "blockbuster drugs" and other therapies aimed at millions of patients. The ability to test thousands of compounds on cells from a single patient and assess which combination of treatments might yield the most effective outcome for that patient will require a new approach. Because of the very small sample sizes involved in many treatment regimes, the approval process will need to shift from a focus on the treatment itself to a focus on the reliability and efficacy of the processes used to screen and administer treatments.

Sixth, pharmaceutical companies will soon include bio-marker information with many of their drugs to indicate whether a given patient will respond well to them. Sixteen of the twenty largest pharmaceutical companies surveyed by McKinsey and Company said that 30 to 50 percent of the drugs they're developing have a bio-marker program, and they predict that the percentage will rise.[9] Expect to see personalized genetic data being matched with medications in the near future to achieve maximum benefit for the patient.

Seventh, personalized medicine will also open the door for a range of new start-up companies in the diagnostic testing field. Despite the overblown claims of some of today's direct-to-consumer testing companies, this will eventually become a mainstream technology. Since drug development itself is so expensive, smaller firms can't afford to get involved in that area. However, they could step in to produce low-cost diagnostic tests for particular drugs that have biomarkers, and thereby lock up the market on certain diseases. The hot research projects to watch will focus on cancer, immune system disorders, and infectious diseases. Other personalized therapies, including anti-coagulants and treatments for depression and schizophrenia, are also ripe for development.

Eighth, mass-market blockbusters will still exist, but they'll represent a far smaller share of revenues. Drugs for typical individuals with common maladies will still represent big opportunities for pharmaceutical companies; in these cases, personalized medicine will help predict those who will have adverse side-effects. By 2030, it's likely that half or more of industry-wide profits will come from personalized solutions and the rest will still come from standardized blockbusters.

Ninth, stem cell therapies will provide commercially-viable, cost-

effective solutions to many of our toughest healthcare challenges by 2025. Already personalized therapies based on stem cells are demonstrating their ability to restore hearts damaged by heart attacks, eliminate the symptoms of Parkinson's disease, repair stroke damage, and rejoin severed spinal cords, at least in laboratory animals. While other stem cell varieties have advantages in certain situations, induced pluripotent stem cells (IPSCs) and conditionally reprogrammed cells (CRCs) seem most are likely to dominate the most niches.

Tenth, tissue engineering will become a $100 billion dollar business by 2030, unless a competitive transplant technology leaps ahead. The rapidly aging populations of North America, Japan, China, and the EU will require many more organs in the coming years than can possibly be provided from voluntary human donors. Aside from coerced donations, the only viable solutions seem to be xenotransplantation and tissue engineering. And, even if xenotransplantation (discussed in Chapter 8) makes the great leaps needed to deliver cheap, compatible transplant organs, tissue engineering will still become a major industry because of its ability to produce simple tissue grafts in a matter of days or weeks.

Eleventh, by the mid 2020s, "liposome microarrays" will permit hospitals to design a personalized chemotherapy regimen for each cancer patient. The result will be more predictable treatment of tumors and greatly reduced side-effects. This will lead to much better outcomes, fewer re-occurrences, and lower overall costs.

Twelfth, the big regulatory challenge of the 2020s will come, not from personalized therapies, but from ensuring the ethical use of personalized medical data. Armed with a person's complete genome and basic medical history, a computer will be able to forecast a person's longevity, likely future illnesses, and biological risk factors. Armed with this information, employers, insurers, and even potential spouses could make decisions that are detrimental to the individual. The challenge will be to set let limits on the accessibility and use of this information, while still getting the benefits associated with personalized medicine. It is likely to be 2050 or beyond before these issues are fully resolved.

9

How could bio-reengineering save our world?

> "Every orchid or rose or lizard or snake is the work of a dedicated and skilled breeder. There are thousands of people, amateurs and professionals, who devote their lives to this business. Now imagine what will happen when the tools of genetic engineering become accessible to these people."
>
> --Freeman Dyson

Bio-reengineering is the term we use to describe the practical applications of gene-splicing, more technically known as "recombinant DNA technology." Gene-splicing has been around since the mid-1970s, but it has only been due to recent advances in bioinformatics that its full potential has begun to be realized. Essentially, bio-reengineering allows scientists to manipulate living matter, including human bodies, by adding, deleting, or changing their "building blocks" at the molecular level, much as children build and rebuild objects with Lego toys.

In this chapter, we'll examine five revolutionary branches of bio-reengineering:

1. Genetically-enabled agriculture at the core of "second green revolution."

2. Synthetic biomaterials.
3. Gene therapy.
4. Biosynthetic drugs.
5. Transgenic animals.

While these represent only a few of the many economic sectors being revolutionized by bio-reengineering, these are the ones that will create tens of trillions of dollars worth of economic value, as well as hundreds of millions of new jobs worldwide, in the coming Golden Age. In the process, these industries will transform the lives of everyone on this planet by 2050.

The bio-entrepreneurial era dawns

It reads like the beginning of a Michael Crichton novel: "Why struggle with cloning when we can build genes to your specifications?" says the ad for a company called Genewiz.

It goes on: "Genewiz can synthesize codon-optimized cDNA, gene variants, artificially designed DNA, or any other sequence for your research. Simply provide a nucleotide or amino acid sequence, and we will ship your desired gene cloned into your choice of plasmid."

But it's not science fiction. Genewiz is a real company selling the components for re-programming life.

For investors waiting for the next big technological breakthrough, bio-reengineering may be it.

Even though scientists have known the structure of DNA since 1953, and they've been splicing genes since 1974, so-called "synthetic biology" is becoming a practical reality only now because of the dramatic progress that has taken place in *gene sequencing* and *gene synthesis*. Let's quickly define those two terms:

- *Gene sequencing,* which is at the core of bioinformatics, is the process of reading the sequence of base pairs from a sample of DNA and storing it in a computer.
- *Gene synthesis* involves creating new DNA, typically based on computer-generated instructions.

140

Between them lies the real value-added in synthetic biology: creating a new and improved genetic sequence which, when synthesized and inserted into an organism, will deliver better, faster, and cheaper results than natural alternatives.

Automating the sequencing and synthesis steps has dramatically lowered economic barriers to entering this new industry. Today, anyone with a budget of $25,000 to $30,000 can have a bacterial genome sequenced and synthesized with modifications by a company like Genewiz or Eurofins MWG Operon, ready to insert in a new host cell. So beyond the limited amount of cash required to purchase these services, all that's really needed is the scientific expertise to drive the overall project and perform some of the key procedures before sequencing and after synthesis.

With the arrival of predefined BioBricks, the design of modified genomes is becoming simpler and quicker all the time. BioBricks are standard sequences of DNA that encode basic biological functions. With them, anyone can program living organisms in the same way that a computer can be programmed.

The vast and expanding library of BioBricks is maintained by the BioBrick Foundation, a non-profit organization founded by engineers and scientists from MIT, Harvard, and UC San Francisco. New England Biolabs is now selling a BioBrick assembly kit, which allows easy assembly of BioBricks to create genetic systems. With it, *anyone* can become a genetic engineer for the amazing price of $235.

An unexpected factor in the growth of interest in synthetic biology among college students is the International Genetically Engineered Machine competition (iGEM), in which undergraduate students are given a kit of these biological parts. They then spend the summer working at their own schools and using the BioBricks or new parts that they design themselves to build biological systems and make them function in living cells. This competition has grown from 5 teams in 2004 to 245 teams in 2012, involving more than 3,000 participants from 34 countries. They have designed everything from cells that blink to a biosensor for arsenic.[1]

One of the more remarkable developments came from half a dozen undergraduates from the University of California at Berkeley

141

and three high school students. They developed an artificial red blood cell made from E. coli that produced hemoglobin and carried oxygen in the bloodstream. With chronic shortages of donated blood for transfusion, it's easy to imagine the commercial success of a successful synthetic blood substitute.

Human-driven evolution in the blink of an eye

It is stunning how fast all this has occurred.

Synthesis of the first gene in a lab was accomplished by an Indian Nobel laureate in 1972. By 2009, *Bloomberg* was reporting developments at Harvard University that opened the doors to creating synthetic life, man-made organisms, and novel proteins not found in nature. The research was led by George Church, who was a key player in the launch of the human genome project in the 1980s.[2]

This led directly to the breakthrough achieved in May 2010 by Craig Venter's company, Synthetic Genomics. Venter's team of researchers announced, in the journal *Science,* that they had created the "first synthetic self-replicating life form ever created in the lab."[3] Since creating genuine synthetic life is essentially a different enterprise than simply high-jacking the mechanisms of life through bio-reengineering, we'll wait to address *those* implications in Chapter 10.

However, both set the stage for the big story of the coming decade: the dawning of what we call "the bio-entrepreneur era." That era will be enabled by the combination of cost-effective sequencing and synthesis embedded in companies like Genewiz, coupled with the accessible codified knowledge in the form of BioBricks.

Why is this milestone so crucial? The bio-engineering done by Big Pharma and well-funded biotech startups since the discovery of gene splicing in the 1970s is analogous to the digital computing world inhabited by mainframes from 1950 to the mid-'60s. Sequencing the first complete Human Genome in 2003 was somewhat analogous to developing UNIX and solid-state memory: the underpinnings of the minicomputer revolution.

Now, high-speed, low-cost sequencing, coupled with cheap, reliable gene synthesis and libraries of off-the-shelf BioBricks, have put biotech at roughly the same stage where infotech resided just after Intel developed the first true microprocessor in 1971. So, it's likely that some obscure biotech grad students will soon fill 21st century roles analogous to those of a young Steve Jobs or Bill Gates. And just as the companies created by people like Jobs and Gates have revolutionized our lives, the companies created by the new generation of bio-entrepreneurs will do so even more.

The second green revolution: Genetically-enabled agriculture and biomaterials

The Great 21st Century Food Challenge

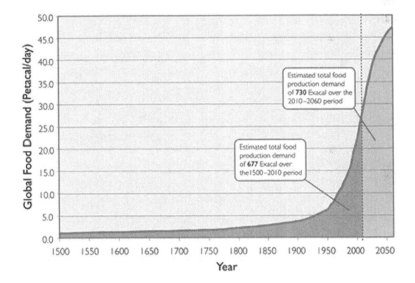

Source: CSIRO Australia, 6 October 2009
The challenge to produce enough food will be greater over the next 50 years than in all of human history.

One of the industries where this revolution will make the greatest impact on our lives is in agriculture. Between 2010 and 2060, the world's cumulative consumption of food will exceed the total amount of food that was consumed since the beginning of agriculture over 10,000 years ago through 2009.

It is estimated that to feed the growing population by 2050, at least 70 percent more food will be needed each year than is produced today. In developing countries, many experts believe this goal will not be met since current investments in agriculture are woefully inadequate. [4]

In 2008, during the financial crisis, the world got a glimpse of what will likely happen if food supplies don't keep pace. When the price of food commodities soared, hundreds of millions of poor people, who already spend up to 80 percent of their incomes on food, were drastically affected. Thirty countries experienced food riots, and two governments fell.

However, there is actually reason for optimism today because breakthroughs in infotech, biotech, and nanotech are already converging on solutions that promise to revolutionize agriculture. Collectively, we refer to this as the Second Green Revolution, because it builds on the foundation of the first Green Revolution, which created a quantum leap in food production beginning in the 1950s.

Specifically, there are five technological forces rooted in bio-reengineering that are driving the second green revolution and giving it the potential to take root and serve populations worldwide:

1. GM crops
2. Smart water
3. Elimination of waste and spoilage
4. Effective recycling
5. Optimized packaging

The first force is the rise of genetically modified crops, also known as GM crops. These crops not only produce more food on the same land, but are:

*   Resistant to plant diseases and insects.
*   More nutritious.
*   More adaptable to environmental conditions such as drought, cold, and heat.
*   Able to thrive in soils containing minerals like salt that would kill traditional crops.

In the 17 years since bio-engineered crops were first commercialized, their production has steadily increased. In 2012, the volume of biotech crops reached a record 170.3 million hectares, an increase of 10.3 million hectares from 2011.[5]

This is a 100-fold increase from the 1.7 million hectares planted in 1996, when the crops were first available commercially. According to Clive James, founder of the International Service for the Acquisition of Agri-Biotech Applications (ISAAA), "This makes biotech crops the fastest adopted crop technology in recent history."[6]

In fact, 17.3 million farmers worldwide are now using GM crops, up 600,000 from the previous year.[7]

In 2012, the U.S. continued its lead in producing bio-engineered crops with 69.5 million hectares, which represents 41 percent of the global biotech crop. However, 2012 was the first year in which developing countries surpassed industrial nations in biotech crop area, with 52 percent of the global total.[8]

According to the latest analysis published in the *International Journal of Biotechnology*, genetically modified (GM) agriculture has added 83 million and 130 million tons, respectively, to global production of soybeans and corn, and net farm level economic benefits amounted to almost $11 billion in 2009 alone. More importantly, 53.1 percent of the farm income benefits went to developing country farmers, and the vast majority of those income gains were from GM insect-resistant cotton and GM herbicide-tolerant soybeans.[9]

Farmers are naturally risk-averse. So, they are embracing GM technology for one simple reason: Bio-engineered crops deliver substantial and sustainable socio-economic and environmental benefits. Four of the biggest benefits include:

1. Bio-engineered crops contribute to food, feed, and fiber security and self-sufficiency. Between 1996 and 2010, even as food became more affordable and agriculture increased in productivity, $98 billion in profits was generated at the farm level due to biotech crops.[10]

2. Bio-engineered crops help save land. Because of their higher productivity, less land is needed for growing GM crops. Between 1996 and 2010, 91 million additional hectares were not needed because of this type of food production.[11]

3. Bio-engineered crops help reduce poverty and hunger. Foods

are not the only GM crops. In developing countries such as China, India, and Pakistan, biotech cotton provided more than 15 million small resource-poor farmers cash income in 2011. This biotech cotton is genetically engineered to produce its own insecticide to protect it from destructive caterpillars.[12]

4. Bio-engineered crops help save the environment. In 2011 alone, CO_2 emissions were reduced by 23 billion kilograms, which is equal to the exhaust generated by 10.2 million vehicles; and 473 million kg a.i. of pesticides did not have to be used. (kg a.i. means the number of kilograms of the actual active ingredient in the pesticide, as opposed to the total pesticide solution.)[13]

Blight-resistant potatoes and "golden rice" that are genetically-modified to provide high levels of beta carotene are just two examples of the way foods are currently being engineered to perform better and offer more nutrition. And, according to a 2013 report by the ISAAA, farmers will soon be able to plant rice with enhanced Vitamin A, soybeans that are free of trans fats, and soybeans that are enriched with omega-3.[14]

As awareness of these benefits grows, consumer attitudes toward genetically modified foods are changing. For example, a study by Iowa State University revealed interesting results. Generally, people are willing to pay *more* for GM foods if the modifications enhance consumer traits, such as taste, coloration, and vitamins. However, if the GM food contains enhanced traits only of value to the farmer, such as pest and drought resistance, consumers expect to pay 15 percent *less*. So, it appears consumers are *not* uneasy buying modified foods as long as the foods provide health or aesthetic benefits.[15]

Nevertheless, despite the total absence of reported links between GM food and adverse health or damage to the environment, there are still many who oppose bio-engineered crops. Europeans have for years resisted this technology, although that bias appears to be waning. Recently, 41 Swedish scientists wrote an open letter to politicians and environmentalists emphasizing the need to rethink European legislation that restricts the use of GM crops.

The second force helping drive the food revolution is "smart irrigation," which rests on the twin foundations of IT and bio-engineering.

Currently, 70 percent of worldwide fresh water usage is allocated to farming. The vast majority of that water is wasted through run-off and evaporation.

By 2050, with a population of 9 billion people, this water usage pattern will not be sustainable.

We already have many tools that will let us fix this problem. One is computerized irrigation systems that use sensor networks to direct water where it is needed, when it is needed. Other systems have been developed that actually pull water out of the air in humid countries, lessening the demand on in-ground water supplies.

Another answer will be bio-engineered crops that require dramatically less water or can even grow in salt water. By the end of 2013, the first biotech maize hybrids that provide a degree of tolerance to drought will be commercially available in the U.S. Then, in 2017, a tropical, drought-tolerant biotech maize is expected to be made available for sub-Saharan Africa. These advances will particularly help developing countries where drought occurs more often.[16]

The third technological force will be elimination of waste and spoilage.

Historically, more food is wasted than is consumed. The culprits are pests and spoilage, resulting in far less than half of the food grown in the world being consumed by either people, farm animals, or pets. In some cases, the pesticides needed to protect these crops are causing harm as well as doing good. One example is the recent decline in useful bee populations, which may be due to pesticides.

A combination of solutions will be required. Plants are being bio-engineered to be resistant to pests, and better pesticides and herbicides are becoming available. Insect pests are also being controlled by genetically modifying insects to thwart reproduction as well as attacking microbes and parasites.

Meanwhile deploying new harvesting, storage, packing, and shipping methods will protect food from pests and spoilage once it's ready to harvest.

The fourth force is effective waste processing and recycling. Not only are we seeing a huge increase in agricultural demand for food crops, but there is an enormous shift from plant to animal protein as the world becomes more affluent. With this increase in animal production comes an increase in animal waste generated by feedlots, fish farms, and meat processing plants. An important issue is how to deal with this waste.

Rising Affluence Drives Shift to Meat

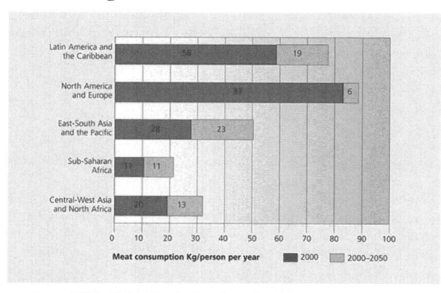

Source: IFPRI—IMPACT projections, September 2007
Global affluence is driving a dramatic shift from plant to animal nutrition. The result is a dramatic rise in the demand for animal feed grains and corresponding explosion in animal waste products.

One long-term solution is "in vitro meat production," which eliminates the need for animals. Instead, muscle stem cells are grown in an ultra-clean food processing plant to produce very healthy ground meat suitable for hamburgers, sausages, and tacos. This "cultured meat" is not destined to totally replace conventional meat. However, it will provide some relief from the growing waste issue, while helping to feed the growing world population.[17]

Another part of the equation is using bio-tech to clean up

conventional meat production. Synthetic life research, which we'll examine in the next chapter, is on the verge of delivering microbes that turn animal waste and remnants into useful by-products that can be used to generate energy, produce crops, or act as industrial feedstocks.

New uses for waste products are also being devised. A new method is being developed for converting billions of pounds of chicken feathers into plastic. Inexpensive and abundant, feathers are a source for keratin, a tough protein, which has been found to provide strength and durability for plastics. An added benefit is that this plastic features a high degree of bio-availability.[18]

Finally, the fifth force involves optimization in the packaging, transportation, and distribution chain for food. One important shift already taking place in the U.S. is the elimination of the transportation bottlenecks created by trucks and trains. Because of poor coordination, perishable foods have, at high expense, been shipped on trucks from "farm centers" such as Florida, central California, and the Midwest to "consumption centers" on the West Coast and in the Northeast.

Today, information technology is permitting farmers, grocers, and intermediaries to tightly coordinate their activities to make low-cost shipping possible. Much of this is a return on heavy investments in IT-intensive logistics, driven by retailers since the late 1970s.

At the same time that we're realizing the power of optimizing the long supply chains, it's also becoming increasingly possible to shorten the supply chain everywhere. That's why the biggest impact from streamlining won't come in the developed world; it will come in the developing world. Specifically, in countries with poor logistics infrastructure such as India and China, it often makes more sense to move the food processing capital equipment to rural areas and encourage people to both produce and consume locally.

However, where this idea of shortening the supply chain intersects trends toward massive urbanization and new materials technology, it's leading to a totally different paradigm: vertical urban farming. This is an avant-garde concept with many proponents. The question is not whether it could work, but whether it can become a cost-effective solution for the developing world within 30 years.[19]

Closer to realization is the idea of better food packaging optimized to make food easier to transport and store. One innovative development, known as modified atmosphere packaging, is being used to reduce food spoilage by controlling the growth of organisms. The result is a longer shelf life and safer foods.

Another new type of packaging changes color to alert customers when food is starting to go bad as the result of broken packaging or poor refrigeration.[20] Packaging is also being designed with an eye to low-impact disposal; cheap bio-engineered plastics that break down quickly in landfills are already in development.

To understand how bio-reengineering contributes to resolving issues of packaging and waste-handling, consider two examples:

Researchers at Europe's Delft University of Technology have succeeded in breeding bacteria that turn the main sugars in agricultural bio-wastes left over from food production into environmentally-friendly products, including bio-plastics. This means that potato peels can be transformed into sunglasses, and cane sugar can be converted into car bumpers.

The Delft researchers used two genes from *E. coli* bacteria that make sugar digestible. Further, they kept choosing the bacteria that performed the process with the least waste, and then using them for the next generation of bacteria. The team ended up with a new type of bacteria, which is more efficient than any previously used bio-reengineered solution.[21]

Meanwhile, researchers at the UK's University of Wolverhampton figured out how to create bio-plastics from waste cooking oil. The researchers found they could cut the cost of using glucose as a raw material in growing bacteria by substituting the used oil. Not only did they create 300 percent more PHB with oil than with glucose, but they also discovered that the bioplastic was more suitable for making high-value medical implants.[22]

These five forces of technology promise to meet the world's sharply escalating food demands as we move into the 21st century. In the process, they will create hundreds of millions of low- and medium-skilled jobs where they are needed the most.

Drug manufacturing made easy

A large number of pharmaceutical compounds are relatively simple "small molecules" that can be easily synthesized by routine chemical operations on an industrial scale. That includes drugs like ibuprofen.

A second category of drugs involves large complex molecules that are produced easily in large quantities by living organisms under factory or natural conditions. The first antibiotic, penicillin, falls into that category.

However, many of the most promising drugs for cancer therapy are very rare in nature and impossible to directly synthesize in the laboratory at any kind of reasonable cost. The cancer drug Taxol falls into this category. Fortunately, bio-reengineering solves that problem. By splicing a gene extracted from a plant or animal into a prolific and well-understood bacterium, we can create a *drug bio-factory* that produces the rare and expensive drug, cheaply.

The result has been a proliferation of life-saving drugs that would not have otherwise been possible. As we move further along our path toward widespread personalized medicine, the importance of this avenue will only increase.

The power of gene therapy

For people in the developed world, no application of bio-reengineering is likely to have as big an impact as "gene therapy." Gene therapy is defined as "the transplantation of normal genes into cells in place of missing or defective ones in order to correct genetic disorders in those cells." Although it's been around since the early 90s, gene therapy has, until now, been reserved for severe diseases with few other treatment options.

However, gene therapy has recently been proven capable of competing with and disrupting traditional forms of treatment. The best example to date is the recent report that gene therapy was successful in treating hemophilia B. This means that it could replace the need for lifelong protein replacement infusions for people with this condition. If successful in subsequent clinical trials, this treatment for hemophilia

B, and a similar approach in development to treat hemophilia A, could take over the $6.5 billion a year market for hemophilia therapies.

And this is not the only success. As documented in the journal *Human Gene Therapy*, the technical feasibility of gene therapy "has been established in multiple diseases and with different technology platforms." Now that the technology is working, the next phase is to develop commercially viable models for gene therapy in the health care marketplace, so that these therapies can be delivered to the patients who need them.[23]

To understand why this is so important, consider just a few examples of on-going research:

- In a study published in the journal *PLoS-One*, University of Missouri researchers found that gene therapy, using a proven "longevity" gene, energized mice during exercise and might be applicable to *humans*. After gene therapy with the "longevity" gene, the researchers studied how well the mice performed on treadmill exercises and found that the mice could run farther, faster, and longer than other mice of the same age and sex. The researchers attribute this performance enhancement to the gene called MCAT; they believe the gene is responsible for removing toxic substances, known as free radicals, from the mitochondria of the cell. These results suggest that similar therapy may one day improve the life quality of the elderly. As such, it could have important implications for many diseases, such as muscular dystrophy, heart disease, diabetes, and neuro-degenerative diseases.[24]
- An innovative genetic strategy for rendering T-cells resistant to HIV infection without affecting their normal growth and activity was described in the journal *Human Gene Therapy*. A team of researchers from Japan, Korea, and the U.S. developed an anti-HIV gene therapy method in which a bacterial gene called "mazF" is transferred into "CD4+" T-cells. The MazF protein is an enzyme that destroys gene transcripts, preventing protein synthesis. When HIV infects treated T lymphocytes, MazF is induced, blocking HIV replication and, essentially, making the T-cells HIV resistant.[25]
- Even more exciting is an experimental cure for Type 1 diabetes

152

that has shown a nearly 80 percent success rate in curing diabetic mice. The results, presented at The Endocrine Society's 93rd Annual Meeting in Boston, offer hope of curing a disease that affects 3 million Americans. The investigators added a gene called CD274 that inhibits the activity of cells that destroy islets cells in patients with Type 1 diabetes. With just one injection of this gene therapy, the mice remained diabetes-free long term, and their bodies returned to normal insulin levels.[26]

Going forward, these examples represent just the most basic beginnings of what can be achieved with gene therapy.

Transgenic replacement organs

In Chapter 8, we discussed the shortage of organ transplants, which only promises to get worse as the population ages. By 2025, we're likely to see widespread availability of organs manufactured using stem cells and bioprinters. However, these may prove to be expensive.

Fortunately, there is an alternative solution that is likely to be less expensive and available even sooner. This technology, based on bio-reengineering techniques, is called *transgenic xeno-transplantation.* This is the transplantation of organs and tissue from one species to another. For humans, the most likely animal donors are pigs, due to their comparable size, their rapid growth, and the physiological similarity of their organs to ours.

A major hurdle with any transplantation, but particularly xeno-transplantation, is the rejection of organs as the result of antibodies in the recipient's immune system, which attack the donated tissue. Strides have been made to overcome this problem, but other serious roadblocks remain, including incompatibilities between human and pig anti-coagulation mechanisms, and the potential presence of pathogens that can be deadly to humans, such as those that lead to "mad cow disease."

Now, however, a novel new approach has been developed that would eliminate all of these problems. What is this "game-changing" new approach? It's a futuristic idea called "blastocyst complementation."

Put simply, it's a technique in which the organs of one species are grown in a different, yet similar, species by injecting stem cells into embryos of the second species. Thanks to the efforts of researchers in Japan, this technique is no longer just theoretical.

Recently, scientists at the Center for Stem Cell Biology and Regenerative Medicine at the University of Tokyo have successfully engineered mice to grow rat organs. The mice had been genetically altered so they could not produce their own pancreases.[27]

When stem cells from rats were injected into the mice embryos, they grew rat pancreases. The Japanese team believes this technique can be used to grow any type of organ in a compatible species. Professor Hiromitsu Nakauchi, director of the center, is confident we'll soon be able to apply this technique to produce human organs in other species. As of this writing, the center is seeking permission to use human stem cells; but, in the meantime, they have been able to generate human blood in pigs by injecting human blood stem cells into pig fetuses.

Understandably, this possible breakthrough is getting a lot of attention. Professor Chris Mason, Chair of Regenerative Medicine at University College London, paints an exciting scenario when he states, "For something like a kidney transplant where it is not urgent, it would be highly attractive to be able to take cells from a patient, grow them in this way, and deliver a personalized kidney."

Similarly, to treat people suffering from diabetes, human stem cells could be injected into a pig to grow a replacement pancreas.

Bio-terrorism thwarted

Another critical implication of bio-reengineering is its capacity to both enable and thwart bio-terrorism. In the coming era of bio-entrepreneurship, the ability of well-educated terrorists to engineer new strains of pathogens is clearly a problem. However, we argue this downside threat is more than offset by the new resources available to counter the threat.

154

As genomic pioneer J. Craig Venter explained at a late-2012 conference sponsored by *Wired* magazine, the conventional response to bio-terrorism and natural pandemics relies on an outdated model from the Mass Production era. When scientists identify a pathogen threat, it takes days to identify the pathogen, weeks to develop and test the antigen, and months to manufacture and distribute the doses. Then, if the crisis is averted, tens of millions of doses costing hundreds of millions of dollars sit in warehouses until they expire and must be destroyed.[28]

Venter suggests a new 21st century model that harnesses infotech, bioinformatics, and bio-reengineering. How does it work? As soon as a suspicious outbreak occurs, the pathogen is isolated and sequenced. Bio-informatics is used to identify candidate antigens, which are tested *in vitro* and *in vivo* against the pathogen.

The antigen with the best results and minimum side effects is quickly synthesized from digital data in a lab close to those who can benefit most from treatment. The antigen is inserted into a host organism that mass-produces it. Finally, purified doses are administered to those who might be, or have been exposed to the pathogen, stopping the crisis in its tracks. Cost and response time are minimized.

More importantly, coupling this neutralizing response with a retaliatory capability will make even the most fanatical terrorist think twice. Just as the doctrine of "mutually assured destruction" thwarted a nuclear confrontation in the Cold War, the idea that any bio-terror attack would have limited impact and lead to retaliation on one's allies by conventional means would create a huge barrier to such activities. In fact, the lack of bio-warfare and chemical warfare in World War II largely stemmed from such a scenario growing out of experiences in World War I.

Putting in place the kinds of capabilities that Venter suggests would provide an excellent first line of defense against naturally-occurring epidemics that could cause millions of deaths.

What lies ahead?

First, the Second Green Revolution will dramatically improve the lives of over half the people on this planet by 2050. Since the dawn of mankind, people have worried about having enough to eat and drink. And even in the 21st century, over half the world's people spend the majority of their incomes on the basic necessities of life. However, the five forces propelling bio-reengineering and the complementary technologies we've discussed will create a huge agricultural productivity leap, dramatically improving the affordability and quality of food. This revolution will employ a range of technologies to transform sunlight, water, air, waste products, and abundant minerals into cost-effective nutrition.

Second, bio-factories will transform "bio-wastes" into "bio-treasures." By hijacking the mechanisms of life, scientists have already turned a wide range of micro-organisms into bio-factories. Much of the early progress has involved high-value pharmaceuticals and specialty chemicals, but this technology will spread across the economy in the coming decades. As it matures, its scope will broaden dramatically. By 2040, almost all of the organic waste from cities, farms, and factories will be reprocessed into useful products. For example, scientists have already developed microbe-based systems that generate fuel and electricity as they purify water on a laboratory scale. And best of all, these solutions will prevail, not because of coercive regulations, but because they make economic sense.

Third, by 2025, gene therapies will go mainstream, curing disease and paving the way for life extension. Like so many technologies, gene therapy has had a long, slow "ramp up." Part of the problem is that scientists have not understood enough about genomics and cellular mechanisms to use it effectively. For instance, they've focused almost exclusively on the narrow set of medical conditions brought about by single genetic mutations. Secondly, they've relied on a few retro-virus-based "delivery vectors" for deploying the therapy. But, in the past few years, researchers have gained greater insight into more complex genetic conditions as well as safer, more reliable delivery mechanisms. As a result, science is now poised to make enormous leaps in terms of gene therapy applications. And some of the most exciting possibilities include research on extending humans' healthy life spans well beyond

156

today's norms.

Fourth, look for a booming market for products and methods related to BioBricks. Companies that target would-be entrepreneurs—especially the ones who are now in high school or college—will do well. Two such companies already in existence are Ginkgo Bioworks and New England Biolabs. Expect to see more companies in this product space, soon.

Fifth, xeno-transplantation based on "blastocyst complementation" is likely to beat out "tissue engineering" in the organ transplant market through the mid-2020s. Like "blastocyst complementation," tissue engineering has a lot of hurdles to overcome before it can seriously compete with human donors. However, they'll both become targets for commercialization as part of a broader effort to deliver better outcomes, while containing the overall cost of healthcare. Although developing donor animals will not be cheap, and this approach will involve surgical costs comparable to conventional transplants, there will be a big savings when the costs of long-term care and treatment are compared to transplantation. While the cost of growing organs will likely be higher with tissue engineering, the harvesting and implanting may actually be less costly than with xeno-transplantation. In either case, the real benefit of both technologies will come in not having to wait on a human organ donor who may never arrive.

Sixth, ethical issues are certain to be raised about breeding animals simply to be used as a source of human organs. Animal rights activists will surely go into full swing, even attempting to block research and development through the courts. Although they have succeeded in discouraging many people from wearing fur, they will face a steeper uphill battle arguing against a technology that promises to extend the length and quality of life for ailing humans. One obvious counter-argument is that we already raise animals for life-sustaining food, so it is logical to raise them for life-sustaining and life-enhancing organs.

Seventh, in many countries, adoption of xeno-transplantation will undoubtedly be delayed by government regulations. It will start from safety concerns, which are legitimate, since well-established procedures will need to be followed. This oversight will make procedures burdensome and costly, meaning that fewer people will benefit. This promises to open up another lucrative market for medical tourism. [For more on medical tourism, visit the *Trends* piece **MEDICAL TOURISM** (http://www.audiotech.com/trends-magazine/medical-tourism).]

10

How will synthetic life forms impact our economy and our lives?

"What I cannot build, I cannot understand."

--Richard Feynman

On May 20, 2010, the prestigious journal *Science* published a scientific paper that is certain to have a bigger effect on history than landing men on the moon or breaking the sound barrier. In that scientific paper, J. Craig Venter and his colleagues announced, "the first self-replicating *synthetic* life form ever created."[1]

Venter, an American biologist, led one of the two scientific efforts that resulted in the first successful sequencing of the human genome in 2000. In 2005, he founded Synthetic Genomics, with the goal of creating man-made life forms and applying them to real-world problems. It took Synthetic Genomics just five years to achieve its first major breakthrough. How did Venter's team do it?

They started by sequencing the genome of an existing bacterium, and storing the digitized sequence in a computer. Then, they used a computer-driven machine that assembles DNA sequences from amino acids to synthesize a genome nearly identical to that of the original organism. Finally, they inserted this synthetic genome into a different bacterium. With the new DNA on board, the recipient bacterium followed the instructions of that synthetic DNA, immediately transforming itself into the same type of cell as the donor.

From that moment forward, the organism began to reproduce billions of copies of itself. Although the *recipient* bacterium was not synthetic, once the synthetic DNA was on board and the cell began reproducing, within 20 or 30 generations, there was none of the original protein left in any of the progeny cells. At that point, it had become a legitimate man-made product.

As Venter put it, "We call it synthetic because the cell is totally derived from a synthetic chromosome, made with four bottles of chemicals on a chemical synthesizer, starting with information in a computer."

When the scientists were creating the synthetic DNA, they made a few changes. One change was to include a so-called "watermark" in a section of non-essential DNA. The "digital watermark" clearly identifies the DNA as Synthetic Genomics' intellectual property. And it clearly shows up in the proteins of the billions of new cells, indicating that they are *synthetic*, not naturally occurring.

The implications of synthetic biology

This represents a major milestone in the biological sciences. No longer are we restricted to observing nature. We are now able to control the very code that defines living things. Now, the race is on to define the synthetic biology game and dominate it.

As explained in Chapter 1, civilization is about to enter the Deployment (Prosperity) period of the Digital revolution. In the Deployment period of each Boom, the major opportunities shift from the *core* technology to its ability to fundamentally transform other economic sectors.

Synthetic biology, also called "artificial life," involves applying information technology to program and transform living things. In the process, we will be able to transform industries like agriculture, health care, and energy in the coming 25 years more than

160

we have in the past 5,000 years.

To understand what's happening and why it's happening now, consider the fact that the *ability* to decode and digitize genomes has been slightly more than doubling every year for the past quarter of a century. As a result, the power to extract genetic information from living systems has increased 100 million times in that scant 25 years. Similarly, the *cost* of synthesizing DNA has been falling at its own exponential rate.

It's difficult to overstate the importance of these developments. A BBC report on the implications of the first synthetic life form used phrases like "the new industrial revolution." That's not far off. Synthetic life is to the computer revolution what computers were to electricity. We are now witnessing the very earliest stages of it.

Just to give a hint of what's in store, Venter and his partners are already working with pharmaceutical and oil companies, such as ExxonMobil, to build life forms that could produce fuel and medicines. Venter's team is specifically working on designing man-made algae that can take carbon dioxide out of the atmosphere and turn it into fuel.

Biology becomes a practical engineering discipline

But the most earth-shattering transformation may not be the recent reprogramming of an organism, but the more prosaic tasks involved in transforming *synthetic biology* from "pure research" into a "practical engineering discipline." From the day Crick and Watson determined the structure of the DNA molecule to the present, most of the work in biotech has been analogous to what Volta, Faraday, and Henry did with electricity.

Now, we're finally moving into an "era of standardization," like the one pioneered by Edison, Tesla, and Steinmetz. That means using standardized, interchangeable parts rather than handcrafted, one-off designs.

But instead of vacuum tubes, coils, transistors, capacitors, and resistors, synthetic biologists will use well-defined segments of DNA, RNA, and proteins, as well as metabolites, such as lipids, amino acids, nucleotides, and carbohydrates, as their building blocks to produce a specific desired functionality in a biological system.

By assembling those biological components in specific ways, they will produce living devices that carry out biochemical reactions and that control the flow of information to make the necessary physical processes occur.

For example, researchers at MIT are already building a library of these devices, which they call BioBricks. As we discussed in Chapter 9, BioBricks are standard sequences of DNA that encode basic biological functions, which allow living organisms to be programmed. There is a registry for these standard parts that is expanding weekly.

The researchers assemble these BioBricks into what they call modules, which are likened to integrated circuits in computers. By connecting the modules together inside of living cells, they can potentially program those cells to carry out any function of which a living system is capable.

This is possible because a living cell is a machine that carries out chemical reactions to sustain and reproduce itself. In the course of doing so, it follows a set of instructions contained in its DNA, and then manufactures substances such as proteins, which are its own building materials, and sugars, which are its fuel.

Synthetic biologists take advantage of this existing electro-mechanical platform and then alter the instructions to suit their purposes. So, for example, a biologist at the University of California in Berkeley was able to program cells to produce artemisinin, an anti-malarial drug, at a much lower cost than conventional methods.

Not surprisingly, applications for patents on new life forms are already overwhelming the U.S. Patent and Trademark Office. It seems like everyone is getting on the synthetic biology bandwagon. The Department of Energy is investing hundreds of millions of dollars in an effort to produce ethanol using artificial life forms.

In addition, an organization called Synthetic Biology Engineering Research Center, (SynBERC), was recently started by students, faculty, and staff at MIT and Harvard. It has already evolved into a consortium of researchers and laboratories from various institutions who are working on engineering biological systems.[2]

The SynBERC community has six stated aims:

1. To create standard biological parts that can be used to build biological systems.
2. To develop the design methods and tools for the biological engineering lab.
3. To reverse-engineer existing biological parts so that they can be used as off-the-shelf devices.
4. To reverse-engineer a simple generic bacterium as a platform for many biological devices.
5. To define the minimal genome needed to sustain life.
6. To expand the genetic code to use more base pairs and increase its diversity.

While the SynBERC community is one of the most active organizations in the field of synthetic biology, the field is rapidly crowding with other initiatives. For example, the Riken Research Institute in Japan known sponsored the "GenoCon International Contest of Genome Design" to tap into the power of crowdsourcing.[3]

The first challenge, announced early in 2010, was "To design a DNA sequence conferring to the *Arabidopsis thaliana* plant the functionality to effectively eliminate and detoxify airborne formaldehyde." During the following summer, 66 participants, including nine high school students, used Riken's SciNetS Scientists' Networking System to design a genome to solve the challenge.

Next, RIKEN chose five entries for further study. Two of those entries were submitted by high school students. Its research scientists then used each of the five designs to actually synthesize the DNA of the designs and grow real plants from them, and tested them to see whether they were tolerant to formaldehyde. Based on the results, the company awarded prizes and discovered new insights—such as the potential for to use genes from a fungus to detoxify formaldehyde— but perhaps more importantly, discovered new talent it can rely upon for future research projects.

The second GenoCon challenge, announced in 2012, closed in February 2013. It invited anyone, regardless of experience or education level, to use RIKEN's Web-based DNA design tool to "Design a plant promoter DNA sequence using the PromoterCAD software to search for functional regulatory DNA. Make a promoter which controls specific expression in a plant tissue such as leaf, stem, or root, or only at a particular time of day."[4]

RIKEN isn't the only organization that is using the "wisdom of the crowd" to solve complex problems in synthetic biology. Venter's two organizations, his non-profit J. Craig Venter Institute and his biotech firm Synthetic Genomics—are sponsoring a contest to design a genome completely on a computer. As he told the *Financial Times* early in 2013, "Three different versions of the genome are being constructed now, and we hope to know by the end of the summer whether any of these designs will work as a living cell."[5]

Venter is striving to find what he calls the "minimal genome"—the smallest number of genes that can keep an organism alive. By stripping genomes down to just the essential ingredients, Venter believes it will become easier, cheaper, and faster to synthesize microbes that will do exactly what we want them to do, including:

- Producing fuel that burns without creating pollution.
- Growing bigger, more nutritious crops on less land.
- Serving as vaccines against viruses.

Because of long development and regulatory approval cycles, especially in health care, the earliest economic winners will be companies making the tools needed for synthetic biology. The decoding and digitizing of genomes is improving at break-neck speed. Those companies that stay ahead of the curve in this technology will reap huge profits as synthetic biology finds its practical applications. Shrewd investors will keep an eye on the winning hardware and software platforms. When the tools become so cheap that a high school student can do synthetic biology, there will be an explosion of demand for these machines.

What lies ahead?

First, it's highly probable that "do-it-yourself" synthetic biology will become commonplace in the 2020s. Think of a 21st century Steve Jobs with a gene machine. This will spawn thousands of start-up companies, potentially dwarfing the waves of innovation seen in computers and the Internet in recent decades. While companies like Exxon are focusing their efforts on creating bacteria that can produce diesel fuel, curious students at high schools and colleges around the world will be creating life forms that perform functions that no one can now imagine. Expect major game-changing innovations to come out of obscure countries. A hint at this potential was seen recently when a team of students from Slovenia won the BioBrick trophy at MIT in two out of three years.[6]

Second, because of the growing popularity of this new science, universities will begin offering degrees specifically in "synthetic biology." In 2011, MIT offered a graduate Synthetic Biology course aimed at industry leaders in biotech, pharmaceutical, and chemical firms. The tuition for this single course was $3,250. Expect such courses to proliferate across the educational landscape, as engineering and life sciences departments cross-pollinate their faculty and staff. Already, we are seeing ads for post-doctoral researchers who are wanted at the Imperial College of London to "work in the Center for Synthetic Biology and Innovation." Young people with a view toward the next big wave will be immersing themselves in this field in the years just ahead.

Third, by 2040, synthetic life will merge with nanotechnology, which we'll discuss in Chapter 12, to create completely new engineering disciplines. The processes in biological systems are far more sophisticated and efficient than man-made mechanical processes. Even the dazzling inner workings of computers can't compare to the complexity and elegance of living systems. By harnessing the power of biology and combining it with the special properties of nanotech systems, inventions we can barely dream of now will become commonplace. For example, bio-synthetic robots that can patrol the bloodstream for invading organisms or for harmful substances, such as cholesterol and toxic chemicals, will revolutionize medicine. This will raise a host of new moral and ethical issues revolving around the potential of people to achieve a virtually endless life span. It will also raise questions about who should have access to these technologies.

Fourth, most commercial synthetic life forms will have genomes that make it *impossible* for them to survive outside the commercial setting. A key environmental advantage of synthetic life forms over naturally occurring organisms bio-reengineered for commercial applications is that they can be designed to ensure that they won't escape into the ecosystem or exchange genes with naturally occurring organisms. This is guaranteed by substituting a synthetic amino acid in the genome to take the place of one of the four standard amino acids found in naturally occurring DNA. Unlike genetically modified natural organisms, these synthetic organisms are easily isolated from the outside environment. This approach was experimentally validated in research recently reported in the journal *Angewandte Chemie.*[7]

Fifth, before 2030, synthetic organisms will be completely reengineered for dramatically improved safety and commercial results. Today's synthetic life forms have reprogrammed genomes, but their organelles and cell membranes come from an existing organism. However, researchers are busily working to optimize synthetic ribosomes, mitochondria, and cell membranes that will remove serious constraints to their commercial performance. This means the volume of food, fuel, or drugs that can be produced from a finite amount of input could be greatly increased, while undesirable by-products could be eliminated. Just as importantly, the new synthetic cell membranes will make the synthetic organisms easily identifiable from natural cells inside another living organism or in a production environment.

Sixth, look for venture capital to move into synthetic biology, often from the ground up. With thousands of hobbyists cooking up biological systems at home with cheap components, new devices for doing everything from producing biofuels to killing garden pests will be cropping up. There will be a mad rush, and for a time it will be difficult to make sense of the free-for-all. But groundbreaking disruptive technologies are likely to come from this sector.

Seventh, a "biology bubble" will inevitably develop involving the stocks of synthetic biology companies. Investors are naturally overly optimistic and overly enthusiastic. In the time frame of 10 to 15 years, we can expect to see an unrealistic bubble in biotech and synthetic life companies similar to the "vaporware" firms of the 1990s. Savvy investors will keep a close watch on unrealistic price-earnings ratios and watch for signs of the bubble bursting and the subsequent painful shake-out.

Eighth, well before 2030, major advances in healthcare and

166

medicine based on synthetic life will be commercialized. When used in conjunction with stem cell therapies and certain medical devices, synthetic biology offers a promising path to "bending the healthcare cost curve" in the right direction. Already, advances in biotechnology are bringing us closer to understanding aging and diseases in ways that will truly change the way people live as—as well as how long they will live. It is not out of the realm of possibility to imagine the end of disease as we know it.

Ninth, by the mid-2020s, synthetic organisms will be deployed as weapons against invasive species. Chemical insecticides often kill desirable native species like honey bees as readily as they kill harmful pests like mosquitoes. Even worse, we lack realistic technologies for dealing with many invasive species like zebra mollusks and Burmese pythons. Therefore, genetically targeted bio-weapons that infect and kill only specific species based on their genomic signatures will be created and deployed. Then, once those species are decimated, the organism will lack a host and become extinct, just as the poliovirus became effectively extinct.

11

What happens when we begin to understand how the brain works?

"The mind is its own place, and in itself can make a heaven of hell, a hell of heaven."

--John Milton, *Paradise Lost*

Scientists are just beginning to analyze and understand the activity of the 100 billion neurons within each human brain. The quadrillions of connections between these neurons enable us to sense, compute, imagine, and remember. The functioning of complex chemical pathways determines how we perceive and respond to the world around us. Hence, our quality of life has more to do with what's happening within the brain than what's happening in the world around us.

For thousands of years we've sought to understand our brains, and for the past three centuries we've tried to figure out how they might work. Yet, only now, for the first time, are we able to understand even superficially how the brain functions and potentially use this knowledge to deliver life-changing solutions. For example, between now and the early 2030s, we'll see:

- *Brain-machine interfaces* that will let our minds directly control our environments.

- *Neuromarketing techniques* that will enable marketers to design products, channels, and advertisements tuned precisely to achieve a desired response from the target consumer.
- *Chemical and mechanical performance-enhancers* that will enable us to be more effective at many levels.
- *Treatment and/or prevention of diseases of the brain,* including Alzheimer's disease, Parkinson's disease, chronic depression, and ALS.
- *Breakthrough virtual reality applications* that will leverage brain-science to let us experience "total-immersion adventures and fantasies," as well as letting us "*be* there without having to be there."

This will be possible not simply because we understand the brain better, but because that knowledge will enable us to apply the tools of infotech, biotech and nanotech (discussed elsewhere in this book), to deliver unprecedented brain-related *solutions*. This will make it possible, for the first time, to cost-effectively interact with the mechanisms within the brain. Yet, despite the enormous advances we'll examine here, mankind will only begin to tap the potential of brain science during the coming Golden Age. Even bigger advances await us in the next Technological Revolution, beginning around 2030.

In this chapter, we'll examine the underlying science, the commercial implications, and the broader societal impact of these technologies. As you'll see, brain science itself will open the door to applying other technologies in ways that have, until now, only existed in science fiction. The results will be nothing short of magical.

High-tech "mind reading"

Ever since it was discovered that the brain works by generating electrical impulses, (which manifest themselves as brain waves), the possibility of reading those waves has been tantalizing. But only in the past few years have scientists begun to master the ability to record brain activity and then apply that knowledge to useful ends.

What began in the late 1950s as an ability to record a single neuron at a time has progressed to today's ability to record the activity

170

from hundreds of neurons simultaneously. In a meta-analysis of 56 studies conducted since the 1950s that recorded the activity of neurons in both animals and humans, researchers at The Rehabilitation Institute of Chicago discovered that the number of simultaneously recorded single neurons has doubled every seven years due to continued improvements in technology and data analysis.

This increase is significant in the move toward "reading the mind," since more data points offer a better understanding of what's happening at any given moment in the brain.

Scientists at the Rehabilitation Institute are themselves involved in ground-breaking research to restore connections in the brain that are lost due to stroke or spinal cord injury. Using data from neurons, researchers are working on ways to reestablish those connections through cutting-edge technologies such as brain-machine interfaces, functional electronic stimulation, and virtual reality.[1]

Other work is proving that it is indeed possible to record information from the brain and then use it to mimic natural neuronal activity. Researchers at the Tel Aviv University have successfully implanted a robotic cerebellum in a brain-damaged rodent that restored its ability for movement.[2]

The chip in the robotic cerebellum was designed to receive, interpret, and transmit sensory information from the brain stem, allowing it to provide communication between the brain and body. Simple blinking movements in response to stimuli are the early results. Without the robotic cerebellum functioning, this movement was not possible.

When we hear about research into mind reading, it is difficult not to think in nefarious terms, picturing someone eavesdropping on our thoughts or stealing our ideas. The research today is much more humanitarian in its vision, from making life more convenient, to helping those who are paralyzed regain the capacity for movement.

The goal is to harness the power of brain waves to deliver a positive outcome. For example, researchers at the University of California in Berkeley have conducted research into ways to help patients with brain damage speak again. The results showed it is possible to decode the complex patterns of electrical activity that the brain forms from audible words, and then translate those patterns back into a very close approximation of the original words.[3]

As volunteers listened to 5 to 10 minutes of conversation, brain activity was recorded using electronic telepathy, where electrodes are placed on the surface of the brain. When patients heard a single word, their brain activity was analyzed by a computer program and researchers were able to deduce which word the volunteers had heard.

Neuroscientists have long suspected that the brain translates spoken words into patterns of electrical activity. The study shows that it is possible to translate these patterns back into the original sounds, which is an important step toward helping stroke victims regain the ability to speak.

Perhaps just as remarkable is the progress being made on using thoughts to control the motions of a car. At the AutoNOMOS innovation labs of Freie Universität Berlin, a computer-controlled vehicle was linked through an interface to newly-available commercial sensors that measure brain waves.

The computer was trained to interpret bio-electrical wave patterns from the brain as commands for "left," "right," "accelerate," or "brake." The goal of the researchers is to create autonomous vehicles of the future, and today's brain-sensor controlled model is what they refer to as a "hybrid control approach," where people and machines work together.[4]

In another new study, at the Washington University School of Medicine in St. Louis, scientists demonstrated that a cursor on a computer screen could be controlled by people speaking words out loud, or thinking them in their heads.[5]

Volunteers quickly learned how to control a computer cursor by thinking or saying specific words, which generated brainwave patterns that an interface had been programmed to recognize.

According to Eric C. Leuthardt, MD, of Washington University, "We can distinguish both spoken sounds and the patient imagining saying a sound, so that means we are truly starting to read the language of thought. This is one of the earliest examples, to a very, very small extent, of what is called 'reading minds'—detecting what people are saying to themselves in their internal dialogue."

In a similar study, researchers at the Duke University Center for Neuroengineering trained two monkeys to move a virtual avatar hand using only brain activity. However, in this study, a significant element was added: feedback.[6]

The texture of virtual objects was fed to the monkeys' brains as patterns of electrical signals, which enabled the monkeys to identify and differentiate the virtual objects. According to the study, this was the first time there was a bi-directional link between a brain and a virtual body.

These developments could be life changing for victims of injury and stroke. The results of the Washington University study, for example, hold great possibilities for enabling a person who has lost mobility to move a robotic arm using the same portion of the brain that used to serve that function.

The Duke study could lead to a robotic exoskeleton that would not only allow severely paralyzed patients to move using their thoughts, but would also offer feedback from their surrounding world regarding the texture, shape, and temperature of objects.

Echoing the work being done at Duke, a study from the University of Chicago revealed that by adding kinesthetic feedback information about movement and position in space for a robotic arm, monkeys that were using a brain-machine interface were able to greatly improve their ability to control the arm.[7]

This type of feedback has great implications for the future of mind control over robotic prosthetics. With this type of kinesthetic sensing, tasks such as buttoning a shirt or even walking will be much easier to achieve than they would be if visual cues were used alone.

In another noteworthy effort, a team of scientists at the University of Maryland has developed a brain cap that offers a non-invasive way to read brain waves. For some time, it was believed that the human skull was too thick to be able to detect enough useful brain activity through it, and that sensors needed to be placed directly on the brain.[8]

The Maryland study achieved decoding results that rivaled those obtained from implanted electrodes. The team envisions their sensor-lined cap, paired with interface software, soon controlling computers, robotic prosthetic limbs, motorized wheelchairs, and even digital avatars. The health and comfort benefits of using a non-invasive method for detecting brain waves are compelling.

Another minimally invasive, low-power approach for connecting the brain to external devices is being developed at the University of Michigan. An implant is positioned under the skin, but does not penetrate the cortex. The body's skin acts like a conductor to wirelessly transmit neural signals from the brain to control a computer.[9]

The implications of this research are profound. Just as increasing processor speeds ushered in the computing revolution in the last century, the increasing ability to simultaneously record single neurons marks the beginning of a neuroscientific revolution.

Over the next few years, as more results are obtained from our improved ability to read the brain, we will gain a better understanding of the functional principles, development, and operation of the brain. Each new discovery will lead to even greater insights, causing knowledge of the brain to grow exponentially.

With this increased knowledge will come new and better ways to help those who are disabled from neural disorders or mishaps. Methods will be developed for rerouting messages to parts of the body that have been shut off from the brain because of injury or stroke. It will become common to restore functionality to patients who have suffered paralysis.

Meanwhile, touchscreens, keyboards, trackpads, and computer mice will be relics of the past, and we'll interface with devices through thought.

The primitive interfaces we use today will initially be made obsolete by voice recognition technology. But mind-machine interfaces will ensure they are gone forever. This will also make speech recognition unnecessary since our devices will pick up directly on our thoughts.

We will use our brain activity to not only interface with computers, but also to control and be linked to virtually all of our devices, from household appliances to cell phones. To call someone, we'll simply think of the person's name, and to search the Internet, we'll simply think about what we want to find.

Marketing to the human brain

One of the age-old dreams of marketers has been to divine, as if by magic, what people really think about products and services. This has led to a proliferation of businesses that probe and prod customers, conduct focus groups and surveys, and otherwise try to devise ways of discovering people's opinions.

But, in too many cases, there remain big gaps between what people *say* they think about a product and what they *really* think about it. As a result, marketing professionals are always left with the sense that they can never truly know what is on the customer's mind.

This has been rapidly changing in recent years. And, two areas of science are largely responsible for this change:

1. Neuroimaging
2. Behavioral psychology

In the case of neuroimaging, new technologies were introduced that ultimately allowed researchers to look into the workings of the brain in real time. Computed tomography, or CT scanning, was invented in the 1970s, and magnetic resonance imaging, or MRI, was developed in the 1980s.

This set off an explosion of related technologies and refinements in recent years that brought us to the present state-of-the-art, in which scientists can ask a patient to perform a task—say, looking at a variety of product images—and can then see how the brain responds.

Thanks to such breakthroughs, so-called neuromarketers are now hard at work to crack the code on what customers are really thinking. For example, scientists at Duke University and Emory University recently published an article in the journal *Nature Reviews Neuroscience*, offering advice on how to hire a neuromarketing firm. NeuroFocus, a Nielsen subsidiary, offers brain scanning services to study the response to ads and buying trends of potential consumers.[10]

While there is already heated discussion of this trend in the

175

blogosphere, with concerns about privacy and fears that the ad business will take things too far, there are clearly good reasons why this technology could make itself useful, not only to companies, but to individuals who wish to buy better products and to receive more relevant advertising.

Brain imaging has already done something that no one was able to do before: Prove that a "brand" frequently makes more difference than the product itself. In the famous "Pepsi Challenge," people liked the taste of Pepsi more than Coke when they couldn't see the cans or identify which product was which. Yet, people continued to buy more Coke, and that brand stayed on top.

Why would people buy one soft drink when they preferred the taste of another? To answer this important question, scientists at the Human Neuroimaging Lab at the Baylor College of Medicine repeated the Pepsi Challenge while scanning the brains of volunteers.[11]

Again, most people preferred Pepsi if the soda was not labeled—as in the original challenge. A scan of a brain area associated with rewards, called the *ventral putamen*, responded five times more powerfully to Pepsi than to Coke.

But, when the researchers repeated the test with the cans clearly visible, almost all the subjects preferred the drink in the familiar red Coke can. Significantly, different areas of the brain responded. The *medial prefrontal cortex*, which is associated with logical thinking and reasoned judgment, lit up when Coke was selected. In other words, the preference didn't have to do with the physical response to the taste so much as to the *idea* of Coke. Clearly, brand perception matters more than product quality.

As a result of such a profound demonstration, people in all realms of business and science are piling onto the brain imaging bandwagon. The BrightHouse Institute for Thought and Science recently established a Neurostrategies Division specifically to conduct brainscanning research in association with Emory University Hospital.

A BrightHouse press release states that it uses information from brain imaging "to more accurately measure consumer preference, and then apply this knowledge to help marketers better create products and services and to design more effective marketing campaigns."

The other scientific discipline that is mining our brains for clues to new marketing strategies is behavioral psychology. Using the traditional testing tools of the psychology lab, researchers are discovering, essentially, how people make decisions and what factors influence those decisions—especially factors that would be counter-intuitive. The short version of the story is this: We think we are logical creatures, but most of our decisions are *not* based on logical processes.

For example, a report in the *Journal of Consumer Research* shows that people respond more favorably to abstract language than to concrete information when making a purchasing decision. This is linked to the human preference for using more abstract language to describe a good experience with a product, and more concrete language to describe a bad experience. So, when an advertising message describes a positive experience with a product or service in abstract terms, people are more favorably disposed toward the offering than if the positive message about it had dealt with specifics.[12]

Similarly, researchers have found that something as simple as whether an ad directs a person's attention to the present or the future can influence his behavior and his purchasing decisions. Before sending them grocery shopping, Tel Aviv University researchers told half of the participants in an experiment to consider "who you are right now." They told the other half to think about "who you will become in the future." While shopping, those who concentrated on the *present* were more likely to buy pleasure-oriented items, such as chocolate. Meanwhile, those who were thinking of the *future* were more likely to buy healthful foods.[13]

Consumer behavior isn't just influenced by brands and advertising messages. Even subtle sensory cues can be profoundly persuasive.

Consider the sense of smell. New studies, cited recently in the *Trends* article **THE SMELL OF SUCCESS GROWS STRONGER** (http://www.audiotech.com/trends-magazine/the-smell-of-success-grows-stronger), have given us a much better understanding of how scented environments influence consumers to devote more time to shopping and motivate them to spend more money.

In experiments where certain scents were present in a retail setting, people lingered longer while shopping, and they believed that they had spent less time than they actually had. They also gave a higher rating to the store's merchandise, indicated a greater desire to make a purchase, and revealed a willingness to pay a higher price.

These results confirm the findings of an earlier study by Alan R. Hirsch, MD, director of the Smell and Taste Treatment and Research Foundation in Chicago. Hirsch tested people who had examined a Nike running shoe in rooms either with or without a floral scent. About 84 percent of the subjects preferred the shoes displayed in the scented room and valued them, on average, at more than $10 higher than the group in the non-scented room did. In other words, finding the right scent can raise profits.[14]

This subconscious reaction should not be surprising when the following four characteristics of the sense of smell are considered:[15]

- First, according to the Sense of Smell Institute, humans possess the ability to detect approximately 10,000 different odors.
- Second, after one year, people are, on average, able to recall scents with an accuracy of 65 percent.
- Third, scent signals go right to the center of our emotions in the brain, bypassing the centers related to mental judgment and interpretation.
- Fourth, our sense of smell has been found to determine 75 percent of our emotional states.[16]

Understanding how our sense of smell works explains its close connection with emotions. When a scent reaches the nose, odor receptor cells send signals to a part of the brain called the *amygdala*. This area is part of the limbic system, which is the emotion-processing part of the brain that also influences behavior, mood, and memory.

The signals trigger an immediate, visceral reaction. Any conscious thought generated by the higher cortical areas come second, if at all. Pam Scholder Ellen, a Georgia State University marketing professor, summarizes the process this way: "(With) all of the other senses, you think before you respond, but with scent, your brain responds before you think."[17]

The Brain Links Aroma and Behavior

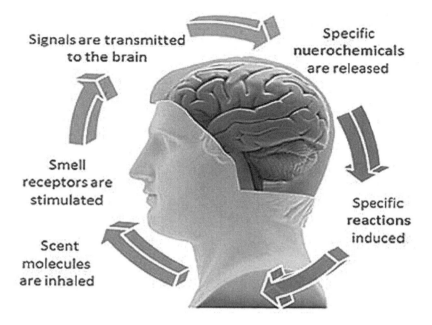

Signals are transmitted to the brain

Specific nuerochemicals are released

Smell receptors are stimulated

Specific reactions induced

Scent molecules are inhaled

This statement sheds light on an important aspect of smell—it acts as a chemical alert system, warning us about toxic molecules that might be in our vicinity. That's why we act rather than think.

But as important as smell is for safety and even survival, marketers are even more interested in the latest research into the emotion-invoking power of scents. According to Rachel Herz, a Brown University neuroscientist, "The emotional power of smell-triggered memory has an intensity unequaled by sight- and sound-triggered ones." It's this kind of deep-seated effect and connection that sellers dream of harnessing in the marketplace.[18]

The brain at work

According to the poet Robert Frost, "The brain is a wonderful organ: It starts working the moment you get up in the morning and does not stop until you get into the office."

Fortunately, research is yielding insights into changes that businesses can make to ensure that employees' brains stay active and productive during the workday. At a time when intellectual capital is one of the few ways to create a competitive advantage, it's critical for companies to create the best conditions for brains to do their best work.

This involves everything from lighting and decor to temperature and aromas. Even the refreshments served at a meeting and the background sounds have been found to positively or negatively impact performance, depending on the specific context.

Consider just a few recent discoveries about how *color and lighting* in the workplace can enhance or hurt people's moods and productivity:

Let's start by considering the impact of *color*. As reported in the journal *Science,* researchers at the University of British Columbia tested the cognitive performance of 600 people under three conditions. One group worked on computer screens with *red* backgrounds. Another group worked on screens with *blue* backgrounds, and the third group worked on screens with *neutral* backgrounds.[19]

Surprisingly, the color of the screen made a big difference in people's performance, as follows:

- People in the *red* group tested better at recall and attention to detail. For example, they scored high on tasks like remembering a list of words, or finding misspelled words.
- People in the *blue* group tested better on using their imagination. For example, they scored high on tasks like turning shapes into toys, or thinking of creative ways to use a brick.

As Juliet Zhu, who co-authored the study, told *The New York Times,* the study has clear implications for workplace performance. She explained, "If you're talking about wanting enhanced memory for something like proofreading skills, then a red color should be used. [However, for] a brainstorming session for a new product. . . then you should get people into a blue room"[20]

This is just the latest study in a long line of research that appears to show that colors can affect people's performance by influencing their moods.

180

For example, the *Times of London* reports on a study at England's Durham University that shows that the color red can improve the performance of athletes because it subconsciously triggers feelings of dominance. The researchers compared the performance of athletes who were evenly matched at the 2004 Olympic Games. In sports such as boxing, tae kwon do, Greco-Roman wrestling, and freestyle wrestling, when one competitor was wearing red and his opponent was wearing blue, the athlete in the red uniform won 60 percent of the time.[21]

However, a different study suggests that athletes who wear red tend to win for a different reason than their own elevated self-confidence. Psychologists from the University of Munster discovered that referees gave more points to people who wore red uniforms in "tae kwon do" competitions.

The researchers showed 42 veteran referees a video of a match in which one competitor was wearing red and his opponent was wearing blue. The referees consistently awarded the athlete in red more points than the athlete in blue. Then the researchers showed the exact same video of the same two athletes, but the colors of their uniforms were digitally reversed. The competitors that *appeared* to be wearing red were awarded an average of 13 percent more points than the blue competitors.

Another visual stimulus that can affect people's performance in the workplace is the *lighting* that is used. Specifically, researchers at the University of Surrey's Sleep Center found that blue-enriched white light increases the alertness of office workers.[22]

When the traditional white light in office ceiling fixtures was replaced with blue-enriched white light, employees' performance and ability to concentrate improved. They also reported improvements in their moods; less fatigue, eyestrain, and irritability during the workday; and better sleep at night.

According to the researchers, the blue light appears to be more pleasing to the brain because it targets a photoreceptor in the eye that scientists have discovered only recently. The study suggests that the white light used in most offices today may be keeping workers from feeling alert and doing their best work.

181

Also, researchers from Jefferson Medical College as well as Brigham and Women's Hospital found that the body's natural clock is more sensitive to shorter-wavelength blue light than it is to the longer-wavelength green light, which is needed to see. This finding supports a growing body of scientific evidence that a second, non-visual photoreceptor system drives the body's internal clock, which sets sleep patterns.[23]

While the researchers' immediate goal is to use the blue light in therapeutic settings, such as treating winter depression or sleep disorders, the finding can also be applied to a business context. Offices and retail stores can use this insight to install lighting that will make people feel energized on the job, and relaxed when they are shopping.

In fact, a new system may make it possible for the lighting in a building to change automatically between different types of light, depending on what the occupants are doing. This system, called Aladdin, was developed by a team of researchers from several European countries with funding from the ICT strand of the European Union's Sixth Framework Program.

The adaptive lighting system is designed to improve the lives of people who spend many hours a day under artificial lighting, such as factory or office workers. It uses data from biosensors worn by people as they move around the room or building. The sensors measure the occupants' heart rate and skin conductance response, which goes up when the body is active and goes down when the body is resting.

The sensors transmit this data through a wireless network to a central control system, which responds by turning on bright lighting in areas where people are actively working, and lowering the lights wherever people are in a more relaxed state, such as when they are engaged in deep thinking or brainstorming.

This is still an embryonic field, but one that will grow rapidly over the next two decades. More information can be found in the *Trends* article **MANAGING THE SENSORY ENVIRONMENT FOR FUN AND PROFIT** (http://www.audiotech.com/trends-magazine/managing-the-sensory-environment-for-fun-and-profit).

How technology is changing our brains

Brain-science is not only showing us how we can market more effectively and make workers happier and more productive; it's also showing us how the technologies of the Digital Revolution are actually transforming our brains in measurable ways. For millennia, mankind has created technologies that have transformed who we are and how we behave. However, with the advent of digital technology, that process has dramatically accelerated. Now, because of modern brain science, we are able to document the relationship and begin to guide it in beneficial directions.

Therefore, technology could be used to enhance and protect people's mental sharpness as they age. Research shows that solving mental puzzles can help postpone the worst effects of Alzheimer's disease. Memory training also enhances our traditional mental abilities. As a result, brain fitness has become a hot area of research.

As Torkel Klingberg, a cognitive neuroscientist at Sweden's Karolinska Institute points out in his book *The Overflowing Brain*, the amount of input we have available to us at all times has now outstripped the brain's capacity to process it. The function of the brain called "working memory" refers to our capacity to hold onto relevant information temporarily while we work on it, such as remembering the next few steps in a complex recipe long enough to execute them. Once working memory is full, you can't add more without crowding something out.[24]

Working memory, in other words, is our bandwidth, and in the human brain, this means that we can remember about seven things on average. By comparison, information technology completely overwhelms working memory.

Another effect that is especially significant for the younger generation is that playing video games can literally "turn off" the frontal lobes of the brain—the part that is used for reason, logic, analytical thinking, and restraint of the emotions.

Researchers at Nihon University in Tokyo showed that the more time adolescents spend playing video games, the less they use that part of their brain. And if they play long enough, the frontal lobes don't turn on even when they're *not* playing.[25]

By contrast, doing simple problems in arithmetic, such as single-digit addition, activates the brain broadly, including the frontal lobes, the limbic system, and areas involved in learning and memory.

Yet, all new technologies come with benefits as well as drawbacks. One of the *benefits* of all the modern digital technology is that it can train us to react more quickly to visual stimuli. We become more adept at searching through large amounts of information and screening out what is irrelevant.

A study at Northumbria University in England showed how fast people could find relevant information. Searching for health information, they spent less than two seconds on each page, discarding what wasn't relevant until they found what they were looking for.

Using the networks in the brain that mediate logic and reason—a step-by-step process—is slower than intuitive, emotional responses, which are nearly instantaneous. This fast response in sorting information suggests that those faster circuits are being recruited to assist in the task—and that represents a rewiring of the brain.

A study conducted by a neuroscientist at Unitec in New Zealand showed that people who played eight hours of computer games each week improved their ability to multi-task by two and a half times.[26]

The bottom line: Digital technologies appear to be making our brains less capable of normal "slow" processing, while improving their ability to handle "fast" processing of stimuli. Is this good or bad? No one yet knows for sure.

Healing the brain: Parkinson's, Alzheimer's, and depression

Research is also revealing promising new treatments for brain-related maladies like Alzheimer's disease, Parkinson's disease, and chronic depression. The costs to society of these conditions, at the individual and national level, are enormous. However, the latest findings from research in brain science, coupled with breakthroughs infotech and biotech, provide reasons for optimism.

According to the Alzheimer's Foundation, the costs of caring for patients with Alzheimer's and other dementias totaled $200 billion in 2012, and will rise to $1.1 trillion by 2050. Furthermore, the cost to the economy in terms of decreased productivity of family members providing care and support may actually double the *total* costs.[27]

Historically there has been almost nothing that could be done to even detect the disease early, let alone prevent, halt, or reverse it. But the latest research indicates that all of these goals are achievable by 2030.

Consider just one exciting example of how we might be able to treat and prevent Alzheimer's: A Canadian research team, working with GlaxoSmithKline, has identified a molecule, known as *MPL*, that eliminated up to 80 percent of amyloid beta plaques in animals with Alzheimer's. It also resulted in a significant improvement in cognitive function.[28]

MPL has been used extensively by GlaxoSmithKline in conjunction with other kinds of vaccines for many years, so its safety is well-established. Assuming that tests in humans match or exceed results in animals, MPS could also be administered as a preventive measure to people with risk factors for Alzheimer's disease as well as to those already showing symptoms. As a preventive therapy, it could become a highly cost-effective application of personalized medicine.

For more details on treating Alzheimer's, please refer to the *Trends* article **HOPE FOR THE VICTIMS OF ALZHEIMER'S DISEASE** (http://www.audiotech.com/trends-magazine/hope-for-the-victims-of-alzheimers-disease).

According to the National Alliance on Mental Illness, the direct and indirect workplace costs of depression are more than $34 billion per year in the United States alone. This calculation involves three elements:[29]

1. Major depression is associated with more annual sick days and higher rates of short-term disability than other chronic diseases.
2. People suffering from depression have high rates of absenteeism.

185

3.   Depression causes people to be less productive at work.

In a study comparing depression treatment costs to lost productivity costs, 45 to 98 percent of treatment costs were offset by increased productivity.

While the economic cost is relatively small compared to many other ailments, this does take into account the burden imposed on families of victims and the 5,000 to 10,000 suicides caused by depression every year.

Consider just one example of how doctors might soon be able to treat depression: Medical researchers from Australia's University of New South Wales and the Black Dog Institute have carried out a definitive study of tDCS, a non-invasive form of brain stimulation, which passes a weak depolarizing electrical current through the brain using electrodes on the scalp while patients remain awake.[30]

The researchers divided 64 patients who were suffering from clinical depression into two groups. The first group received tDCS for 20 minutes every day for up to six weeks. The other group was given a placebo treatment. The study revealed that patients who underwent tDCS felt their depression decrease, while their ability to concentrate and process information increased.

A third major brain therapy opportunity involves Parkinson's disease. It is caused by loss of the neurons that produce the neurotransmitter *dopamine*.   The U.S. National Institute for Neurological Disorders and Stroke estimates that at least 500,000 Americans have been diagnosed with Parkinson's, and about 50,000 new cases are diagnosed each year.[31]

The risk of developing Parkinson's disease rises sharply with age after the age of 60, so the number of cases is likely to grow significantly as populations become older throughout the world. In the U.S., it is estimated that its prevalence will at least double by 2030.

In 2009, researchers estimated the total U.S. cost for Parkinson's at $10.78 billion per year, or about $22,000 per patient per year.

Consider two of the most intriguing examples of how Parkinson's disease might be treated or prevented:

- A new study at Harvard University shows that flavonoids can protect neurons against Parkinson's. Based on a 20-year study of 130,000 subjects, the study found that males who ate the most flavonoids were 40 percent less likely to develop the disease than those who ate the least. And participants who consumed one or more portions of strawberries or blueberries each week were around 25 percent less likely to develop Parkinson's, compared to those who did not eat berries.[32]

- For those who already have Parkinson's disease symptoms, the results of a new study from Japan's Riken Institute are particularly encouraging. The Riken team extracted bone marrow stem cells from test animals. Next, they treated the stem cells with growth factors that turned them into dopamine-generating neurons. Then the animals that donated the stem cells were given a chemical that induced Parkinson's disease. When the animals received a transplant of the new dopamine-generating neurons from their own bone marrow stem cells, they showed significant improvement in motor performance, without side-effects.[33]

Enhanced brain performance

For decades, advances in medical knowledge have enabled athletes and their trainers to legally and illegally administer performance-enhancing drugs and mechanisms that helped them outperform the competition. And now, advances in brain science are opening up the same possibility for research scientists, musicians, and anyone else whose performance relies more on his or her central nervous system than on muscle tissues.

It's increasingly possible to make people "smarter," more alert, and more emotionally adept using various technological approaches. As highlighted in our *Trends* piece BEING ALL YOU CAN BE ON THE JOB (http://www.audiotech.com/trends-magazine/being-all-you-can-be-on-the-job), we've been tracking this phenomenon for over a decade and examining the social and economic implications. Consider just a few examples:

- An article in the *Los Angeles Times* described concert

musicians who take a beta-blocker known as Inderal to prevent stage fright. Inderal controls the effects of adrenaline, so musicians can perform at their best.[34]

- A recently published study proved that the blood-enhancing drug EPO also drastically increases motivation in the brain as soon as it has been injected, without the number of red blood cells increasing. In addition, it has been shown to substantially improve memory.[35]
- New research published in the *Journal of Neuroscience* demonstrates that certain patterns of transcranial magnetic stimulation improve learning ability.[36]

Until recently, the use of performance-enhancing drugs has been confined to the sports and entertainment industries. But now, according to an article in *The Conference Board Review,* it is about to enter the corporate realm.[37]

Foresight, a British think tank, has reported on drugs that can boost scores on exams and enhance memory, and a whole new class of drugs that improve cognition is being developed.

For example, Modafinil was developed to treat narcolepsy, but also improves memory and alertness while avoiding the jittery side effects of amphetamines. Soldiers use it. So, why not consultants who need to pull all-nighters? Why not give it to a design team that's creating the latest computer tablet? Another group of compounds, known as ampakines, will increase alertness and cognition and enhance memory.

Also, the blood hormone *erythropoietin* (EPO), which has been used by some athletes to enhance their performance illegally, may be effective in improving memory. Researchers have long known that patients who were treated with EPO for chronic kidney failure experienced improvements in cognition as a side effect. To investigate the connection, a team of scientists led by Hannelore Ehrenreich of the Max Planck Institute gave mice injections of EPO every other day for three weeks. The mice exhibited better memory than a control group of mice that were treated with a placebo. The improvements in memory were linked to changes in the neurons of the hippocampus, a part of the brain that is associated with learning and memory.[38]

Another development promises to be even more effective—and controversial. Direct mind-machine interfaces are not the stuff of science fiction anymore. According to an article in *The New York Times*, a company in San Francisco called Emotiv Systems sells a headset for under $300 that picks up signals from the brain and facial muscles and uses them to control a computer. In Sunnyvale, California, OCZ Technology Group is selling a similar device, based on eye and facial movements, for only $169.[39]

This is just the beginning of a very big industry that will seek to enhance human performance by coupling the mind and body with machines of various kinds. Increasingly, the machines will participate in decision making and not simply carry out instructions.

Medical implants are becoming far more common as well. In the future, it will become routine for people with diabetes to have an implant that constantly monitors blood sugar and adjusts insulin levels. Why not have an implant that does the same thing for brain chemicals that enhance performance? The drugs and technology are now available to make such an implant that could detect when a person's attention is wandering and refocus it chemically.

Total virtual reality

In its first incarnation, beginning around 1990, virtual reality was a concept that fell well short of its potential. It could not hope to capture "reality" because it was constrained, not only by inadequate hardware and software technologies, but by limits to scientists' understanding of the brain and perception.

As a result, it became "a solution in search of a problem that it could really handle." Aside from flight simulators and a few other training systems, it essentially remained a "novelty."

But, during the coming Golden Age of the Digital Revolution, the technologies of embedded computing, smart machines and service robotics will converge with brain-science advances to create truly realistic virtual experiences.

What lies ahead?

First, by leveraging the power of the latest in computing, wireless and sensory technologies, "advanced telepresence" will show up in hazardous situations within the next five years. We already see the use of similar technologies in today's military drones and robots. Unlike consumer or industrial applications, the "life and death consequences" of military and Homeland Security applications provide a solid business case for developing and deploying advanced avatars. Anthropomorphic robots with advanced sensors would be ideal for disarming IEDs, rooting out terrorists, and cleaning up toxic sites like Japan's Fukishima nuclear plant.

Second, it's likely that major strides in brain science will qualitatively transform the science of virtual reality so that, by 2025, consumers will become fully immersed in machine-generated "virtual worlds." Travel, sports, and pornography are realistically three multi-billion dollar industries that could be disrupted by virtual reality. We can already see this evolution taking place. Consider the following:

- Interdisciplinary labs all over the world are working to crack the code of the mind-controlled computer. As a result, direct access to the brain's neural networks is improving interactivity by letting the system anticipate head and eye movements or create an action based on the person's thoughts.
- Already a company called Mechdyne is offering turn-key hardware and software that permits commercial users and researchers to quickly implement state-of-the-art virtual reality solutions.
- An online service called RealTouch provides a VR service including haptic hardware and software that permits customers to have sex with each other or with paid models.

Third, by 2025, brain-machine interfaces will let our minds control our environments (perhaps employing artificial limbs and computer interfaces), without using our hands or even our voices. Brainwaves will be picked up and sent to wireless routers for the control of every conceivable kind of device in the home or office. Some of the possible applications seem far-fetched, but reality is likely to be much more exotic than anything that can be imagined today. For example, for someone away on vacation, a thought about the dry weather at home could be picked up by a wireless, hand-held device and sent over the Internet to turn on the sprinkler system. The system of text messaging in use today may be replaced by the much more user-friendly method of simply thinking the words you wish to send. All household appliances, as well as computer and electronic devices, could be controlled through this system. And huge advances will be made in the control-by-thought of automobiles, airliners, and fighter planes. In addition, mind-computer interfaces will penetrate deeply into the battlefield environment, where so-called "smart bombs" and smart missiles will get much smarter through direct integration with the human mind. [For more information, refer to the *Trends* article DIRECT MIND-MACHINE INTERFACES OPEN UP NEW COMPUTING POSSIBILITIES (http://www.audiotech.com/trends-magazine/direct-mind-machine-interfaces-open-up-new-computing-possibilities).]

Fourth, in the same timeframe, neuromarketing techniques will enable marketers to design products, channels, and advertisements tuned precisely to achieve an ideal response from the target consumer. Neuromarketing is a powerful new tool that can help shape not only better branding solutions, but better products as people are given a chance to participate in their design before the products ever reach the marketplace. This presents numerous opportunities. We already see a burgeoning business sector devoted to nothing other than using modern psychological and technological means to delve into the minds and emotions of consumers. Some big businesses will bring this function in-house, but a growing number of new ventures, like BrightHouse, are being founded to provide these services to their clients. This, in turn, will change the nature of business consultancies, which will have to institute their own neuro-imaging departments, or forge an affiliation with a research institution, in order to stay competitive.

Fifth, chemical and mechanical performance-enhancers will let people harness knowledge of the brain to become more effective. Savvy business leaders will increasingly monitor the disruptive effects of various performance enhancers introduced into the competitive environment. Not many years ago, the iPhone or Blackberry were considered luxuries. Today, they're considered necessities for mobile professionals who can't live without always-on email and Internet

191

access.   Expect   more   and   more   technologies,   including
pharmaceuticals, to play a similar role.

12

How will nanomaterials, microelectromechanical systems, and digital fabrication end the "Age of Scarcity"?

"To see a world in a grain of sand,
And a heaven in a wild flower,
Hold infinity in the palm of your hand,
And eternity in an hour."

--William Blake

The history of civilization is closely linked to the use of the natural resources that exist all around us. These include nutrient-rich soil, enormous mineral deposits, and fossil fuels. Nearly all progress, from the first cultivated crop to the exploration of Mars, has come from devising game-changing ways to exploit those resources.

Cheap natural resources helped drive economic growth for much of the 20th century; but now, inflation-adjusted prices for many commodities have climbed back to where they were a century ago.

These costs are *not* rising because we are running out of raw materials in an absolute sense. Instead, costs are rising for three reasons:

193

- The raw materials are being harvested from new sources that tend to be much farther from the places of manufacture and consumption, which leads to higher transportation costs.
- Political instability and poor infrastructure in resource-rich locations are making these new sources more expensive to exploit.
- The new sources of materials are often of poorer quality than the sources developed earlier, which means more work is required to obtain the same amount of raw material.

At the same time that the *supply* costs are soaring, the rapid growth occurring in emerging markets is causing an increase in *demand* for natural resources. As demand has risen, so has cost, making it harder for providers to turn a profit.

Inevitably, this means that consumer prices rise and large segments of consumers are priced out of the market. If this pattern continues, it will have a chilling effect on the growth of global GDP, as well as the potential for lifting billions out of poverty.

Already, manufacturers are feeling the effects of rising commodity prices, causing their variable costs to increase. From 2000 to 2010, for example, one steel company saw its variable costs rise from 50 percent to 70 percent, due mostly to increases in commodity prices.[1]

Prices are rising as the constrained supply cited above interacts with *escalating* demand. This demand isn't simply keeping pace with population growth; it's accelerating at a faster rate than at any time in history.[2] Consider energy:

- Between 1800 and 1900, global consumption of energy doubled.
- From 1900 to 2000, it grew over 20 times.
- According to the International Energy Agency, energy use is expected to increase by an additional 50 percent between 2000 and 2030.

Naturally, every resource is finite. But each time it has seemed that we were running out of a critical resource, human ingenuity has found a substitute or adaptation that has enabled our economic growth not only to continue, but accelerate.

194

Despite this fact, a pessimistic mindset known as the "culture of scarcity" has shaped much of the conventional wisdom about natural resources. This mindset was initially championed by observers of the Industrial Revolution like Thomas Malthus and David Ricardo.[3] Their four-part refrain, echoed down to the present, is as follows:

1. We live in a finite world with finite resources that can only produce a limited amount of economic value.
2. Cumulative human activity will upset a natural balance if it grows unchecked.
3. Long-term economic growth is impossible without leading to calamity.
4. The only answers are "fewer people" or "making each person get by with less affluence."

Ironically, the culture of scarcity was, and is, the most virulent in precisely the places where progress has been most rapid. And not surprisingly, the culture of scarcity has always been most strongly embraced by elites who would do well under the status quo, even as the rest of the world suffers.

Today, intellectuals aligned with the environmentalist movement often embrace the "culture of scarcity" with a seemingly "religious" fervency. They argue that the global economy simply has to "stop growing." For example, Richard Heinberg of the Post Carbon Institute contends in his book, *Peak Everything,* that the earth has already reached or exceeded its ultimate capacity. According to Heinberg, and many others, the next generation, and those that follow, will have to live with *less.*[4]

That seems "acceptable" to an elite fraction among the most affluent one billion people who live mostly in North America, the EU, and Japan. In fact, these regions of the world have already peaked in terms of per capita energy, food, water, and mineral consumption. For many in the affluent world, getting by with less matter and energy will hardly be an inconvenience.

However, for the *other* six billion, who live mostly in Asia, Africa, and much of Latin America, economic growth is the only route they have to happiness and security. And, they aren't going to give up on that possibility *willingly.*

195

Why would anyone expect them to do so? Time after time, in every technological upheaval from the Industrial Revolution to the Mass Production revolution, the culture of scarcity has proven itself to be fundamentally wrong.

But, to make our case, we don't have to go back to ancient or medieval case studies. Just consider the most widely read and quoted environmentalist book of all time, *Limits to Growth,* which emerged from the famous 1970s Club of Rome study. *Limits to Growth* was based on a simplistic computer model that considers only eight variables. Its alarming message was that economic growth would require increased consumption of finite resources and generate more pollution. This consumption and pollution would exceed the "carrying capacity of the earth" and lead to the "collapse of our civilization."[5]

Just about every prediction made in *Limits to Growth* has been proven wrong. Why? Because these researchers, like Malthus and Marx before them, underestimated the ability of innovation to achieve three critical goals:

- Finding new ways to access more resources.
- Creating more wealth from fewer resources.
- Transforming waste into new resources.

Wave after wave of innovation embedded in four-and-a-half "technology revolutions" has raised U.S. GDP per capita by 6,400 percent since 1800 and proven the culture of scarcity *wrong* at every turn. Consider the Green Revolution, which we discussed in Chapter 9.

Half a century ago, experts and politicians were panicked by the looming threat of overpopulation. In 1967, President Lyndon Johnson announced that, other than nuclear war, it was the greatest threat to the survival of the world.

That same year, biologist James Bonner wrote in the journal *Science* that, "All serious students of the underdeveloped nations agree that famine among the peoples of the underdeveloped nations is inevitable."[6]

A year later, in his best-selling 1968 book, *The Population Bomb,* Stanford biology professor Paul Ehrlich declared, "The battle to feed all of humanity is over. In the 1970s hundreds of millions of people will starve to death in spite of any crash programs embarked upon now. At this late date nothing can prevent a substantial increase in the world death rate."[7]

The solution, according to Ehrlich, was to implement a proposal in William and Paul Paddock's 1967 book *Famine 1975! America's Decision: Who Will Survive?* The Paddocks argued that there wouldn't be enough food to feed the entire world's population, so certain countries, such as India and Egypt, should be classified as "hopeless" and the U.S. should halt all food shipments to those nations.[8]

Ehrlich's book concluded that, "There is no rational choice except to adopt some form of the Paddocks' strategy as far as food distribution is concerned." Even the head of the U.S. National Academy of Sciences agreed with this assessment.

If this policy had been used, the result would have been a self-fulfilling prophecy: The mass starvation that the Paddocks and Ehrlich predicted would inevitably have occurred in India, Egypt, and the other countries that were deemed "hopeless."

Instead, as Dan Gardner points out in a *National Post* article called "The Nation-Killing Famine That Never Was," the U.S. kept sending food shipments, and India embraced changes to increase its agricultural production. In particular, geneticist Monkombu Sambasivan Swaminathan brought the Green Revolution to India. By planting India's farmland with high-yield strains of wheat, he increased the country's harvest from 12 million tons to 17 million tons in 1968. By 1975—the year the Paddocks predicted the famine would hit hardest—India was producing so much food that it turned down all offers of foreign food aid.[9]

The "population bomb," of course, turned out to be a *dud*. Even though the world's population increased from 3 billion in 1960 to 6 billion in 2000, the result was not worldwide famine and economic catastrophe. In fact, as the World Economic Forum reminds us, over the same time period that the population was doubling, per capita income increased by 115 percent, and life expectancy climbed by more than 15 years.

In fact, because the global food supply has nearly tripled, the per capita food supply is between 30 percent and 40 percent greater than in the 1960s. For that reason, the average human is better fed than at *any* time in history, totally refuting Ehrlich's premise.[10]

To make this point, author and futurist Ramez Naam cites the example of how many people can be fed with an acre of land, depending on the technology employed:

> "Before the advent of agriculture, an acre of land could feed less than a thousandth of a person. Today it's about three people, on average, who can be fed by one acre of land. Pre-agriculture, it took 3,000 acres for one person to stay alive through hunting and gathering. With agriculture, that footprint has shrunk from 3,000 acres to one-third of one acre. That's not because there's any more sunlight, which is ultimately what food is; it's because we've changed the productivity of that resource by innovation in farming—and then thousands of innovations on top of that to increase it even more.

> "In fact, the reason we have the forests that we have on the planet is because we were able to handle a doubling of the population since 1960 without increasing farmland by more than about 10 percent. If we *had* to have doubled our farmland, we would have chopped down all the remaining forests on the planet.

> "Ideas can reduce resource use. . . . In the United States, the amount of energy used on farms per calorie grown has actually dropped by about half since the 1970s. That's in part because we now only use about a tenth of the energy to create synthetic nitrogen fertilizer, which is an important input.

> "The amount of food that you can grow per drop of water has roughly doubled since the 1980s. In wheat, it's actually more than tripled since 1960. The amount of water that we use in the United States per person has dropped by about a third since the 1970s, after rising for decades. As agriculture has gotten more efficient, we're using less water per person. So, again,

198

ideas can reduce resource use."[11]

The culture of scarcity not only fails to consider the transformational power of productivity-enhancing innovation, it also pays little heed to the power of innovation to enable *substitution*.

Throughout history, people have failed to anticipate how replacing horses with cars would eliminate waste from city streets, how replacing whale oil with kerosene would save the sperm whale from extinction, or how tiny silicon chips could do the jobs of electromechanical mechanisms containing tons of metal.

In addition to substitution, innovation undermines the culture of scarcity in another way: in its ability to "transform waste into treasure." This is what we refer to as the "circular economy," as we've covered in the *Trends* article **MAXIMIZING VALUE IN A CIRCULAR ECONOMY** (http://www.audiotech.com/trends-magazine/maximizing-valud-in-a-circular-economy). We'll discuss this in more detail later in this chapter.

Environmentalists spend a lot of time fretting over whether people have sorted their household trash for recycling, but they don't look ahead sufficiently to recognize that such efforts have *marginal* benefits, at best.

The truth is that forthcoming industrial-scale processes based on infotech, biotech and nanotech will transform our mountains of trash into mountains of treasure. Japan's top experts estimate that its landfills alone contain enough gold and rare-earth minerals to satisfy the entire world market for over 10 years.[12]

Similarly, Alcoa estimates that the *world's* landfills contain a 15-year supply of aluminum. To those who understand how to "ride the wave" of innovation, it's clear that much of what has been "consumed" has simply been stored in the form of "trash." Our task is to find the technology to *relocate* the contents of landfills back into valuable commodities. And that technology is already being developed far faster than policy-makers and businesses can understand the implications.

Besides ignoring the potential for revolutionary innovations, the culture of scarcity typically dwells upon the idea of over-population. Obviously, if population outgrows our ability to innovate, it will create a crisis. However, as we detail in a forthcoming book in this series, you need to worry much more about the consequences of a highly probable "population *implosion*," than an increasingly unlikely "population *explosion*."

The facts are that by 2050, the global population will peak between 9 billion and 10 billion, and then start to decline. The graying of human civilization and the depopulation of the planet are likely to be the real threats to our wellbeing in the late 21st century. Japan, Russia, and the EU are already being impacted. Brazil and China will be hit hard by 2020. And while it's likely that innovation will enable us to compensate for *these* long-term problems, the key message is that the population control mantra still coming from the culture of scarcity has already created unintended consequences that will have to be dealt with for generations to come.

Escaping the "culture of scarcity" mindset

Our central premise in this book is that the technologies we've been exploring will eradicate any potential shortages in food, water, and energy, and unleash a new Golden Age of abundance and wealth.

To understand why the era of scarcity is ending, and why and this represents a crucial turning point in history, we need to consider what we've learned so far:

- First, we're in the middle of the Digital Revolution, the fifth "technology revolution" our civilization has experienced since 1771. The first half of the Digital Revolution started with the first microprocessor in 1971 and continued through the dot-com crash of 2000. During that period, companies that made computers, networks, and software were the best places to invest and make money. And for most of that period, things worked pretty well using the "conventional wisdom" about government, business, and life that was formulated for the prior era, called the Mass Production Revolution. But, as we explained, since 2000, we've been in the Transition Phase that happens in every "technology revolution" when the conventional wisdom of the prior revolution no longer works. That's what brought about the Great Depression, and it's the reason we've been unable to put the Great Recession behind us. The Transition phase is when the economy reshapes the conventional wisdom of the prior revolution to fit the new era, creating new institutional norms for both the private and public sectors. New regulations, new business models, and new ways of living inevitably emerge.

- Second, we have used specific trends in infotech and biotech to draw a road map for understanding how these technologies can specifically transform industries. By the early 2030s, this map implies the following:

1. Chip technology, data storage, and network price-performance will increase by a factor of 10,000 or more.

2. Mobile and embedded computing will use these foundational information technologies to deliver *virtually-free* networked intelligence everywhere and in everything.

3. Combined with human intelligence, AI-based smart machines will "optimize our world," but contrary to some forecasts, the machine will not functionally replace the human mind.

4. Leveraging AI and mobile/embedded computing, affordable service robots (including self-driving cars and elder-care companions) will become mainstream.

5. Quantum computers will solve key problems that are impossible for conventional computers, making a particularly large impact on security and scientific applications.

6. Scientists will map the genome of every known species and nearly every human being on the planet for less than $100 each.

7. Genomic data will enable doctors to optimize treatment for each patient and grow custom replacement organs, improving outcomes and lowering total costs.

8. Gene splicing (i.e., bio-reengineering) will enable governments to eliminate hunger and thirst, while preventing bio-terrorism and curing disease.

9. Synthetic life forms will proliferate and prove

themselves safer and more productive than natural organisms in a wide range of applications.

10. Brain science will eliminate most cases of dementia and depression, while fostering whole new industries.

11. These technologies set the stage for the coming wave of nanotech and energy breakthroughs.

- Third, we've worked to dispel the widespread perception that we face an "innovation crisis." It is this perception that has recently increased the credibility of the culture of scarcity, in spite of its historic inability to predict the future. As we explained in the *Trends* article **AMERICA'S DESPAIR OVER INNOVATION** (http://www.audiotech.com/trends-magazine/americas-despair-over-innovation), the so-called "innovation crisis" is nothing new; in the early 20th century and in the 1930s, such perceptions were also prevalent. Then suddenly, basic research that had been proceeding in the background burst onto the commercial scene, bringing a whole new wave of affluence and opportunity.

The Digital Revolution provides the power to fundamentally transform industries, economic sectors, and entire ways of life. Until now, the big story has been the relentless progress of computing infrastructure and, more recently, the rise of embedded and mobile computing, AI-based smart machines, and bioinformatics.

But an even bigger transformation is coming as the technologies of the Digital Revolution begin to shatter nature's constraints on both matter and energy.

- In this chapter, we'll focus on how the basic realities related to *matter,* which have bound mankind for millennia, will be essentially remade over the next 20 years.
- In the next chapter, we'll map out the same sort of transformation as it applies to *energy.*

It's not an overstatement to say that these innovations will transform the lives of *every* human on this planet. And while the transformation that takes place during the coming Golden Age will be profound, it will simply open the door to further change in the subsequent revolution. For that reason, the people born today will witness even more dramatic change and progress than did their great-grandparents who lived from the 1890s through the 1980s.

Rewriting the economic equations

Today, the culture of scarcity assumes that the technological relationships of the Mass Production Revolution will remain in effect for the foreseeable future. However, nothing could be further from the truth. The technologies we've already explored have laid the foundation for a new set of relationships in the Golden Age of the Digital Revolution.

Beyond the flash point cited in Chapter 1, we'll see an enormous leap forward in nanomaterials, Microelectromechanical Systems (MEMS), and digital fabrication. Suddenly, incredibly tiny units of matter will embody enormous amounts of economic value, and the Age of Scarcity will end.

There are five avenues through which the rewritten relationships between matter and value will irreversibly transform our world:

1. Combining **MEMS** with infotech to deliver the same or better functionality with far smaller devices at a tiny fraction of the cost.
2. Substituting **newly invented materials** made from renewable or super-abundant resources for traditional materials that are becoming scarce.
3. Leveraging the differences between matter at the macro-scale and the **nanoscale,** especially in biomedical applications, computing, and aerospace.
4. Utilizing advanced technologies to transform civilization's trash into treasure via the **circular economy**.
5. Reducing waste and maximizing customer satisfaction by using **digital fabrication** technologies to enable cost-effective production of custom products.

1. MEMS and microsensors

One way to use fewer resources is to dramatically shrink the size of the components that are used in everything from medical devices to automobiles to robotics.

Microelectromechanical Systems, or MEMS, are enabling researchers to scale down systems in order to expedite tasks, perform otherwise impossible tasks, and reduce material consumption by many orders of magnitude.

Let's examine a few MEMS applications, which illustrate some of the benefits these devices are now delivering and how they truly are transforming just about every industry.

Just consider the field of medicine. As recently reported in *MIT Technology Review,* Medtronic, the world's leading medical-device maker, is working on a pacemaker smaller than a Tic Tac mint. By contrast, current pacemakers are about the size of a silver dollar.[13]

A key benefit of this greatly reduced size is that the device would eliminate lead wires since the pacemaker could be positioned right where the electricity is needed. These wires cause a pacemaker to require greater power; plus, if they fail, there can be serious complications.

Another promising medical device based on MEMS technology is a prototype model of an implantable artificial kidney. For the 85,000 patients on the kidney transplant waiting list, and the 350,000 on dialysis, it will be life-changing.[14]

With the rapid advancement of MEMS, there's no doubt that someday soon implantable artificial kidneys will be a reality. The goal of the University of California San Francisco researchers is to create a device that is the size of a coffee cup. It will use thousands of microscopic filters and a bioreactor that will serve the metabolic and water-balancing roles of a real kidney. A larger external model has proven that the idea works, so work is now underway to reduce it to an implantable size.

For some MEMS applications, internal computing power is required. The incredibly small scale of this type of computer defies the limits of traditional semiconductor materials.

But now, a team from Harvard and MITRE's nanosystems group may have broken this smallness barrier with a reprogrammable circuit made out of nanowire transistors.[15] Keep in mind that a nanometer is one-billionth of a meter, and nanowires tend to be only 30 to 60 nanometers wide, making this undeniably the smallest computer in the world.

This microcomputer contains only 496 transistors but if Moore's Law continues its relentless advance, that number will double every 12 to 18 months.

For people who don't work in a microscale environment, it would never occur to them how challenging it is to manipulate such tiny objects. An engineering research team from the University of Waterloo understood this challenge and devised "flying microrobots" that now give researchers more control in this environment.[16]

Powered and levitated by a magnetic field, these robots use microgrippers to move tiny objects with great precision. Applications for these microrobots may include microassembly of mechanical components, handling of biological samples, and (as we'll discuss later in this chapter) even microsurgery.

1a. Lab on a chip

To date, most of the biggest MEMS breakthroughs involve either "lab on a chip" applications or microsensors, as discussed in the *Trends* article **THE LAB ON A CHIP REVOLUTION** (http://www.audiotech.com/trends-magazine/the-lab-on-a-chip-revolution).

As far back as the mid-1960s, microtechnology was being applied to chips used as pressure sensors. Soon, that technology was being used for various applications, including making sensors for airbags in automobiles. It was at that point that scientists began using MEMS to handle minute quantities of fluids—a field of research known as *microfluidics*.

In the process, they developed tiny capillary channels, mixers, valves, pumps, and measuring devices. The term "lab on a chip" arose in connection with these experiments. The first actual chip-based analytical system was built at Stanford University in 1974 for gas chromatography.

Intense interest in this field grew throughout the 1980s and '90s. But big advances only came in the mid-'90s, as researchers realized how useful lab on a chip technology could be for genetic research. DNA microarrays for genetic analysis were developed, and DARPA began funding research on portable biological and chemical warfare detection systems.

As computer chip technology, microelectronics, and MEMS increased in sophistication over the past decade, research efforts focused on reducing an entire analytical chemistry laboratory and all of its functions to something that could be carried around and used in the field. But even so, progress was stymied because samples usually had to be prepared separately, in a full-scale lab, before being processed by the miniaturized lab on a chip.

But now, according to the journal *Angewandte Chemie,* a team in Singapore has developed a rapid test for genetic diagnosis that uses a single drop of fluid containing nanoparticles. That drop is moved across a chip by a magnetic field. This not only miniaturizes the entire process, but it reduces the time for analysis from hours to minutes.[17]

For example, a drop of blood can be mixed with the drop containing nanoparticles and then placed on the chip. The nanoparticles contain antibodies that bind to cells in the blood. The magnetic field physically pulls the bound cells out of the fluid and moves those selected cells to the next station on the chip.

Enzymes can then be delivered to the selected cells for various functions. So, for example, a single drop of blood could be used to discover a cancer that would otherwise be undetectable. Best of all, the whole process takes just 17 minutes.

Because of the extreme miniaturization of the channels and small amounts of chemicals in these devices, they can also be used to mimic biological systems. According to a *Chemical & Engineering News* cover story, researchers are using lab on a chip technology to gain a whole new level of understanding of the chemical processes underlying high blood pressure, stroke, sickle cell disease, and other disorders.[18]

1b. MEMS-based sensors

It's hard to overstate the long-term potential of this emerging technology. As a new generation of scientists takes hold of lab on a chip technology, the possibilities for its uses become almost limitless—just as they did when a new generation of engineers and tinkerers took hold of computer chips in the 1970s.

While lab on a chip technology is delivering dramatic improvements in the cost, accessibility, and consumption of materials related to research and diagnostics, MEMS-based *sensors* are replacing a wide range of large and expensive systems. The benefits of these sensors are showing up in areas as diverse as entertainment, medical diagnosis, and national security.

MEMS sensors are appearing in more and more places. Consider just five applications:

1. They measure forces that determine when a car's air bag will deploy.
2. They measure the direction of the force of gravity in an iPhone, enabling the screen to rotate when the phone is turned sideways.
3. They direct smart bombs and missiles.
4. They're used to measure forces in sports, such as the impact a player sustains when being tackled.
5. They can pick up whiffs of chemicals that even a dog's nose would miss.

They are improving all the time, weighing less, getting smaller, and improving their capabilities. According to the *IEEE Sensors Journal,* they are transforming our way of life, and the market for them is huge: just the automotive safety market for MEMS represents hundreds of millions of dollars a year.[19]

An article in the *International Journal of Materials and Structural Integrity* explains how MEMS could be installed in buildings and other structures to monitor cracks and stresses and to prevent deadly collapses, such as the bridge collapse that occurred in Minneapolis in 2007.[20]

Part of the reason that bridge collapsed is that it is too

expensive to inspect such structures frequently enough, in a meaningful way. But MEMS could do it continuously and cheaply, keeping track of moisture, temperature, acidity, and physical forces and sending wireless signals to remote monitoring stations. These sensors could even be installed as the concrete for the structure is poured.

MEMS are particularly well suited to preventing catastrophes such as the BP oil spill in the Gulf of Mexico. Part of the problem that engineers had in stopping the oil after the blow-out occurred had to do with remote sensing; they didn't know exactly what their mechanical arms were doing deep underwater. Installing MEMS on drilling equipment and submersible robots would solve that problem, making it possible to stop leaks much more rapidly, which would reduce costs dramatically and prevent this resource from being wasted.

Another example of MEMS in action involves a 1.7 millimeter-wide device designed to stabilize an SUV. In this application, the MEMS device prevents accidents in which these top-heavy vehicles roll over during sharp turns or during skids on slick roads. The device is actually a microscopic gyroscope that detects when a vehicle is spinning or beginning to roll and then automatically triggers a compensating correction. This inexpensive device could replace more costly sensors made from quartz that are now only available in luxury vehicles.[21]

Similar devices are being developed for healthcare, medical, and surgical applications. At this level, the devices can be turned effectively into electronic noses, capable of sniffing out almost any chemical. This would make it possible to detect trace indicators of diseases long before conventional diagnostics could detect them. The same type of sensors could also make criminal forensics much more effective.

With these super-sensors, basic advances in physics and material sciences will come more easily to researchers who now have no direct way to measure many phenomena in the universe, such as the movement or transformation of sub-atomic particles.

Devices are also being designed to greatly improve space exploration, especially in applications such as the search for life on

Mars. In addition, MEMS will vastly increase the power of atomic force microscopes, which are a basic tool of the nanotechnology revolution.

2. New wonder-materials

Another way to address the finite supply of natural resources is by substituting newly invented materials made from renewable or super-abundant resources for them. In Chapter 9, we looked at the implications of bio-plastics as a natural outgrowth of the technology of bio-reengineering. But revolutionary wonder-materials based on molecular engineering are not limited to this those produced by biological systems.

2a. Metallic glass

Consider the revolutionary properties of metallic glass. For thousands of years, civilizations have crafted metal and glass, creating not only objects of beauty, but also elements for industry. These distinct materials each possess strengths and weaknesses that determine their applications.

Common glass is strong and resists being deformed, but is brittle and cracks easily. This is due to its non-crystalline, disordered atomic structure, called an amorphous structure. Metals, on the other hand, resist cracking, but are subject to bending, stretching, and flattening. Their crystalline structure provides microstructural obstacles that keep metal from cracking and allow it to bend.

In 1960, at Caltech, a new class of material was discovered called "metallic glass." When most people think of glass, they immediately think of window panes. But metal can exist as a glass as well.

Why? Because, by definition, "a glass is any material that goes from a liquid to a solid without crystallizing." Metallic glass is a so-called "amorphous solid," which combines many of the desirable attributes of glass *and* metals.

It wasn't until the 1990s that metallic glass was produced in bulk. Although it offered the tantalizing promise of being stronger and tougher than any known material, two major hurdles have kept metallic glass from being widely adopted for useful applications:

- The size of metallic glass parts that can be produced
- The inherent brittleness that metallic glass exhibits

The *size* limitation for parts is related to the way metallic glass is made. First, the material is heated to its glass-transition phase of between 500 and 600 degrees Centigrade. At this point, the material softens into a liquid state that can be molded and shaped. The challenge is that, in this state, the atoms tend to automatically arrange themselves into crystals—this needs to be avoided to create an amorphous structure, which makes it strong.

Common glasses can take hours to solidify, offering ample time to form and shape the glass. However, metallic glass usually crystallizes almost instantly upon reaching the thick-liquid state.

To avoid this crystallization, the material needs to be heated quickly and uniformly throughout and then injected into a mold where it freezes. The larger the amount of material, the greater the challenge of achieving this quick heating. Consequently, the size of parts that could be produced has been limited.

But now, researchers at Caltech have developed a technique that heats and processes metallic glass extremely quickly, allowing time for injection and freezing before crystallization.[22]

The technique, called ohmic heating, uses an intense pulse of electrical current that delivers energy of over 1,000 joules in about 1 millisecond. As a result, the material is heated 1,000 times faster than before, enabling parts to be made in milliseconds. The result is an inexpensive material that is 20 times stronger and stiffer than plastic.

The second important hurdle that had to be overcome is the inherent *brittleness* that metallic glass exhibits due to its amorphous structure that provides no barriers to the spread of cracks.

Researchers at the University of California at Berkeley, working with colleagues at Caltech, addressed this fundamental problem of poor fatigue resistance in bulk metallic glasses by creating a metallic glass alloy named DH3. This material is made from five

210

elements: zirconium, titanium, niobium, copper, and beryllium. This alloy is the result of inducing a second phase of the metal, which creates narrow pathways of crystalline metal.[23]

These pathways stop any cracks that begin to trickle through the glass. The alloy has proven to be stronger than many structural metal alloys, with a fatigue limit that is more than 30 percent higher than ultra-high-strength steel and aluminum-lithium alloys.

Applications for metallic glass will be plentiful. For instance, researchers at Switzerland's ETH Zurich are using it to develop a new generation of biodegradable bone implants. It will also be found in many products that need to be strong, yet flexible, including airplane wings, golf clubs, and engine parts. [24]

2b. Miracle plastics

It's hard to imagine a modern economy without plastics. They touch virtually every aspect of our lives, and they have become nearly indispensable.

One of the most positive characteristics of plastics is their durability. But the downside is that, after they are discarded, they sit in a landfill virtually forever. That's why recent advances in the area of *biodegradable* plastics are so important:

- One innovation transforms *lignin*, a complex compound derived from wood, into a renewable plastic when combined with resins, flax, and other natural fibers.[25] The substance is called Arboform and it can be thermo-formed, foamed, or molded. It is a durable material that can be cast very precisely, yet degrades into water, humus, and carbon dioxide once placed in a landfill.
- Another biodegradable plastic is being developed by Brazilian researchers at Sao Paulo State University.[26] It is reinforced with nanocellulose fibers from bananas, pineapples, and other pulverized plant fibers, creating a material that is three to four times stronger than petroleum-based plastics, and 30 percent lighter. In addition, it is more resistant to heat, chemicals, and water. Although it rivals Kevlar in strength, it is renewable and

biodegradable.

- Also, a family of new thermoset resins made from renewable raw materials has been discovered by Prof. Gadi Rothenberg and Dr. Albert Alberts of the University of Amsterdam.[27] These materials are fully biodegradable, non-toxic and non-hazardous, and can be made in forms ranging from hard foam to flexible thin sheets. These new thermoset resins will provide safe alternatives for polyurethane and polystyrene, both of which are toxic, and could be used in the construction and packaging industries.

Another important advance in plastics is the creation of *ultra-strong* materials. One example is a super-strong form of polypropylene, a commonly used plastic. It's being developed by Prof. Moshe Kol of Tel Aviv University's School of Chemistry.[28] His team of researchers has produced the world's strongest version of the plastic, using a new catalyst for the polypropylene production process.

This new substance is strong enough to replace steel and other materials that are used to make many everyday products. Specifically, the replacement of steel parts in cars with polypropylene parts would bring down the weight of cars, which would improve gas mileage. Additionally, the cheaper plastic could cut manufacturing costs.

Researchers are also developing plastics with some characteristics that run counter to everything we think of when we hear the word "plastic." For example, they are making them *electrically conductive*. Consider three recent developments:

- Australian researchers have created cheap, strong, flexible, and conductive plastic films.[29] They use an ion beam to mix a film of metal with the polymer surface of a plastic sheet. By controlling the ion beam, the degree of conductivity of the plastic film being created can be determined. These films offer tremendous opportunities in the development of "soft materials" for plastic electronics applications.
- Highly conductive plastic fibers on the order of several nanometers thick have been created by researchers from CNRS and the University of Strasbourg.[30] The fibers' other characteristics of lightness and flexibility make them excellent candidates for meeting the challenge of miniaturizing

components down to the nanometer scale, which is the next
step for electronics in the 21st century.

- The IFAM in Bremen has produced a composite material that
  becomes a fine-meshed electrically conductive network.[31] It is
  lightweight, yet exhibits the electrical and thermal conductivity
  of metals. This material could replace the integration of metal
  circuit boards, since the components could be produced in a
  single work step. This will drastically reduce both the
  production costs and the weight of the material. Automobile
  and aircraft manufacturers, in particular, are candidates for this
  breakthrough material.

Another way in which the new plastics are shattering our
conventional assumptions is that some of them are *self-healing*.[32] A
traditional characteristic of many plastics is that scratches and cracks
are hard or impossible to repair. In a self-healing plastic, any crack or
scratch breaks links between the bridges that span the plastic. This
produces a change in color that warns of the damage. When exposed to
light, pH changes, or higher temperature, the bridges re-form,
reversing the damage. Applications for this material are expected to
range from cell phones to laptops to cars.

Other recent advances in plastics are equally encouraging. For
example, in the medical field, plastics are being created to replace
metal bone implants.[33] Karri Airola, a researcher at the University
College of Borås, explains why a plastic implant would be superior:
"With metal implants, there is sometimes a risk that the patient will
have to undergo another operation, to replace the implant. For
implants made of fiber composite, this risk is smaller, since the
properties of the fiber composite more closely mimic those of the
bone." According to Airola, research has shown that these composite
implants can actually grow together with bone tissue

3. Nanomaterials

Nanotechnology involves the design, engineering, and manufacture of
products at the scale of less than one one-billionth of a meter. Today,
nanotech is mostly limited to nanoparticles added to consumer
products and nanofibers added to fabrics. However, a wide range of

nanotech-based products are making their way through the R&D process, especially in the fields of medicine, security, electronics, and chemical engineering.

In Chapter 2, we explored the forthcoming impact that graphene and carbon nanotubes are expected to have in terms of extending Moore's law. As we've explained recently in *Trends*, batteries, fuel cells, solar cells, and numerous chemical processes are all becoming dramatically more cost-effective, and less materials-intensive due to the application of nanotechnology. The result is that we're getting dramatically more value from each unit of matter and energy we consume, and this trend is only going to accelerate in the coming years.

In fact, two potentially enormous new industries are possible *only* because of rapid advances in nanotechnology:

1. Private-sector space travel
2. Nanomedicine

3a. Nanomaterials in space

Initially, *space travel* only made sense for superpowers who realized synergy between space exploration and defense. But the emergence of advanced composites has increasing made it far more amenable to market competition from niche suppliers.

At the same time, the advance of bioinformatics has revealed a great deal about the molecular mechanisms of life. And this has uncovered new and potentially powerful ways to fight cancer at the molecular scale using nanotechnology.

In space, nanoprobes using ground-based laser propulsion could replace expensive chemical rockets, perhaps heading toward nearby stars. This and other breakthroughs will supercharge the rapid progress now being made in terms of private-sector space technology.

When a SpaceX spacecraft lifted off in December 2010, orbited Earth, and was recovered in the Pacific Ocean, it represented more than just a small step in rocketry. It was one giant leap for the private-sector space industry.[34]

214

This orbital flight was the first for a private venture, and it indicates just how far this industry has come. The fact is, private-sector space firms are poised to move beyond pie-in-the-sky to actual spacecraft-in-the-sky, delivering sustainable, *profitable* operations.

SpaceX is one of these firms; its proven Falcon 9 booster sent the Dragon spacecraft on a trip around the earth.

Also eyeing the sky, and the hopefully lucrative space business, is Virgin Galactic, founded by billionaire Sir Richard Branson. Branson is betting that people will line up for the chance to take a trip into space.[35]

According to Branson, "We are now very close to making the dream of sub-orbital space a reality for thousands of people at a cost and level of safety unimaginable even in the recent past."

So why has private industry spaceflight finally taken wing, *now*? Certainly, it's due in large part to the many recent advancements in materials and other technologies.

But another key component is support from a surprising source: NASA.

In a startling break with the past, the Obama Administration has ordered NASA to focus on an initiative that will effectively outsource most *manned* spaceflights, turning to private industry to design and develop the rockets and spacecraft needed to carry U.S. astronauts to and from the space station.[36]

There are, in fact, two agencies set up within NASA that are working toward this end:

- NASA's Commercial Crew and Cargo Program is investing financial and technical resources to stimulate efforts within the private sector to develop and demonstrate safe, reliable, and cost-effective space transportation capabilities.
- NASA's Commercial Orbital Transportation Services partnership agreements wing, known as COTS, is working with U.S. industry to ramp up sub-orbital flight testing as well as orbital launches and re-entries.

That's why there was a lot more that just spaceflight equipment riding on the Falcon 9 booster test when it lifted off that December. It was the first such flight under a COTS contract. Therefore, its success was a big step for the private space industry.

Demonstrating NASA's commitment to a reliance on private industry, NASA Deputy Administrator Lori Garver is hopeful that a new private-sector launch system for commercial flights to and from the International Space Station could be available by around 2016, if not earlier.

Over the coming decade, commercial technology will revolutionize the economics of space flight. As in every industry where they have been tried, market-driven, private-sector initiatives will provide better, faster, and cheaper solutions than their public-sector counterparts. Driven by competition and the profit motive, expect the costs of low-Earth orbit and geosynchronous launches to drop precipitously.

The big successes are likely to come from partnerships between the public and private sectors. Government agencies like NASA, the Department of Defense, and their non-U.S. counterparts, will continue to be a major source of demand throughout this decade and beyond. Developing low-cost, multi-purpose platforms in partnership with the U.S. government could give U.S.-based commercial spaceflight companies an early advantage.

This new generation of cost-effective spaceflight will open up a wide range of new space-based industries. Growing semiconductors, synthesizing drugs, and other—as yet unimagined—zero gravity technologies are likely to dwarf attention-grabbing industries like space tourism. Longer-term, it may enable a quantum leap in space-related economics by paving the way for so-called "space elevators."

Space elevators will inexpensively propel humans and cargo hundreds of miles above the Earth's atmosphere at the push of a button. The idea goes back to at least the 1800s, but modern technology has brought it out of the realm of fringe science fiction and into the engineering mainstream.[37]

The five basic design elements of an operating space elevator are as follows:

1. A platform, resembling an offshore oil rig, featuring a very tall tower, will be constructed at the equator, most likely in the

216

middle of the Pacific Ocean.

2. A thin ribbon stretching into space will rise from the platform to the sky.
3. A massive counterweight will be located on the other end of the ribbon, 62,000 miles away.
4. Climbing vehicles, equipped with solar panels to produce electricity from light and power the electromagnetic propulsion system, will ascend and descend the ribbon.
5. High-powered, ground-based lasers aimed at the climbing vehicle's solar panels will provide power.

Conceptual Drawing of the Space Elevator

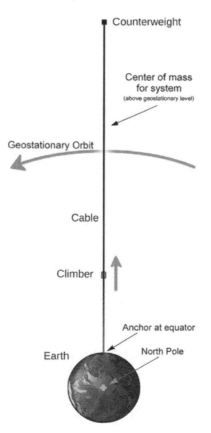

Source: www.spaceelevator.com

The laser and power transmission technologies for the space elevator already exist and are known to work. The ribbon is the key to making the project feasible, and it is under development in labs around the world. It will most likely be made of carbon nanotubes, because they promise the highest strength of any material known and can withstand the stresses involved in tethering an object in space to the earth over an extended period.

The reusable climbing vehicles will be about the size of railroad cars and will travel hundreds, or potentially even thousands, of miles an hour. At top speed, they could reach geosynchronous orbit in as little as five hours. However, at more realistic speeds, it might take from five to seven days to make the trip.

The climbing vehicles will shuttle people and cargo up to a platform poised at an altitude of 22,300 miles, which is the height at which a satellite always stays in a fixed spot relative to a spot on the Earth's surface. At this point, the ribbon will be moving at the same speed as objects in orbit at that distance from the Earth.

At less than $100 a pound, the estimated cost of transporting materials and people to orbit would be roughly 100 times less expensive than the cost of using space shuttles or other rocket technology today.

That's why the lure of the space elevator is likely to become irresistible. Putting a useful payload into geosynchronous orbit today costs about $10,000 a pound. Based on the cost of energy today, the variable cost of launching the 26,000-pound payload of the space shuttle would cost less than $17,000 using the elevator.

Once the fixed costs have been fully amortized, this will open space not only to businesses, but even to ordinary people who are curious to go there. For example, it would cost the carrier about $200 to send up a passenger.

3b. The enormous promise of nano-medicine

The second new industry that will emerge because of rapid advances in nanotech is *nano-medicine*.

218

One of the greatest advances in medical history was the development of surgery. However, after more than 150 years, it is still a wrenching and brutal process.

According to *Medical News Today,* about 300,000 people have coronary artery bypass surgery each year. It seems almost miraculous, for example, that someone on death's door from cardiovascular disease can be granted a new lease on life through bypass surgery. On the other hand, that procedure comes at a tremendous cost and often with serious side effects, such as pain and diminished cognitive abilities.

That is why researchers have long dreamed of finding an alternative to surgery. And one does appear to be on the horizon at last. It was imagined in a 1966 science fiction film called *Fantastic Voyage*, in which scientists were able to reduce doctors and submarines to microscopic size so that they could be injected into the bloodstream and travel through the body, fixing whatever was wrong.

Although none of today's scientists envision shrinking their colleagues, *The Jerusalem Post* announced not long ago that researchers at the Judea and Samaria College in Ariel, Israel, and from the mechanical engineering department of the Technion-Israel Institute of Technology have designed a robot that can crawl through the bloodstream to treat conditions, such as tumors, that are too difficult for conventional surgery.[38]

The robot, called ViRob, is powered by a harmless external magnetic field and has the ability to crawl upstream against the flow of blood. In principle, numerous such robots could be injected into the body simultaneously to treat widely invasive forms of cancer. The researchers say that the robot could remain in the body indefinitely to carry out medical procedures as needed.

For example, ViRob can clean the plaque from blood vessels in patients suffering from cardiovascular disease. It can also cut off samples of tissue for biopsies. It can be fitted with a camera so that the inside of the body can be viewed in real time. And, because the ViRob makes deep incisions unnecessary, it reduces recovery time for the patient.

The robot is equipped with tiny arms that allow it to grab onto the walls of blood vessels and push itself along. The hair-like arms

219

stretch or retract to fit the size of the vein or artery.

ViRob is not alone. Other technology teams around the world are also having success with microscopic medical robots, also called "medical micro-bots."

A Web site called Thefutureofthings.com details a robot, created by the Chonnam National University in South Korea, that has similar capabilities to ViRob.[39] The Korean microbot also performs diagnostic tests and releases drugs where needed. It can, for example, find and dissolve blood clots blocking arteries. It's made primarily of a biocompatible elastic material called *polydimethylsiloxane*.

Unlike ViRob, it can only remain in the body for about 10 days. It differs from the Israeli robot in another important way: The Korean robot is powered by actual living muscle fibers. The microbot has a rectangular body with three legs on each end. Heart muscle tissue is grafted onto the elastic skeleton.

The front legs are short (about 400 micrometers) and the rear legs are longer (at 1,200 micrometers). When the heart muscle fibers contract, they bend the legs and the microbot moves at an average speed of about 100 micrometers per second. It can move about 50 meters in a week. The robot takes its fuel directly from the bloodstream of the patient in the form of sugars, oxygen, and other nutrients that are naturally present there.

The plan for this microbot involves clever measures to prevent the immune system from attacking it, since it is a biologically active device. Stem cells are taken from the patient's own bone marrow and then grown into heart muscle fibers. Each robot is custom-made for the individual patient so that his immune system will recognize the microbot in the same way it recognizes the body's own components.

Meanwhile, according to *The Boston Globe,* Japanese scientists are working on another microbot design. Referred to as a "robotic snake," the two-centimeter-long device has a swimming tail to propel it through the gastrointestinal tract, as well as the bloodstream. The tail also functions as its steering mechanism. This Japanese medical microbot can also take video images.[40]

Not to be outdone, American researchers are also busy creating their own medical micro-bots. *New Scientist* published an article about a microbot developed by scientists at Carnegie Mellon University. Known as the Heartlander, it is inserted through a small incision and attaches itself to the surface of the heart, where it injects drugs or installs medical devices to control such ailments as congestive heart failure.[41]

In tests on pigs, the Heartlander installed pacemakers and injected dyes for making images of the heart. The Heartlander attaches to the surface of the heart by suction and moves its segmented body in order to crawl.

According to a report in *Technology Review,* an even more advanced effort is underway at the Swiss Federal Institute of Technology in Zurich. Scientists there are turning to nanotechnology to solve the microbot riddle for medical science.[42]

They have developed a propulsion system that mimics the flagella that efficiently propel some bacteria. That propulsion system is just 27 nanometers thick and 40 micrometers long. This means the Swiss researchers will be able to create medical microbots far smaller than anything seen before, and the bots will be capable of going into the tiniest blood vessels and even inside cancerous tumors.

The flagella are made up of tiny coils of nanomaterials. The researchers made them by layering extremely thin strips of gallium arsenide, using the same sort of photolithographic techniques used in chip fabrication. The bottom layer was doped with indium, which puts a stress on the gallium arsenide and causes it to twist into a helix.

Using magnetic coils that switch their field rapidly, the scientists were able to cause the nanocoils to rotate, and they have proved that the bots can swim in water that way. This offers great promise for drug delivery systems, because the very high accuracy of this propulsion system would mean very precise targeting, which increases the ability to use much higher doses of a drug. This is especially important if the drug is a toxic chemotherapy agent for fighting cancer.

Another flagellum-based propulsion mechanism has been designed for medical microbots by a team at Monash University, near Melbourne, Australia. It uses piezoelectric crystals that change shape in the presence of an electric field. By rapidly alternating the electric field, the flagellum starts to vibrate, and that vibration can be used to spin a tail for propulsion.[43]

A third flagellum-based solution is under development at Carnegie Mellon University's NanoRobotics Lab. Bacteria with flagella are being used to propel small spheres through fluids. The Carnegie Mellon researchers are using chemical signals to operate the bacteria. The bacteria, known as *S. marcescens*, are only 20 nanometers in diameter and 10 micrometers long.[44]

Attached to polystyrene micro-spheres by electrostatic forces, they rotate their flagella to push the micro-spheres forward. The scientists can stop the motion by introducing copper ions into the solution. To start the motion again, they introduce a chemical called *ethylenediaminetetraacetic acid*, which traps the copper ions attached to the rotor of the flagellar motor, allowing it to resume its motion.

Numerous other efforts are underway to develop the important new technologies needed for commercially successful medical microbots. Among them are projects for steering bacterial robots toward tumors using magnetic fields, pioneered by the École Polytechnique in Montréal, Canada. Under this scheme, the bacterial microrobots would attack and kill the cancer cells once they reach the site of a tumor.

The European Union is also funding a partnership among Italian, French, German, and Spanish institutions to create what the scientists are calling an "operating room inside the body." The aim is to build components that can be ingested and then self-assemble inside the stomach. The assembled robotic system would then be operated remotely by doctors without cutting through the skin.[45]

And finally, scientists from the Institute of Robotics and Intelligent Systems in Zurich are planning to steer tiny robots inside the eye to perform delicate surgical procedures, such as repairing a detached retina.

In the coming decade, medical therapies will undergo another technological revolution, which will be comparable to the biotech revolution. Across the globe, scientists are pursuing ways to work inside the body as never before—and without the negative effects of invasive surgery.

This means that there will be a deluge of new start-up companies launching efforts to come up with a winning medical microbot. In the short term, expect to see a number of dedicated microbots that are aimed at specific therapies, such as unclogging arteries or attaching pacemakers. In cases like this, there will be a significant first-mover advantage, as insurance firms pressure hospitals to adopt the technology and thereby save billions of dollars on surgical procedures.

In the 2020s, a subsequent wave of development of medical microbots will involve the start-ups being acquired by major pharmaceutical companies, medical technology companies, and diversified healthcare giants like Johnson & Johnson. At the same time, researchers will make continued progress toward more general-purpose microbots that can perform a range of tasks from drug delivery to surgery. Look for a rush to set the standard, as a sector shake-out occurs, with many technologies falling by the wayside as a winner emerges.

But in all likelihood, there will be a wide variety of approaches that will find acceptance in different geographic markets as well as in different medical specialties. For example, there may be a general-purpose bot dedicated to drug delivery, another for biopsies, and yet another for diagnostic tests, just to mention a few.

As nanotechnology matures, medical microbots will become ubiquitous. They will be so small that they'll have no side effects and will be able to drift harmlessly inside the body until needed. Because of that, it's entirely possible that they will be routinely given to children in the same way vaccinations are now dispensed.

In fact, in many cases, microbots will take the place of vaccines and may prove the solution to many intractable problems. A microbot programmed to find and dismantle the HIV virus, for example, may ultimately defeat that disease-causing agent.

By 2030, a complete revolution in surgery and dentistry will take place as medical microbot technology becomes mainstream. Microbots that can remain for long periods of time inside the body could, for example, work to scrub plaque from arterial walls continuously, not just when it becomes so thick that it causes heart disease. Likewise, nano-sized microbots could constantly clean bacteria from teeth, virtually eliminating the problem of decay and gum disease. Nanobots could even work inside the body to remove fatty tissue in people who are obese.

3c. Nano-war on cancer

Scientists who work on cancer research have long struggled with a painful choice: If they make the treatment powerful enough to have a fighting chance at destroying cancer cells, it is likely to destroy the surrounding tissue. But if the treatment isn't strong enough, the cancer cells will survive and possibly spread.

Now, nanotechnology is offering hope for new treatments that overcome this dilemma. Nanotech is the science of working at an incredibly small scale; a nanometer is less than one-ten-millionth of an inch. Evidence is mounting that cancer treatments based on nanoparticles can target cancer cells with a degree of precision that was unthinkable just a few years ago.

Researchers are making progress along several paths simultaneously. Let's take a look at some of the most promising new developments.

At Yale University, researchers led by Professor W. Mark Saltzman have developed an innovative way to deliver cancer-fighting drugs to brain tumors by injecting therapeutic nanoparticles into the brain with a catheter, and then using pressure to guide them to the tumor.[46]

As reported in the journal *Nature Materials*, the nonviral nanoparticle developed at Yale is able to act like a virus to introduce a specific gene into diseased cells in order to kill or repair them.[47]

This is a big improvement over conventional nonviral gene therapy agents, which often carry a positive electric charge that can kill healthy cells. It is also safer than *viral* gene therapy treatments, which can cause significant immune reactions.

Saltzman's team overcame the problem of excessive charge by

224

making the new nanoparticle more hydrophobic (water-repellant) and thus less likely to form chemical bonds with water molecules. Specifically, the team incorporated safe, water-insoluble units into the polymer that generates the nanoparticles. This reduces the positive charge and increases stability. The result is an efficient mechanism for gene delivery that is also extremely safe.

Meanwhile, at the University of Southampton, scientists have developed smart nanomaterials that can disrupt the blood supply to cancerous tumors.

The team of researchers, led by Physics Professor Antonios Kanaras, showed that a small dose of gold nanoparticles can activate or inhibit genes that are involved in angiogenesis—a complex process necessary for the supply of oxygen and nutrients to most types of cancer.

The team focused on endothelial cells, the cells that make up the interior of blood vessels and play a pivotal role in angiogenesis. As the researchers explained in the journal *Nano Letters*, they use a technique called laser irradiation. The team shines light on the gold nanoparticles with a laser beam, which is able to destroy the endothelial cells and cut the blood supply to the tumor.[48]

Researchers at Cornell University are using a similar approach. Led by Professor Carl Batt, the researchers synthesized nanoparticles made of gold sandwiched between two pieces of iron oxide. They then attached antibodies, which target a molecule found only in colorectal cancer cells, to the particles. Once bound, the nanoparticles were engulfed by the cancer cells.[49]

To kill the cells, the researchers pointed a laser at the nanoparticles. The gold in the nanoparticles absorbed the radiation from the laser, which caused the cancer cells to heat up and die. As described in the journal *Nanotechnology*, the surrounding healthy tissue was not harmed.[50]

The researchers are now working on a similar experiment targeting prostate cancer cells.

Of course, there's one shortcoming to techniques using lasers: If the cancer occurs in a place where a laser can't reach, it won't work. To remedy that problem, scientists at the Georgia Institute of

Technology have coated gold nanoparticles with a chemical that brings them inside the nucleus of the cancer cell and stops it from dividing.

In the *Journal of the American Chemical Society*, Professor Mostafa El-Sayed, director of the Laser Dynamics Laboratory at Georgia Tech, explains that once a cancer cell stops dividing, apoptosis sets in and kills the cell. According to El-Sayed, "In cancer, the nucleus divides much faster than that of a normal cell, so if we can stop it from dividing, we can stop the cancer."[51]

The researchers tested the hypothesis on cells harvested from cancer of the ear, nose, and throat. They decorated the cells with a peptide called RGD to bring the gold nanoparticles into the cytoplasm of a cancer cell. They also used a peptide called NLS to bring the gold into the nucleus.

Previous studies had shown that just delivering gold into the cytoplasm has no effect on the cancerous cell. The new study revealed that implanting the gold into the nucleus effectively kills the cell.

The gold works by interfering with the cells' DNA, although the researchers aren't sure exactly why it works. That will be the subject of another study.

What matters is that it works—and it works even on cancer cells that can't be reached with the laser.

Another ingenious method involves heating gold nanoparticles with alternating magnetic fields rather than with a laser. At the University of Georgia, scientists have found that head and neck cancerous tumor cells in mice can be killed in half an hour without harming healthy cells.

The findings, published recently in the journal *Theranostics*, mark the first time to the researchers' knowledge that this cancer type has been treated using magnetic iron oxide nanoparticle-induced hyperthermia, or above-normal body temperatures, in laboratory mice.[52]

The team, led by Assistant Physics Professor Qun Zhao, found that the treatment easily destroyed the cells of cancerous tumors that were composed entirely of a type of tissue that covers the surface of a body, which is also known as epithelium.

226

For the experiment, Zhao injected a tiny amount of nanoparticle solution directly into the tumor site. Next, he placed the mouse in a plastic tube wrapped with a wire coil that generated magnetic fields that alternated directions 100,000 times each second. The magnetic fields produced by the wire coil heated only the concentrated nanoparticles within the cancerous tumor, and left the surrounding healthy cells and tissue unharmed.

Similarly, Virginia Tech researchers are investigating the use of magnetic fluid hyperthermia to heat and destroy cancerous cells. The procedure has been used successfully in prostate, liver, and breast tumors.[53]

According to the researchers, who presented their findings at a recent meeting of the American Physical Society Division of Fluid Dynamics, they injected magnetic nanoparticles into the body intravenously. The nanoparticles then attached to the cancerous tissues. When the researchers added a high-frequency magnetic field for 30 minutes, the particles heated up, raising the temperature of the tumor cells.

Just as in the other studies, the heated cancer cells died, with no adverse effects to the surrounding healthy tissue.

To further perfect the technique, graduate student Monrudee Liangruksa and her colleagues tested the effects of different types of magnetic nanoparticles. The most promising varieties were iron-platinum, magnetite, and maghemite. But because iron-platinum is toxic to humans, the most biocompatible agents are magnetite and maghemite.

4. The circular economy

While nanotech, MEMS, and wonder-materials all offer the promise of new, smaller, and cheaper resources for making products, there is another growing challenge at the other end of the product lifecycle. It's the question of how to deal with a growing mountain of waste.

On a global basis, we have plenty of space that can accommodate all of this trash. However, the transition from rural to urban living means that we can only dispose of most of this waste cost-effectively in a small radius around the world's top 50 urban centers.

Both the natural resource issue and the waste issue will need to be resolved effectively if global affluence is to grow. Not surprisingly, human ingenuity is already at work finding a way around these barriers. According to a recent project managed and developed by McKinsey & Company, both of these problems can be solved by a "circular economy."[54]

In contrast to today's economy, where natural resources are extracted, used to make products, and then generally discarded when a product's usefulness has ended, in a circular economy today's goods are tomorrow's resources. To a much lesser degree, that is happening already, as recycled material reduces the need to extract new raw materials. But in a full-fledged circular economy, there is a closed resource loop where large volumes of finite resources, such as metals and minerals, are pulled from products and reused.

One example is gold. On average, only five grams of gold can be extracted from a ton of ore from a gold mine. In contrast, up to 150 grams of gold could be extracted from a ton of discarded mobile phones.

In addition to recycled resources, plant-based materials are used in a circular economy to form some "product parts" that then biodegrade at the end of the product's life. Other components of this model include:

- The use of cost-effective renewable energy.
- Avoidance of toxic chemicals that are not reusable.
- An emphasis on superior designs of materials, products, and systems that eliminate waste.

The implementation of a circular economy would involve adaptation at each phase of a product's life, including design, manufacturing, sales, and disposal.

- The **design** phase is critical for the success of this economic model. The reusability of product parts is dependent on materials selection, standardization and modularization of components, purer material flows, and designs that enable easier disassembly. Engineers will be expected to create "supply circles" where materials that are reclaimed from products at the end of their lifecycles are looped back into the production process. R&D will be called upon to develop sustainable materials, such as plastics made from plant-derived feed stocks rather than fossil fuels. With proper design, products could also be easily repaired and reused instead of being tossed into landfills. This new emphasis on designing products for sustainability will create a profound shift in the way materials are used across the economy.

- At the **manufacturing** level, structural changes will be needed to complement the integration of efficient technology. For example, in heavy industry settings, the "waste" stream from one factory could be used as a resource for other companies or even consumers. Proximity, of course, will be a major factor. The result would provide a local system based on multiple closed loops. Those companies that commit to process design and equipment changes that deliver greater energy efficiency will contribute greatly to the circular economy.

- **Sales** dynamics in the circular economy will evolve toward durable goods moving into consumers' hands as rentals rather than direct purchases. This performance-based payment model will allow manufacturers to maintain control over the components that make up their products, making it easier to reclaim them at the end of the product lifecycles. Some business models will allow manufacturers to retain ownership of the materials in the products via rental-type arrangements, and other models will involve more conventional sales with incentives for customers to return old products to manufacturers at the end of the product's life.

- End-of-life **disposal** and "rebirth" is the most challenging chapter in the story of the circular economy. Efficiently recapturing components and raw materials from products through cost-effective collection and treatment systems will need to become a core competence of suppliers all along the supply chain. This focus on recapturing raw materials will become a major driver for locating manufacturing in close proximity to consumption.

The benefits of a circular economy would be far-reaching:

- For manufacturers, there would be substantial net savings on materials, plus a significant drop in volatility and supply risks. A McKinsey analysis for the Ellen MacArthur Foundation reports that a net materials cost savings of up to $630 billion per year by 2025 could be realized if a subset of the EU manufacturing sector employed circular economy business models.[55] Included in this subset are the automotive sector, machinery and equipment, electrical machinery, other transport, furniture, radio, TV and communication, medical precision and optical equipment, and office machinery and computers.
- Positive multipliers would take effect due to innovations, including increased employment opportunities. Not only would there be direct employment from new companies that spring up, but those jobs would spawn other jobs. Studies have shown that a manufacturing job creates 1.6 local jobs in service industries, such as barbers, waiters, doctors, and lawyers. An innovation-related job has an even greater multiplier effect, creating five such jobs.
- Both developing and developed countries would see gains from a circular economy. Developing countries would benefit from an increased ability to industrialize, because their dependence on imported materials would drop. They would not be at the mercy of greatly fluctuating prices for materials, which would free companies to focus their resources on growth and innovation. At the same time, the recycling of materials would create new industries and new jobs. These same factors would also enable developed countries to experience a long-term, resilient economy. Simply knowing that the costs of materials will remain relatively constant will encourage companies to take more risks on new products and projects. This stability would lead to ever-increasing standards of living, all without putting a stress on natural resources.

5. Digital Fabrication

We've been discussing the exciting potential of 3D printing in *Trends* for many years. Our 2006 analysis titled THE ERA OF

ABSOLUTELY FABULOUS MANUFACTURING IS COMING (http://www.audiotech.com/trends-magazine/the-era-of-absolutely-fabulous-manufacturing-is-coming), provided one of the earliest looks at this new technology. For our most recent reports on this subject, please refer to NANO-PRINTING AND BIO-PRINTING: THE NEXT FRONTIER (http://www.audiotech.com/trends-magazine/nano-printing-and-bio-printing-the-next-frontier), and BIO-NANOPRINTING: DIGITIZING THE LANGUAGE OF LIFE (http://www.audiotech.com/trends-magazine/bio-nanoprinting-digitizing-the-language-of-life), in our October 2012 and January 2013 issues, respectively.

Our focus in our latest analysis is on how 3D printing technology will impact the manufacturing sector and the overall economy. Specifically, "will the ability to print parts and entire products disrupt established manufacturers?" And, "will it provide an opportunity for entrepreneurs and small niche producers to compete with big corporations?"

The answers to both questions is a resounding *yes* if you believe the argument laid out in *Makers: The New Industrial Revolution*, by former *Wired* editor-in-chief Chris Anderson. Anderson's book promises that "the collective potential of a million garage tinkerers and enthusiasts is about to be unleashed upon the economy, driving a new age of American manufacturing."[56]

Our response: *Well, maybe.* Make no mistake, the impact of 3D impact on manufacturing will be big, but it won't be quite as big as Anderson imagines it will be.

Before we get to that, let's outline the parts of Anderson's vision with which we agree.

1. In the United States and in other developed nations, high labor costs have made traditional manufacturing so expensive that companies have been forced to outsource production to off-shore producers in countries such as China, Indonesia, and Bangladesh.

2. As a result, millions of American manufacturing jobs have been lost. According to the Economic Policy Institute, 2.1 million U.S. manufacturing jobs have been off-shored or eliminated since 2001, which has created a drag on the

economy as a result of high unemployment and reduced consumer spending.

3. However, the prices and performance of 3D printing technologies are reaching the point at which they are becoming affordable to individual purchasers.

4. Meanwhile, a so-called "Maker Movement" has emerged, based on three principles:

   • People use desktop tools to design new products.

   • People share those designs with each other for free, and collaborate with each other in Maker communities on the Internet.

   • People use standardized file designs that enable individuals to send their designs to factories that will accept such jobs.

5. What this means is that factory production is now possible without a factory. An individual inventor no longer needs to find a corporation to develop his idea and distribute his product; he can simply push the "make" button on his printer to create a prototype or a customized product for an individual buyer, or he can send the design to a factory that will mass-produce the product for him.

So far, so good. However, we believe Anderson carries his idea *too far* when he extends it to much of the world's population. He assumes that almost everyone will want to create products for themselves or sell them to everyone else. He also assumes that people will choose to design their own products to print at home rather than buying a proven product from a company that has been in business for decades.

For example, Anderson relates a story in which his daughters wanted to redecorate their dollhouse. Instead of buying new dollhouse furniture, Anderson and his children went on-line to Thingiverse, a site where people upload 3D designs they've created. They selected a set of Victorian chairs and couches, changed the scale to fit the size of their dollhouse, and clicked on "build." Using a 3D printer called a MakerBot Thing-O-Matic, the family printed their new furniture in 20 minutes.

As Anderson concludes, "If you're a toy company, this story

should give you chills."

Perhaps, to some extent. But toys, like many other products, are not just commodities that are easily interchangeable. Anderson's vision ignores a few basic principles of marketing.

- First, the onslaught of television advertising over the past seven decades has created a nation of consumers who recognize brand names and associate them with certain positive qualities. Research shows that marketers spent $1.4 billion on advertising toys in the U.S. in 2011 alone. A home-designed, home-printed generic toy might be enough for a very small child, but it won't satisfy a child who has been barraged with ads for branded products—as any parent who has tried to feed a child a homemade hamburger instead of a McDonald's Happy Meal could attest.
- Second, products are linked to status. For a child in grammar school, owning a toy that all of his classmates covets conveys a sense of self-worth. Similarly, a Gucci handbag gives its owner a sense of luxury and prestige that would be hard to duplicate with a do-it-yourself purse.
- Third, a product's perceived value is increasingly influenced by the experience of the purchase. American Girl Stores and Nordstrom stores give shoppers an experience with the product and related services that a generic product could never provide.

For these reasons, it seems unlikely 3D printers in the home will lead to the demise of toy companies like Mattel and Hasbro, or to businesses that manufacture products in which brands, expertise, fashion sense, and R&D truly matter. In this application, 3D printers are no more a threat to manufacturers than the SodaStream home soft-drink dispenser is to the Coca-Cola Company.

However, the implications of the other potential application—involving the "Send" button rather than the "Make" button—are far more promising. The ability for individual inventors, or entire organizations, to design innovative new products on a computer screen and then send them to dedicated manufacturing services could be a game-changer. In this model, the product isn't a cheap knock-off of a better product for sale elsewhere; it is a product that offers a genuinely better solution for a "job to be done."

For example, Anderson's grandfather invented an automatic lawn sprinkler system and patented it in 1943. However, he could not bring it to market himself; he had to convince a manufacturer to license his invention. Fortunately, he beat the long odds that keep many innovative ideas from being noticed and licensed. But even though he received royalties for what became a very successful product, he lost control of his invention because he did not control the means of production.[57]

Today, if Anderson's grandfather were alive, he could print out a prototype of his design, test it, make modifications, and print it again, all without leaving his workshop. But once the design was perfected and patented, he would not have to plead with manufacturers to license it. Instead, he would simply upload his design files to companies that would fulfill his order to produce anywhere from a dozen to a million units or more.

Suddenly, all of the following is feasible:

- First, even firms as small as those with just one skilled expert will be able to design a product, then prototype and test it in a home workshop.
- Second, they'll be able to get small batches of those prototypes made cost-effectively for performance testing and market testing.
- Third, they'll be able to almost instantly scale production up for introduction to niche markets.
- They'll also be able to avoid inventory obsolescence exposure by avoiding large batches of products; make-to-order will become the norm.
- Finally, they'll be able to very quickly respond to market feedback by incorporating changes into the hardware, as well as the software.

All of those developments promise to conserve resources. By making only the amount of products that will be consumed, producers can avoid the wasted inventory that too often ends up in landfills when customer tastes shift.

Where do we go from here?

First, as MEMS technology continues to evolve and improve, many new opportunities will arise. For example, MEMS will improve medical diagnostics. Research scientists at the Fraunhofer Institute in Dresden, Germany are developing a microscopic image sensor that promises to accelerate cancer diagnosis by speeding up the detection of tumors. Fitted to the tip of an endoscope, this sensor is just eight millimeters in diameter, which allows it to be inserted into the body through minimally invasive surgery.[58] By providing magnifications down to the cellular level, this technology can make accurate diagnoses of cancers in real time. This eliminates the time-consuming need to remove tissue and examine it under a microscope, as well as the stressful wait by patients.

Second, many industries will be transformed in ways that are almost impossible to imagine today. Consider the winemaking industry. In growing grapes to make wine, one of the challenges vintners face is achieving the precise balance between drought and over-watering. Either extreme will diminish the quality of wine grapes. To help growers maintain a perfect level of soil moisture in the vineyards, a team from the Cornell Nanofabrication Facility in Ithaca is developing a microsensor that can be embedded in a vine and will measure in real time the water stress in the plant. This sensor will transmit its reading wirelessly to a central server, where the data will be summarized for the grower. The team hopes that micromanufacturing will bring down the cost of the device to allow even the owners of small vineyards to benefit from the technology.[53] Of course, grapes aren't the only crop that could benefit from such a breakthrough. Microsensors could be used throughout the agriculture industry to conserve water and boost crop yields.

Third, several factors are falling into place that will accelerate the migration to a circular economy. The linear model of natural resource usage with its "extract, use, and dispose" approach has reversed the long-term downward trends in raw materials costs, making that a key decision driver for many industries. At the same time, three key factors are evolving in such a way as to encourage implementation of an end-to-end circular economy:

1. Advances in information technology allow the tracking and optimized use of resources along global supply chains, a necessary ability for the cost-effective reuse of materials in products.
2. Nanotechnology and biotechnology are providing new and advanced materials that exhibit increased strength, reduced weight, biodegradability, and other properties that are highly valued in a circular economy.
3. "Life-cycle materials management" for high-tech manufacturing industries is gaining support from governments, as they also become more proactive in policies related to resource efficiency.

Fourth, "complex medium-lived products" will benefit the most in a circular economy. Products fall roughly into three categories: fast-moving consumer goods, such as food and clothing; longer-lasting products, such as phones, washing machines, and light commercial vehicles; and *long-life* products, such as houses. It's the middle category of products that will derive the most benefits in the circular economy. It has been estimated that if mobile phones were easier to take apart and if there were incentives in place for returning phones to manufacturers, the cost to remanufacture them could be reduced by 50 percent. It has also been determined that leasing high-end washing machines instead of buying them would save consumers approximately one-third the cost per wash cycle.

Fifth, while 3D printing has primarily been limited to plastic products until now, as prices drop, the technology will increasingly encompass all types of materials. For instance, the most effective technique for printing with metal is *selective laser sintering*, which involves depositing layers of metal powder that contains a binding material. The material is then melted to hold the metal layers in place until the item is heated in an oven to permanently weld it together. When the ability to print in steel and even precious metals is perfected and the costs plummet, there will be no limit to the types of useful products that can be manufactured by this method.

Sixth, the emergence of what Anderson calls "makerspaces" will make the technology affordable and accessible to the masses. Such venues allow people to use shared printers and facilities without investing in their own 3D printer. It seems likely that such places will appeal mostly to craftspeople and hobbyists rather than commercial enterprises.

Seventh, the link in the new manufacturing value chain that offers the greatest potential for both risk and reward is that of the flexible production facility. These facilities will turn inventors' digital files into finished products, much as online photo services like Shutterfly transform customers' digital images into printed photographs. For example, a company called Shapeways has installed 30 industrial-scale 3D printers in a "factory of the future" in Queens, New York. It accepts orders to print items in plastic, stainless steel, or glass. Companies like Shapeways could profit by leveraging economies of scale across thousands of client orders, but it also runs the risk that the technology in which it has invested will quickly become obsolete.

Eighth, 3D printing will boost the economy by enabling a much wider range of innovative ideas to reach the market. Thanks to cheap prototypes, rapid redesigns, and easy outsourcing to "digital production facilities," innovators will be able to bring new solutions to the marketplace with a minimum investment in time and money. Inevitably, the result will be many more product failures, but those failures will come without huge sunk costs in R&D and vast warehouses of unsold inventory. Innovators will race along the learning curve, building upon fast failures without exhausting their resources until they ultimately design tomorrow's *winning* products.

Ninth, digital fabrication will transform the business model for manufacturers in the healthcare industry. For an industry that requires a high degree of customization because everyone's body is different, digital fabrication is tailor-made. Natural applications include 3D-printed hearing aids and 3D-printed dental implants. Already, fabricators are being used to turn CT and MRI scans into 3D models for improved insight. In the future, artificial bones, blood vessels, and even kidneys will be created via digital fabrication, built layer by layer from living tissue.

Tenth, as soon as 2020, nanotechnology will begin to deliver cancer therapies with unprecedented power and fewer side effects than chemotherapy. The success of the experiments we've discussed points to what promises to be a highly effective, precisely targeted approach to destroying cancer cells, and only cancer cells. If the results of clinical trials on human subjects, which are a few years away, prove to be just as successful, we will finally have a therapy that can completely eradicate the cancer from a patient's body—and without the painful, debilitating side effects of current treatments, such as chemotherapy. Combined with advances in gene therapy, nanotech could make the treatment for cancer as routine and effective as LASIK eye surgery.

13

How will the American energy revolution unleash the wave that changes the world?

"There is a tide in the affairs of men
Which, taken at the flood, leads on to fortune;
Omitted, all the voyage of their life
Is bound in shallows and in miseries.
On such a full sea are we now afloat,
And we must take the current when it serves,
Or lose our ventures."
--*Julius Caesar* Act 4, scene 3, 218-224

Throughout this book, we've examined the implications of several breakthrough technologies for every aspect of our lives and businesses. But one key element in our model has been missing, until now. What is needed is a catalyst that will create the impetus for transforming all of the wondrous possibilities we've considered into real-world products and services.

Throughout history, the catalysts of technological revolutions have created a dramatic shift in both the mindset of decision makers and the resources available to innovators. Abruptly, all of the great ideas that were confined to drawing boards were rushed into production; all of the prototypes that were slowly working their way through the development process were suddenly evaluated with a new urgency.

We needn't look far back in history to see the most recent example of this phenomenon. When Japan attacked the United States at Pearl Harbor in the early morning hours of December 7, 1941, a dramatic change in priorities occurred instantaneously. That change not only transformed the economy of the United States, but nearly every aspect of life in the developed world for the next half-century.

Within a matter of days of the attack, Germany declared war on the United States on the basis of a reciprocal treaty with Japan. Quickly, the U.S. military was expanded, civilian factories were converted to military use, and domestic consumption of goods was rationed. Unemployment quickly went from double digits to zero, even as the labor force participation rate soared. Full employment and rationing combined to fill depleted bank accounts with cash.

Overnight, the nation made huge investments in training and capital goods, which restored an economy that had languished since the stock market crash of 1929. A generation of basic research breakthroughs in areas ranging from telecommunications, to medicine, to nuclear fission was suddenly thrust into high-speed development. Within four years, the global geopolitical landscape was reshaped and the entire international economic infrastructure was transformed.

Today, we find ourselves once again in a state of despair resembling the mood in 1941. Then, as now, we had just gone through 12+ years of weak economic growth following a market bubble. And, like the apparent recovery in the first FDR term, we saw hopeful trends, led this time by housing, evaporate in a second downturn.

In 1941, experts lamented the slow incrementalism of advances in automobiles, radio, railroads, airplanes, and the electrical grid. It seemed that there were no great new inventions to rival the telephone, automobile, or radio. Today, many pundits are similarly warning of the "death of innovation."

The Mass Production revolution was built on a combination of capital-intensive assembly lines, extreme division of labor, and economies of scale that were enabled by demand that was focused on a

240

few standardized products created by mass media. Just seven decades later, the Digital Revolution rests on a foundation of intelligent machines enabling cross-trained knowledge workers to serve highly customized niches identified and managed via interactive, targeted media. And, just as the economy of the 1930s was hollowed out by the deterioration of the capital base (i.e., machines wearing out and empty factories sold for scrap), the economy we see today has been hollowed out by short-sighted off-shoring and a failed education system creating an enormous "skills gap."

But the important message in this story is that the greatest wave of prosperity that humanity has ever known was unleashed as World War II ushered in the new "conventional wisdom," which enabled Mass Production to change every aspect of our lives. The rebuilding of both physical and human capital that began in that moment paved the way for a "Golden Age" that ended with the oil crisis of the early 1970s.

Clearly, the economy and the technologies of the Digital Revolution are fundamentally different from those of the Mass Production Revolution. Therefore, the prescription that will enable us to emerge from the current transition phase is different from what World War II did to bring us out of the last transition.

So, don't expect a *literal* Pearl Harbor. Obviously the attacks of September 11, 2001, raised our awareness of the need to end our dependency on Middle Eastern energy sources, and the subsequent "war on terror" has pumped billions of R&D dollars in advancing technologies like service robotics, artificial intelligence, bioinformatics, and embedded processors, as well as MEMS-based sensors and nanomaterials. But our problems are not ones that can be solved by the kind of bureaucratic, command-and-control thinking that brought us the Manhattan Project, the Jeep, and the K-ration.

Leveraging the power embedded in infotech, biotech, and nanotech requires a bottom-up resurgence of entrepreneurial creativity and risk-taking within start-ups as well as established enterprises. This will come from the combination of several powerful forces that are already at work:

1. The unleashing of the vast energy resources that have already

been discovered in North America.
2. The impact on the U.S. economy that will result from the new energy industry's creation of millions of jobs.
3. The revitalization of U.S. manufacturing.

Each of these forces is intertwined with the others, but all of them depend on the first force, which kick-starts the two that follow.

The first force: unleashing America's vast energy resources

Today, America is positioned to leave behind all of the energy paradigms of the past 60 years. Since at least the 1970s, pessimism about the nation's energy future has been one of the cornerstones on which the culture of scarcity has rested.

Yet now, thanks to breakthroughs in energy technology, we will no longer have to worry about running out of oil, or about having our supply of fuel cut off by a hostile foreign government.

To the surprise of many, the abundance of energy that will drive the economic growth engine in the 21st century will not be based on the sun, wind, or water.

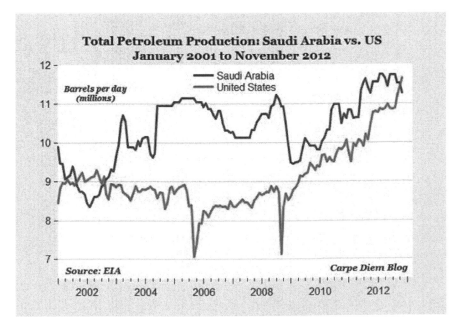

What is this amazing new source of energy that will meet all of our needs at home—and even allow us to export it to other countries?

Oil.

Yes, you read that correctly. According to the U.S. Energy Information Agency (EIA), the United States actually produced more oil than Saudi Arabia did in November 2012 (see chart). Thanks to the significant increases in shale oil production in North Dakota and Texas, total oil output in the U.S. expanded by more than 7 percent between August and November, while output in Saudi Arabia fell by 4 percent during that period.[1]

Those trends brought U.S. petroleum output in November to 11.65 million barrels per day, versus Saudi Arabia's production of 11.25 million barrels per day. This upward trend in U.S. oil output will continue, and the EIA predicts that the U.S. will be the world's largest petroleum producer at 13 million barrels per day, starting in 2018.

Today, the United States already has access to more oil deposits than Saudi Arabia, Iraq, and Iran combined. Our friendly neighbor to the north, Canada, has even more oil than the U.S., which provides another source of energy without the geopolitical risk of buying oil from despots.

Much of this newly discovered oil is in the form of *oil shale*—a type of sedimentary rock that contains kerogen that can be converted into *shale oil* through horizontal drilling and hydraulic fracturing, known as "fracking." Fracking involves pumping pressurized mud into the shale formations that store oil and gas.

A report by the U.S. Government Accountability Office in May 2012 concludes that as much as 3 trillion barrels of shale oil could be extracted from a single location that spans parts of Wyoming and Utah. For perspective, consider that if only 50 percent of the oil in this one deposit could be extracted, it would be equivalent to duplicating all of the oil *reserves* in the entire world.[2]

Edward Luce, a commentator for the *Financial Times,* recently noted:

"So dramatic are America's finds, analysts talk of the U.S.

turning into the world's new Saudi Arabia by 2020, with up to 15 million barrels a day of liquid energy production (against the desert kingdom's 11 million barrels per day this year). Most of the credit goes to private sector innovators, who took their cue from the high oil prices in the last decade to devise ways of tapping previously uneconomic underground reserves of 'tight oil' and shale gas. And some of it is down to plain luck. Far from reaching its final frontier, America has discovered new ones under the ground."[3]

That's not all. The U.S. also has vast reserves of natural gas and hydrocarbon fuels, which means that the country can return to its status as an energy-independent nation—and as a net exporter of fossil fuels to the rest of the world.

The second force: the impact of energy jobs on America's economy

The abundance of accessible energy beneath the U.S. will reinvigorate America's domestic economy. Other countries, such as Canada, Israel, and China, will also benefit from tapping into their own rich shale oil deposits.

But the greatest impact will be felt in the U.S., as the new energy bonanza is about to change the American outlook far more dramatically than most executives, politicians, and investors yet realize. In fact, it will become the *catalyst* that triggers the Golden Age of the Digital Revolution.

As analyst Walter Russell Mead wrote in a 2012 landmark essay series for *The American Interest*, "This is a Big One, a game changer, and it will likely be a major factor in propelling the United States to the next (and still unknown) stage of development—towards the next incarnation of the American Dream."[4]

The American Dream, of course, depends on having a stable job with a high income. For the 23 million or more "under-employed workers" in the U.S., opportunities for such jobs seemed to disappear years ago. All of this leads to predictable consequences:

- Without a good job and a good income, consumers will be afraid to spend on new products and services.

244

- Without the possibility of a job opening in a different field, out-of-work Americans will be reluctant to invest in upgrading their vocational skills.
- Without the confidence needed to bet on new ideas, especially those with long R&D horizons, investors will avoid risks in order to secure their savings.
- Because it will reverse this mindset for consumers, workers, and investors, the energy revolution will be a critical part of a virtuous self-reinforcing loop that will unleash the power of technology to remake the global economy.

This will happens because the energy revolution will make a positive impact on unemployment. We are still in the very early stages, but according to the *Financial Times*, since the financial crisis of 2008, fracking alone has already created more than 600,000 new jobs in the United States. That's just one type of job, however. Many more Americans will be employed in jobs that involve extracting the oil shale and refining the shale oil.[5]

According to a study by UK-based Wood Mackenzie Energy Consulting, the energy revolution will create 1.4 million new U.S. jobs directly in the oil and gas industry by 2030, in addition to the 600,000 already created.[6]

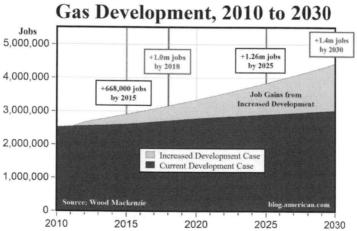

U.S. Employment: Oil and Natural Gas Development, 2010 to 2030

If those 1.4 million new jobs were already open today, filling them would reduce the unemployment rate from 7.7 percent to 6.7 percent.

It is also important to note that jobs in the energy industry tend to pay well above the national average. That means that blue-collar workers will, for the first time in decades, have better opportunities for higher wages. Including overtime, some employees will earn incomes of $100,000 or more. Suddenly, the proverbial "income gap" will begin to shrink even as top earners enjoy even higher incomes.

Furthermore, job growth in the energy industry launches a significant "multiplier effect" in other industries, from manufacturing to transportation to accounting. In fact, one analysis from PricewaterhouseCoopers found that each oil and gas job indirectly supports three other positions in the rest of the economy.[7] So, it's safe to say that those 1.4 million oil and gas jobs will create 4.2 million other jobs, which would theoretically drop the 2030 unemployment rate to 4.8 percent. And this total of 5.6 million jobs would go a long way toward getting America's 12 million unemployed, and 23 million underemployed, people back to work.

For this and other reasons, we expect the new era in energy to help resolve the immigration dilemma. The highest-paying jobs for blue-collar workers in the oil and gas fields will require the ability to speak English and a technical education at a two-year vocational college or a strong vocational high school. Recent immigrants who are not fluent in English and who lack technical training won't qualify for those positions, so they won't be in competition with American workers for them. However, they will still find solid jobs in providing services to higher-paid workers. They could, for example, work in construction, maintenance, or restaurants while they improve their skills by taking classes after work.

The beneficiaries of the energy boom won't be just those who find work and the companies that hire them. The growth in jobs will provide a windfall to the government. Economists estimate that these new employees and their companies will pay $36 billion in taxes and fees to the government by 2015. By 2030, as the industry expands, the government will collect more than $100 billion. In addition to income taxes and taxes on corporate profits, the government will generate revenues from opening access to parts of the U.S. that are currently restricted from oil and natural gas development, as well as allowing the Keystone XL pipeline and subsequent area infrastructure to be built.

This stream of revenue offers a ready solution to the looming shortfall in funds in Social Security and Medicare to support America's aging population in the decades ahead. It provides yet another example of a technological innovation that can address a seemingly impossible demographic challenge.

The third force: the revitalization of American manufacturing

The numbers that we've discussed so far reflect job growth in the oil and gas sector itself, as well as "supporting jobs" in industries like retailing, personal services, transportation, construction, and hospitality. However, the energy revolution will create an extraordinary potential to rewrite the value-added equation for manufacturing and trigger an unprecedented manufacturing renaissance in the United States.

With a reliable supply of affordable, abundant energy, it will once again make economic sense to manufacture goods in the U.S.

That means we can halt the relentless off-shoring of American manufacturing that began in the 1980s. This off-shoring was premised primarily on the idea of exploiting low-cost labor and minimizing regulatory constraints. Beginning around 1978, China and several other countries seemed to offer both advantages. However, the following eight factors that made off-shoring so attractive are rapidly disappearing:

- Direct labor was a large component of the delivered costs, and foreign labor rates were a tiny fraction of U.S. rates. Today, capital equipment and materials represent an increasingly large cost component of most manufacturing categories, eclipsing direct labor.
- Demand forecasts could accommodate long supply chains. Product life-cycles have become shorter and customer demand less predictable, creating big advantages for facilities that can

respond to demand in a matter of days, rather than months.

- Energy used in the manufacturing process was as cheap or cheaper in foreign countries than in the United States. The availability of low-cost natural gas in America's manufacturing heartland has suddenly created a big advantage vs. many Asian sourcing options.
- Raw materials in other countries were at or below domestic costs. Just as with energy, the availability of low-cost American materials derived from the energy revolution will largely offset overseas labor cost advantages.
- Quality standards were such that the foreign producers could be trusted to meet them. Increasingly, foreign producers—especially in China—have been guilty of manufacturing substandard products that inevitably damage the brand perception of the product.
- Adequate feed-back loops between design and manufacturing could be maintained across large physical and cultural distances. Research at MIT and elsewhere has shown that multinational manufacturers are losing their distinct competencies related to design and development because the links between R&D, marketing, and the shop floor have become too tenuous.
- Management and administrative resources at contract manufacturing facilities were competent enough to deliver the designated product within budget and on time. China in particular is undergoing a demographic crisis in which it is not able to fill its management and technical ranks, and this is becoming more true as technologies like digital fabrication, MEMS, and nanotech become increasingly important. Because of language and cultural barriers, it's increasingly preferable to rely on American workers than foreigners working 8,000 miles or more from headquarters.
- Manufacturing and product-based intellectual property could be adequately safeguarded. Increasingly multinationals are finding that their intellectual capital is being pilfered by their contract-manufacturers. When off-shoring represented a crucial cost differentiation and the contract manufacturer lacked the marketing expertise to compete on a global scale, this may have been an acceptable trade-off; but it will become

increasingly untenable in the years ahead.

Consequently, while most U.S-based firms will continue to source a large share of products for developing markets from off-shore manufacturers, there will be a dramatic shift of production for OECD markets back to the heartland of the United States.

Using figures from the U.S. Bureau of Labor Statistics, the Boston Consulting Group now estimates that the average wage for Chinese workers will be 17 percent of the average American worker's wage by 2015.[8] In 2000, that figure was 3 percent. From 2000 to 2009, 6 million manufacturing jobs vanished in the U.S., as tens of thousands of factories were shuttered. But since then, American manufacturing has experienced a resurgence. Consider the following examples, which are increasingly typical of the new economy:

- Exxon Mobile is planning to build a multibillion-dollar chemical facility in Baytown, Texas, that will employ 6,000 workers.[9]
- U.S. Steel has added a $95 million plant in Ohio that will manufacture drilling rigs. The company has also just recently opened a mill at a factory in Ohio that will supply steel pipe for the drilling industry.[10]
- NCR has reported it will be producing its ATMs in a Columbus, Georgia plant that has hired 870 workers.[11]
- The Coleman Company will be making its 16-quart wheeled plastic cooler in Wichita, Kansas, pulling production back from China.[12]

Other companies that have already moved production, and therefore, jobs, back to the U.S. include Caterpillar, Wham-O, Otis Elevator, Buck Knives, Farouk Systems, and Sleek Audio Systems, plus many more.

Beyond the negative impact of rising Chinese labor costs, there are a number of positive factors that explain why manufacturing is returning to the U.S. These factors provide clear signs of America's move toward a golden age of affluence.

As we highlighted earlier, a major factor is the cost advantage that the United States is developing over other affluent industrialized nations when it comes to energy and certain crucial raw materials.

There's probably no better example than the development of horizontal drilling and hydraulic fracturing, or "fracking."

Today, this technology is already unlocking vast supplies of natural gas that, up until now, have been trapped in shale. Fracking has made access to natural gas so abundant that the U.S. is now sitting on a 100-year supply. As a result of the lowered cost of extraction, natural gas prices have plummeted.

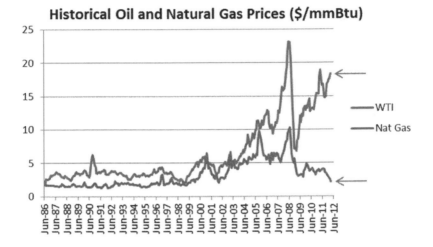

In 2005, domestic natural gas prices made the U.S. a high-cost location for energy-intensive manufacturing processes. But, because of the drop in prices, this disadvantage has been totally reversed, and U S. companies that had set up shop in other countries are moving back to benefit from this low-priced energy source.

Consider just two examples:

- The Nucor Corporation plans to build a $750 million facility in Louisiana for manufacturing direct-reduced iron in a process that relies heavily on natural gas. As recently as 2004, the company had relocated a similar Louisiana plant to Trinidad.[13]
- Major chemical companies are relocating plants to the U.S. to manufacture products that are derived from natural gas feedstocks. Dow Chemical is one of them, with plans to build a plant on the Gulf Coast that will produce ethylene and propylene, both products cost-effectively made from shale gas.

250

Dow's new plant will employ 2,000 workers. [14]

According to Dow Chemical CEO Andrew N. Liveris, "The discovery of shale gas is [the basis of] an American manufacturing renaissance, if handled well. It makes America a low-cost jurisdiction for any energy-intensive manufacturing of the value-add kind."[15]

Dow's engineers estimate that for every dollar of natural gas used for energy or as a raw material, eight dollars is added to our economy.

According to Bob McCutcheon, industry leader for U.S. industrial products and metals at PricewaterhouseCoopers, the low cost of natural gas will have an extraordinarily positive effect on manufacturing in the years ahead. As McCutcheon asserts, "The manufacturing sector could save $11.6 billion in cost, and could create up to 1 million manufacturing jobs attributed to shale gas."[16]

Another positive factor is an increase in U.S. productivity. This surge in productivity has been made possible by superior management methods, information technology, and reengineered business processes. As these factors help expand the economy, new products and new industries will create even more new jobs.

The beginning of this manufacturing renaissance is already being felt. 2011 was the best year for manufacturing in a generation. Three key measures of economic performance were up: profits, output growth, and employment gains.

This growth in manufacturing, coupled with innovations arising from the Golden Age of the Digital Revolution, will propel America into a new golden age of affluence that will benefit people in virtually every demographic group.

The initial wave has just begun. As the costs of labor, land, materials, and energy continue to rise in China, the equation for locating or relocating factories in the U.S. will be very simple to solve, even before factoring in transportation costs, import duties, delivery delays, and quality issues. Except for cheap commodity products or those requiring lots of hand-assembly, companies will find it more cost-effective to manufacture goods in the U.S. rather than in China. Consequently, in the next 10 years, as many as 3 million new manufacturing jobs will be created in the U.S.

Of course, these manufacturing jobs will have their own multiplier effect, with each creating roughly 3 additional jobs across the economy, of which 1.6 jobs are expected to be local service jobs in retailing, personal care, and hospitality. That's 12 million new jobs created directly and indirectly by the manufacturing renaissance, in addition to the 5.6 million jobs created directly and indirectly by the oil and gas industry. These 17.6 million jobs will go a long way toward giving America's 23 million "underemployed" a solid prosperous future.

The geography of U.S. energy jobs

A disproportionate share of the jobs created directly and indirectly by oil and gas, as well as newly resurgent manufacturing, will be located in America's traditional heartland. As Walter Russell Mead explained in his superb series in *The American Interest:*

> "The hollowing out of Middle America has been one of the tragedies of the last generation. Looking at the depopulation of the northern Great Plains, planners began to speculate about returning large chunks of whole states to the wild: The 'Buffalo Commons' idea that would have taken up to 20 million acres out of private hands. The buffalo will have to move over now for the oil rigs and the people who work them; North Dakota will not be reverting to the wild anytime soon.

> "But there are large oil and/or gas reserves in other downtrodden areas. Western New York State and much of Pennsylvania and Ohio appear to have commercial quantities of fossil fuel. The revival of the Rustbelt may be getting under way. And Dixie will not lose out: The U.S. share of the Gulf of Mexico is now believed to have the potential to produce 2 to 3 million more barrels per day than the 1.2 million that it currently pumps.

> "Overall, the new energy geography points toward a revival of the Mississippi-Ohio-Missouri river system as the axis of American growth.

252

"Put cheap and secure energy in the Middle West, and build large new cities and centers of economic demand in the neighborhood, and the energy revival in a few states will support general economic growth in many more."[17]

The long-term outlook for the dollar and the trade deficit is particularly good. Oil imports are going to decline, and natural gas exports will offset them, making the United States a net energy exporter. As we've already mentioned, the federal government will generate revenues from the new energy production, as well as from taxes on the rising incomes of the employers and employees that will profit from the surging energy industry.

Under this scenario, the United States will be an even more attractive place for foreign investment than it is now. Building the infrastructure required to get the new energy industry up and running and to transport its products to the market offers some very profitable and secure investment opportunities. And with the U.S. dependent solely on Canada for a limited amount of foreign oil, the U.S. economy will be much less exposed to the risks associated with turmoil in the Middle East or Latin America. That is the kind of thing investors look for: high growth in safe places.

Few, if any, places in the world are going to look like safer bets for the balance of the 21st century than the center of the United States. For investors, a better combination of benefits is hard to imagine: safety from the threat of military attacks, a stable system of government, and a tradition of upholding property rights for both American and foreign-owned businesses.

Closing the loop

In a real sense, the new North American Energy Revolution could only have emerged in the context of the infotech and materials breakthroughs that characterized the first phase of the Digital Revolution. Consider just a few examples:

- Mapping of unconventional hydrocarbon deposits thousands of feet below the surface was only possible due to the rise of supercomputers running advanced seismological models.

- Hydraulic fracturing and horizontal drilling were enabled by breakthroughs in chemistry and metallurgy.
- New technologies are making it possible to remove the chemicals used in fracking, as well as the natural salts that emerge for gas wells.

The United States has very large reserves of the new fuels, but we are not alone on the planet in having these resources. However, unlike competitors such as Russia and OPEC, the United States has both the R&D and execution capabilities needed to actually derive payback from these breakthroughs. As a result, North America has enjoyed a first-mover advantage. U.S. oil companies have taken the lead in creating the technologies that have transformed the potential of shale oil and natural gas into reliable new sources of energy.

America's unique innovation advantage will play a big role in recapturing its premier position in the energy sector. As Vince Beiser wrote in *Pacific Standard,* "Nano-engineered materials, underwater robots, side-scanning 3D sonar, specially engineered lubricants, and myriad other advances are opening up titanic new supplies of fossil fuels. The problem for domestic oil has never been a lack of supply, surprisingly. It's been the inability to tap into that oil."[18]

That's been changing rapidly. While the U.S. was producing 320 billion cubic feet of shale gas in 2000, by 2011 production soared to 7.8 trillion cubic feet.[19]

Of course, the biggest reason for the increase is the growing use of fracking. Although the technology's impact on the environment is poorly understood, there is no question that it is effective at unleashing energy. Whether the alleged damage is worth the benefits of energy independence is a question that will be hotly debated.

Meanwhile, other technologies are being developed to efficiently extract oil and gas. For instance, a Texas company called FMC Technologies plans to deploy robots that will drill for oil on the ocean floor.

By commercializing these technicians to increase production, the U.S. will harness the powerful jolt of economic vitality coming from the emergent energy sector to transform the *potential* described

254

in the first eleven chapters of this book into a tsunami of affluence that will reengineer the entire world economy. And that's exactly what we'd expect based on the history of the last four Golden Ages.

The U.S. (or North American) energy revolution will be such a huge success *because* it applies the infotech, biotech, and nanotech breakthroughs accumulated since the 1970s to discovering, extracting, and utilizing fossil fuels in cost-effective and environmentally friendly ways. Like biomass (i.e., forests and animal waste) before them, conventional coal, oil, and gas dominated the economy because they could be cost-effectively extracted from discoverable resources using current technology. However, this stage of history is ending after about 150 years. These will soon be largely replaced by shale oil and gas, oil sands, clean coal, and even methane hydrates.

But, what about climate change?

As we predicted as far back as 1994, *"The debate over anthropogenic climate change no longer rests on a foundation of objective scientific evidence and solutions selected on the basis of a quantifiable cost-benefit criteria. For the truly committed on either side, it has devolved into a true "religious battle," pitting the forces of righteousness and truth against those of evil and lies."*

Since we made that forecast in *Trends*, it appears that the world has indeed suffered from a *man-made* climate crisis. By that, we mean that man has intentionally, or unintentionally, manufactured a crisis based on concerns for the climate. In turn, that crisis of perception has undermined the world economy, human health, and the wellbeing of billions of people on this planet.

Specifically, we argue that this man-made "crisis of confidence in technology" has unduly delayed, but not prevented, the beginning of the Golden Age of the Digital Revolution. And it's all been based on *outdated* evidence.

Before you dismiss this argument, consider the most recent data:

First, the Nobel Prize winning team of climate experts behind the science of anthropogenic climate change is the UN's

Intergovernmental Panel on Climate Change, or IPCC. Its chairman is Rajendra Pachauri. Recently, Dr. Pachauri acknowledged a 17-year pause in global temperature rises; Britain's Meteorological Office confirmed this pause and predicts no further increase through 2017. If correct, that would extend the pause to 21 years.[20]

In the U.S., there has not been a single new statewide maximum temperature record set since 1995 and, despite claims to the contrary, July 1936 remains the warmest month on record. Notably, that record was set when the global CO_2 level was less than 300 parts per million versus 395 parts per million today.

The IPCC's warming models have consistently failed to show *any* predictive value with respect to temperature. To understand just how badly flawed are the models on which the IPCC experts insist mankind bet tens of trillions of dollars in resources over the next generation, take a look at this graph taken from the preliminary draft of the IPCC's upcoming report.

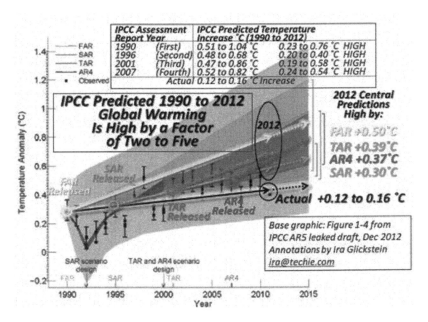

It makes clear that the midpoints of the various models predicted that the world would warm by between 0.5 degrees Fahrenheit and 0.9 degrees Fahrenheit between 1990 and 2012.

However, according to IPCC's own data, actual warming was much less than that: roughly 0.28 F.

This provides unequivocal evidence that either CO_2 is not nearly as strong a climate driver as the IPCC has been assuming, or that some factor, which they don't understand, is at work. In either case, it's clear that the forecasting models have been utterly meaningless for use in making large-scale commitments of resources.

And, when assessing the models for 1990 or 1996, this is understandable. Frequently, models are initially flawed because they do not consider some important variable or capture some important relationships. However, the quality of the IPCC models has *not* improved. Specifically, the predictive quality of the 2001 and 2007 models are not markedly better than the 2001 model. So we are left to ask why anyone still takes these forecasts seriously?

Other metrics have also failed to indicate a long-term causal relationship between CO_2 levels and other adverse climate conditions. Specifically, analyses of rising sea levels, the frequency of storms or droughts, and other weather and climate events have demonstrated *no* statistically significant difference between the past 20 years and what the Earth and mankind have experienced over the past 100-plus years.

For example, the "overwhelming scientific judgment of science" was confirmed in November 2012, when a study published in the peer-reviewed journal *Nature* concluded that "there has been little change in drought over the past 60 years."[21]

But what about storms? The National Oceanic and Atmospheric Administration reports a long-term decline in strong tornadoes striking the United States. The National Hurricane Center reports that the past 40 years have seen the fewest major hurricane strikes since at least the mid-1800s.[22] Even Hurricane Sandy reminds us that the U.S. Northeast has experienced only one other major hurricane strike since 1960, but it experienced six major hurricane strikes during the 1930s, 1940s, and 1950s, when global temperatures were cooler.

Not surprisingly a newly published survey of 1,077 geoscientists and engineers showed that only 36 percent "express the strong belief that climate change is happening, that it is not a normal cycle of nature, and humans are the main or central cause."[24] Meanwhile, two recent surveys of meteorologists revealed similar skepticism of alarmist global warming claims.

In fact, an objective examination of the facts leads us to conclude that the researchers, activists, and government officials who demand that economic growth be sacrificed on the altar of climate change are suffering from an extreme "confirmation bias," reinforced by an almost unprecedented case of "group think."

It is now becoming increasingly clear that this and the other aspects of our "culture of scarcity" have redirected countless billions of dollars from demonstrably productive sectors of our economy, and given it to politically connected institutions that promote climate alarmism and renewable energy technologies that are unready to compete.

Given what was known in the early '90s, the climate change debate was typically framed as a choice between *preemptive mitigation* and *doing nothing*. This led to the 1997 Kyoto Protocol, which was rejected by the United States, disavowed by Canada, and imposed no meaningful constraints on India and China.

As a result, this initial attempt to implement preemptive mitigation was largely unsuccessful. And now, after the expiration of constraints on Russia at the end of 2012, the world is left with a hodgepodge of unilateral and multilateral commitments, not taken seriously by any the world's fastest-growing economies.

However, just as the *Trends* editors forecast nearly 20 years ago, the false dichotomy of the early '90s has given way to three alternatives:

- Preemptive mitigation
- Doing nothing
- Contingent adaptation

Alternative #1: Preemptive mitigation of greenhouse gases implies less economic growth, a transition to so-called renewable energy sources, and potentially, sequestration of greenhouse gases, where produced. What are the practical implications of preemptive mitigation? So far, this approach has been used to justify:

258

- Thousands of regulations
- Carbon trading schemes
- Carbon taxes
- Inefficient renewable energy programs
- Other initiatives that increase the cost of everything we make, grow, ship, eat, heat, cool, wear, and do

In the process, these supposed remedies have impaired job creation, economic growth, living standards, human health, human welfare, and even ecological values. In the U.S., EPA rules have closed numerous coal-fired power plants, and the agency plans to regulate most of the U.S. hydrocarbon-based economy by restricting carbon dioxide emissions from vehicles, generating plants, cement kilns, factories, malls, hospitals, and other *significant* sources.

Were it not for the hydraulic fracking technology that has made natural gas and gas-fired generation abundant and cheap, U.S. electricity prices would be skyrocketing, just as they have in Britain and Germany.

Almost daily, EU newspapers carry articles about "fuel poverty," potential blackouts, off-shoring, job losses, economic malaise and despair, and even deforestation for firewood in European countries.[23] In California, electricity prices are already the highest in U.S., thanks to its EU-style carbon schemes. Most notably, these programs do nothing to reduce Chinese, Indian, or global emissions, which are the real threat if one exists.

Frustratingly, so-called *renewable* energy is nowhere near being economically viable, eco-friendly, or sustainable. Consider the facts about the three most commonly cited sources of renewable energy:

- First, *wind energy* requires perpetual subsidies as well as "backup" fossil fuel power plants that typically produce 80 percent of the electricity attributed to "wind." More tragically, this technology blankets wildlife habitats with turbines and transmission lines that kill millions of birds and bats every year. In fact, industrial wind facilities remain viable only because they are exempted from many environmental review, wildlife, and bird protection laws that are enforced with heavy penalties for all other industries.[24]

- Second, *solar* has proven to be even less viable. The truth is, photovoltaics are nowhere near being cost-competitive with North American natural gas or the latest clean-coal technology. Whether we're talking Europe, China, or the United States, this technology has only made minor market penetration, despite large subsidies. Even in China, many solar firms are now in or near bankruptcy. Like electric automobiles, photovoltaics may be viable in 15 to 20 years, but not now. And, by that time, safe, carbon-free alternatives like thorium and traveling-wave nuclear reactors will be commercially viable.

- Third, *biofuels* have not proven themselves. To date, this industry has mostly succeeded in diverting crops and cropland from food production, as well as replacing abundant and cheap fossil fuels with more expensive alternatives. In the future, advances in biotech are likely to make biofuels from algae and farm wastes competitive. However, that day has not yet come.

Worst of all for the economy, many climate activists and regulators see impeding the implementation of fracking for natural gas, as well as preventing development of energy resources off-shore and on government lands, as key components of preemptive mitigation. Since this development is crucial to jump-starting the Golden Age of the Digital Revolution, we argue that preemptive mitigation has the potential for dooming billions of people worldwide to lives of grinding poverty, ill health, and early death.

Researcher Paul Driessen refers to this willingness on the part of Western elites to sentence billions in Africa and other poor regions to lives of misery through the policies of preemptive mitigation as "eco-imperialism."[25] This was fully on display when Ghana started building a new power plant that would burn natural gas that previously was wasted through "flaring." President Obama told Ghana's government that it should instead use unproven "wind, solar, geothermal, and biofuels energy, instead of fossil fuels that 'threaten' global warming."

Similarly, eco-imperialism motivated the United States to refuse to support loans for South Africa's critically needed, state-of-the-art Medupi coal-fired power plant. These actions cruelly ignored both the livelihoods and living standards that electricity has brought to the world, and the millions of deaths from lung infections and intestinal diseases that these power plants would prevent.

Alternative #2: Doing nothing involves simply adopting the most economical solutions in order to maximize short-term growth and return on investment on specific projects. This scenario will clearly reduce greenhouse gas emissions in the OECD, as North America and the EU replace conventional coal and oil with low-cost natural gas as well as new 99 percent-clean coal technology.

In fact, this scenario alone could reduce North American emissions by as much as 40 percent.

GDP Under Various Climate Change Scenarios

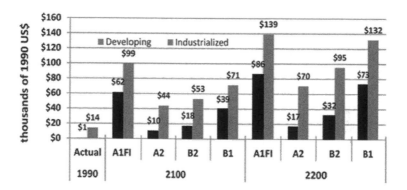

Source: *Is Global Warming the Number One Threat to Humanity?,* Indur Goklany, Global Warming Policy Foundation, 2012)

This chart shows net global GDP per capita in 1990, 2100 and 2200, after accounting for the upper bound estimates of losses due to global warming under four major IPCC emission and climate scenarios. For 2100 and 2200, the scenarios are arranged from the warmest (A1FI) on the left to the coolest (B1) on the right. The average global temperature increase from 1990 to 2085 for the scenarios are as follows: 4°C for AIFI, 3.3°C for A2, 2.4°C for B2, and 2.1°C for B1. A1F1 is roughly comparable to our "Do Nothing" scenario, while A2, B2 and B1 represent various "Preemptive Mitigation" scenarios.

And contrary to what you have probably heard, even environmentalists—like Lord Stern, who led the UK's attempt to quantify the impact of global warming—have found it difficult to prove that "preemptive mitigation" is superior to a "do nothing" strategy. This conclusion is documented by estimates of future net GDP per capita.

This chart labeled "GDP Under Various Climate Change Scenarios" was originally developed by the Global Warming Policy Foundation was derived using the results of the Stern Review. It indicates that net GDP per capita in both developing and industrialized countries would be highest under a "do nothing scenario" (A1F1) in which temperatures rise 4 degrees by 2100. Meanwhile, the most comparable "preemptive mitigation" scenario, where temperatures only rise 2.1 degrees (B1), results in substantially less affluence.

Specifically, assuming comparable populations through 2100, GDP per capita in the *developing* world will rise by nearly 62-fold from 1990 levels, due to "free market" use of energy resources. On the other hand, under a "preemptive mitigation" scenario, developing world GDP per capita would increase only 39-fold. For poorer people in the developing world, this is the difference between genuine affluence and still being poor.

Alternative #3: Contingent adaptation addresses the World Economic Forum's concerns regarding "failure of climate change adaptation." To do so, it enhances the best aspects of the so-called "do nothing" approach with development and selective implementation of technologies for minimizing the adverse effects of climate change, if and when they appear.

Under this plan, market-driven conversion to new cost-effective energy sources, coupled with a rapid rise in affluence, provides the resources needed for adaptation that would minimize hardships brought about by climate change over the coming decades, regardless of its cause.

Unlike preemptive mitigation, which always seems to boil down to fewer people and slower economic growth, contingent adaptation looks for the least-costly, most humane way to achieve a satisfactory outcome.

262

For example, rather than placing emphasis on cutting CO_2 emission through reduced economic activity, contingent adaptation favors more growth-compatible solutions, such as eliminating ordinary industrial "soot." Recent research indicates that this one low-cost adaptation would virtually erase all of the effects of warming that has occurred to the Arctic sea-ice during the last 100 years.

By preventing this melting, it ensures that the dark heat-absorbing water is not exposed to the sun. Furthermore, it's a lot faster than CO_2 mitigation; soot's contribution to warming could be reduced by 90 percent in 5 to 10 years with aggressive national and international policies that would involve minimal impact to the global economy.

In a presentation at the 242nd National Meeting & Exposition of the American Chemical Society, Mark Jacobson, PhD, explained that controlling soot could reduce warming above parts of the Arctic Circle by almost 3 degrees Fahrenheit within 15 years.

Soot or "black carbon" consists of particles, nearly invisible on an individual basis, released in smoke from combustion of both fossil fuels and biofuels. Major sources include exhaust from diesel cars, buses, trucks, ships, aircraft, agricultural machines, construction equipment, and the wood or animal dung fires that hundreds of millions of people in developing countries use for cooking and heating.

Black carbon particles become suspended in the atmosphere and absorb sunlight, just like a black t-shirt on a sunny day. The particles then radiate that heat back into the air around it. Black carbon also can absorb light reflected from Earth's surface, which helps make it such a potent warming agent. But unlike carbon dioxide, which remains in the atmosphere for years, soot disappears within a few weeks, so that there is no long-term reservoir with a continuing warming effect.

Fortunately, the technology for controlling black carbon is already available at relatively modest cost. Diesel particulate filters, for instance, can remove soot from car and truck exhaust. And governments and other entities can make a big impact by introducing low-soot cook-stoves in developing countries.

Best of all, the increasing use of natural gas will have a profound effect, because soot is only produced by natural gas in the event that the burner is not optimized to ensure complete combustion.

Of even more significance, other adaptation mechanisms under the category of geo-engineering offer the promise of cost-effective solutions. Some, like underground sequestration of gaseous carbon dioxide in rock and in water, may not be suitable for long-term storage in some locations because of leakage; further research is needed to verify where and when this makes sense. And, other techniques, like space-based solar shields, turning the oceans into large carbon-sinks, and adjusting the reflectivity of the upper atmosphere, may not be ready for safe, cost-effective deployment for several decades.

However as legendary physicist Freeman Dyson observes, adaptation via "land management" is likely to be by far the most cost-effective route to managing atmospheric carbon dioxide and consequently, global warming. One particularly attractive approach involves planting and harvesting forests. The wood from the forest is then used for building materials or turned into charcoal, which is buried to enrich the soil and thereby sequester the carbon. If today's trees are selectively replaced with "bioengineered trees" optimized for maximum growth and carbon absorption on poor quality land, the result would be a self-supporting industry that also dramatically reduces greenhouse gases. Concerns about the adverse effect of warming on crops can be addressed by adopting crops engineered for hotter, and perhaps drier climates.

Finally, contingent adaptation should be recognized as an interim step between an economy based on fossil fuels and one based on advanced nuclear fission or fusion. The first three generations of nuclear power grew out of the nuclear weapons industry and relied on enriched uranium.

This technology could only be made reliable and safe by investing billions in redundant systems, radiation shielding, and security. Even then, nuclear waste has presented a vexing problem.

However, new thorium-fueled reactors and so-called "traveling-wave reactors" fueled with depleted uranium are dramatically cheaper, safer, smaller, and pose no "weapons proliferation" threat. They also produce hardly any long-lived radioactive waste.

By the 2030s or even sooner, both of these technologies should be ready for full commercial deployment. In the interim, Russia, China, and India are reportedly moving ahead with fast-breeder reactors that are carbon-free, but less safe than future nuclear technologies. Even more important for our long-term transition from fossil fuels, we're likely to see the first nuclear fusion prototypes break even by 2014, and by the 2040s, such plants, fueled by seawater, could be commercialized, allowing the world to produce cheap electricity for centuries.

So what's ahead?

First, "contingent adaptation" will become the default choice for dealing with climate change moving forward. The economic case is simply too compelling to think otherwise. Already, mitigation efforts are being abandoned and "green energy companies" are on the verge of failure, even in China. Recent elections in Australia were driven largely by a repudiation of preemptive mitigation. The real question is how long advocates of preemptive mitigation will be able to stand in the way of economic growth. In the United States, this will depend largely on the outcome of the 2014 Congressional Elections.

Second, the North American Energy Revolution will move forward rapidly, with or without the cooperation of the current U.S. administration. Development of oil and gas fields on private land in the U.S. heartland is already having a big impact.

Third, within five years, low-cost natural gas will largely replace oil and conventional coal for electricity and industrial boilers. This is likely to cut U.S. CO_2 emissions by up to 40 percent. However, new clean coal technology that captures over 99 percent of CO_2 is likely to retain significant market share.

Fourth, Canadian oil sands will be developed in this decade and most likely shipped via pipeline to U.S. refineries. Just as Canada renounced the Kyoto Protocol, it will not hesitate to sell this oil to China, if U.S. pipelines are not approved. However, pressure from business and labor organizations will make rejection of the proposed Keystone XL pipeline politically suicidal.

Fifth, many climate adaptation efforts are likely to move forward in the coming decade, regardless of whether a warming trend reemerges. Once started, most of the adaptations will be self-funding. For example, a forest products industry launched with the help of global philanthropy would become self-sustaining as trees are harvested for building materials and so-called bio-char for the soil. Similarly, a large share of captured CO_2 will be used for the extraction of oil from old fields and in the manufacture of certain synthetic materials. And these applications will proliferate as innovative companies strive to put the nearly-free raw material to use.

Sixth, the surge of demand and investment that will result from the abundant energy supply will accelerate commercialization of the other 11 transformational technologies that will define the Golden Age of the Digital Revolution. As explained earlier, these will not only change the medium-term outlook for Americans, but they will also utterly transform the prospect of every human on this planet in the 21st century.

266

14

How will you take command of your future?

"You see things; and you say 'Why?' But I dream
things that never were; and I say 'Why not?'"
--George Bernard Shaw, *Back to Methuselah*

Up to this point, we've explored 12 crucial trends in technology. But
understanding each of these trends isn't enough. To truly profit from
this knowledge, you need to determine how each technology will
impact people's lives over the coming months, years, or decades. Only
in this way will you be able to foresee the trend's potential to disrupt
industry business models and create wealth for those who capitalize on
each technology.

This brings us to three critical questions:

1. How will you stay on top of evolving trends, not just in
   technology, but in geo-demography and psycho-social
   systems?
2. How will you translate those trends into forecasts and
   insights that could provide your business a competitive
   advantage?
3. How do you translate your forecasts into profits that actually
   show up on the bottom line?

Staying on top of rapidly evolving trends

Let's start by answering the question, *"How will I stay on top of evolving trends?"*

If you own a small business, this responsibility may be yours alone. In a larger organization, however, you will most likely have a team assigned, at least part-time, to this important task. Either way, it's an overwhelming responsibility.

Just consider the facts. Experts estimate that cumulative human knowledge is doubling roughly every 7 years. That means that from July 1, 2007 through June 30, 2013, the amount of knowledge generated was equivalent to all the knowledge generated prior to July 1, 2007. And most of that incremental knowledge involves science and technology.

Fortunately, most of this information is noise, which has little to do with your business. However, your objective is to filter the "noise"—the continuous buzz of news stories and announcements of changes in the environment—to find the "signal" representing the opportunities and threats that will make a significant difference.

By reading this book, you have taken the first step. The next step is to stay continuously alert for the signals that can bankrupt your business if you don't see what's coming. . . or take it to the next level if you see what will happen, before your competitors.

Most business professionals do a pretty good job of seeing the same thing their competitors see. That is, understanding the trends that impact their industries, in the areas where they currently operate and within their own professional specialty. The problem arises when we consider longer-term trends emerging from other countries or industries, and requiring cross-functional insights. That's why so many companies are crushed by new entrants or substitutes with disruptive business models.

An easy and inexpensive way to supplement or kickstart your trend tracking effort is to join the thousands of executives who subscribe to *Trends* to get this vital intelligence every month. A corporate subscription is a great way to create a baseline dialog for any company. It not only provides useful forecasts and insights, but it tees-up questions that will undoubtedly motivate you to probe more deeply with an eye on the relevant implications for your business. Because it continuously sifts through mountains of data looking for key trends in geo-demography and technology, as well as attitudes, perceptions and values, it can save you and your staff a great deal of time and effort that can be applied elsewhere. As a reader of this book, you are eligible for a free trial and special discount pricing. To find out more, visit http://www.trends-magazine/challenge

Beyond this, the most effective mechanism is to reward employees for identifying relevant trends. We suggest a monthly "trend of the month" winner voted upon by the members of your own "trends forum."

How to catch the wave

Regardless of how you monitor, accumulate, and rank key trends, simply knowing about the trends is really just the beginning. You're still left with the second fundamental question, *"How can I translate those trends into forecasts and insights that could provide our business a competitive advantage?"*

The answer is to use what you've learned from this book and from your ongoing trend-tracking efforts, as a starting point for an ongoing action-oriented *management dialog.* These discussions should center on how these trends could open disruptive opportunities for your company and its competitors, as well as new entrants and potential substitutes.

A particularly useful approach is to direct high-potential trends to *a business intelligence team that assesses the company's strategy in light of the monthly flow of new trends and forecasts.* Not only does this on-going effort reduce your year end budgeting and strategic planning effort, but it also ensures that important trends are brought forward in a timely manner.

In a small firm, the team can simply be the core management team and a few "objective outsiders" supported by a moderator. However, the *ideal* team should be drawn from across the functions of the organization, from a variety of generations, ethnic cultures, and educational backgrounds. While an insider can serve as the moderator, third-party professionals prove particularly useful. Why? Because they bring to the table experience with the methodology, a lack of organizational bias, and knowledge from outside the company and industry.

Regardless of the other criteria used, remember that all members should have skills in creative thinking, collaboration, and interpersonal communication.

The team's mission is to review each trend that comes to their attention, identifying the implications for your industry and developing or validating forecasts leading to clear specific actions. If nothing else, the team's mission is to insure that you're never blind-sided by a disruptive business threat you did not consider.

It's the moderator's job to bring forward specific trends and relevant forecasts from various sources. Once a forecast is brought forward, each member of the team should answer two primary questions:

- First, "If this forecast is correct, what are the possible implications for our customers and our industry?"
- Second, "Given the available evidence, what *alternative* forecasts are plausible and what are the implications of each of those?"

For each forecast, this means considering how it could impact your business model, business processes, resource allocations, and marketing mix (i.e., pricing, promotions, distribution, and products). At this point, the objective is not to *falsify* the forecast; that comes later.

Too often, everyone in a company relies on the industry-centered conventional wisdom about the company and the industry. The tendency is to extrapolate the present into the future. But, by starting with the forecasts in *Trends*, the team can consider a much broader range of scenarios. Then, the team can work backwards from the imagined future to the present, outlining the steps that will need to be taken to profit from the trend.

Rather than compressing this work into a hectic once-a-month

270

meeting, team members take some time each day to **contribute forecasts, assessments, and validations to a secure, online, moderated forum**. The objective is to tee-up the what-ifs so everyone can think about them, ask questions, and do additional research. This is where industry, professional, and technical experience makes a big difference.

To minimize the influence of a few individuals, we advocate a "Modified Delphi Technique." It builds on a proven approach originally developed by the Rand Corporation for defense analysis during the Cold War. Participants log-in to the forum anonymously. Then a moderator collects the forecasts and organizes the content for the group so that the opinions are not identifiable by individual. Next, everyone is asked to critique the first round of forecast assessments, which are then presented back to the group in summarized anonymous form. Finally, the participants are asked to make new forecasts taking into account the various critiques.

The third step takes place at the month end. Based on the urgency and magnitude of the forecasts, the team ranks them for further evaluation as part of an evidence-based strategic planning approach.

Implementing this process raises three important questions that we'll answer in the balance of this chapter:

1. How should team members think about trends and forecasts?
2. How does a modified Delphi group achieve results?
3. How do you turn high-potential forecasts into bottom line results?

How should team members think about trends and forecasts?

How should the team members go about understanding generic trends and forecasts and transforming them into actionable insights that are both industry specific and firm-specific? Obviously, there are many potential ways to evaluate trends and validate forecasts, however, we've found the following framework to be particularly useful.

The first step is to **identify whether the trend is cyclic or linear.**

As Daniel Burrus details in his book *Flash Foresight, cyclic change* is based on predictable cycles, such as those that govern the weather, the seasons, the growth of living things, and the market bubbles. For example, night follows day, spring follows winter, and recessions follow bubbles. By understanding cycles, you can avoid the trap of seeing only the current situation and making decisions without anticipating what will come next. For example, stock market P/Es expand and contract, but there is always a reversion to the mean. The same thing is true of home prices relative to rents and food prices relative to production costs. A particularly useful form of a cyclical trend is called a diffusion-curve; you may know it as an S-curve. It describes the adoption of a technology and the well-known "product life cycle."

The other type of predictable change is termed a *linear change*. Linear change always moves in the same direction, without reversing itself. For example, the age of the planet is an example of linear change, because it is constantly increasing and will never decrease.

Patterns of linear change can be readily seen in technologies. As we discussed in Chapter 2, Moore's Law states that computer processing performance per unit cost doubles every 18 months. Eventually, Moore's Law for silicon will come to an end because of atomic and quantum constraints; however, analogous laws for other materials (graphene, molybdenite, etc.) are expected to extend technological progress well beyond that point. Similarly, Metcalfe's Law declares that the number of connections, and consequently, the *potential* value of a network, increases in proportion to the number of nodes (such as Internet devices or Facebook users) squared. Metcalfe's Law and similar relationships are often misinterpreted because analysts fail to appreciate the difference between "actual value" and "potential value."

To anticipate the future accurately, it's important to distinguish between linear and cyclical change. For instance, the popularity of individual smart phones like the iPhone 5 and the Samsung Galaxy III are examples of cyclic change; they will follow a predictable product lifecycle (S-curve) in which they will continue to rise in sales volume until a better product comes along or the product achieves market saturation. Ideally, each firm will introduce an innovation rendering its own products obsolete before a competitor, or market saturation, terminates the upward trend.

The second step in assessing a forecast is to **evaluate it in light of predominate conventional wisdom of the Digital Revolution.** Every technology revolution is defined by an underlying set of rules based on the nature of the dominant technological paradigm. During the investment phase of the Digital Revolution, infotech itself was driven by a new conventional wisdom suited to the unique characteristics of the digital paradigm. However, most of the industries *using* IT were still guided by the economics of the Mass Production Revolution. But, in the Golden Age just ahead, the "conventional wisdom" of the Digital Revolution will also guide the successful firms that disrupt industry after industry, whether they are IT-based or not.

Daniel Burrus identified eight principles that define the conventional wisdom of the Digital Revolution, and every forecast should be evaluated in light of the following eight principles:

1. **Dematerialization.** Technologies become more efficient even as they become more powerful. Computers and smart phones, for instance, will use increasingly less material to create an increasingly better user experience. The same thing is true in almost every industry: less mass will be used to generate each successive unit of GDP. Eventually computing will be everywhere, all the time, nearly invisible and practically free. Ask yourself, "Is the forecast consistent with the dematerialization principle? And, what could dematerialization mean for your customers and the economics of your business in this context?"

2. **Virtualization.** We'll do more and more things in the virtual world that we once did in the physical sphere. We buy online, read e-books on tablets, and test business decisions using software programs rather than real-world employees and customers. Ask yourself, "Is the forecast consistent with the virtualization principle? What could virtualization mean for

273

your customers and the economics of your business in this context?"

3. **Mobility.** Instead of needing to stay in one place, digitally based solutions will go anywhere with us. Ask yourself, "Is the forecast consistent with the mobility principle? And, what could mobility mean for your customers and the economics of your business in this context?"

4. **Product intelligence.** Embedding artificial intelligence and sensors into everyday products and into the objects that surround us will create a world in which everything is connected to everything else and can leverage almost unlimited knowledge, data, and processing. As we saw in Chapter 3, the direct implications of AI are huge, but the indirect implications referred to in Chapters 5-13 are far bigger. Ask yourself, "To what extent could AI undercut the value you create or permit you to undercut the value created by your competitors? Is the forecast consistent with the product intelligence principle? And, what could product intelligence mean for your customers and the economics of your business in this context?"

5. **Networking.** Through technologies and social networks, people are increasingly linked to each other in real time. This includes threats and opportunities related to crowdsourcing of innovation change creating a more responsive marketing mix, and cocreation of products or services with customers and suppliers. Ask yourself, "Is the forecast consistent with the networking principle? And, what could networking mean for your customers and the economics of your business in this context?"

6. **Interactivity.** Instead of just using technologies, we will interact with them and help shape how they perform for us. Are you adapting in real-time to the needs and wants of your customers? Ask yourself, "Is the forecast consistent with the interactivity principle? And, if the forecast is true, what will it mean for your customers and the economics of your business in this context?"

7. **Globalization.** The world will continue to shrink, as consumers are increasingly able to source the products they consume from providers all around the planet. Up to this point, globalization has focused on simplistic off-shoring by

developed countries to developing countries; but the focus will change as developing markets grow and developed countries regain advantages in terms of costs and innovation. Ask yourself, "Is the forecast consistent with the *globalization* principle? And, what could globalization mean for your customers and the economics of your business in this context?"

8. **Convergence.** New solutions will emerge as old ones combine and integrate totally new capabilities. In the same way that today's smartphones combine a computer, a camera, a video camera, a music player, a GPS device, and more, future technology will be multifunctional, where it provides a cost or performance benefit. Ask yourself, "Is the forecast consistent with the *convergence* principle? And, what could convergence mean for your customers and the economics of your business in this context?"

In short, those forecasts that complement these eight principles are "riding the wave" and may merit further investigation. Those whose assumptions go contrary to these principles are "fighting the wave." Just as bond traders seldom win by "fighting the Fed," forecasts that "fight the wave" are unlikely to be correct. Pursue those with caution.

The third step is to **imagine how the forecast could disrupt your industry** and how your business could "change" in order to make the most of the situation. Unlike ordinary incremental change, you can't respond to disruption by simply doing something a little better or a little differently. Instead, it means doing something in an entirely new way.

Why the focus on *disruptive* change? Because the type of incremental change that enabled Toyota to dominate the automobile industry can become a formula for disaster in a world dominated by new business models, globalization, and short product lifecycles. To survive and thrive in such a world, you have to envision how a forecast (based on a trend) could disrupt the competitive context—customers, products, costs, delivery channels, competitors, etc. Then, you have to define a testable hypothesis about how to transform your business to make the most of the situation.

Redbox changed the way DVDs were sold, moving them from

a large retail store to a small, automated kiosk. By contrast, Amazon, Netflix, and others disrupted prevailing industry business models by streaming movies to TVs, laptops, tablets, and smart phones.

Using your specific competitive situation and a specific trend, the team must ask: "How could (forecast X) disrupt our business?"

For example, if your business is an insurance company, and the trend you're considering is the emergence of driverless cars, some of the implications may be obvious. Without a human driver at the wheel, liability is likely to pass to the manufacturer of the vehicle, or to the developer of the software that will integrate the data from the GPS system with the sensors embedded in the roadway, other vehicles, and traffic signs.

For a business that will be less directly affected, such as a restaurant, the implications are less clear and will require more analysis and imagination. Perhaps a different parking lot configuration will be possible: The car can drop off the passengers at the door and park itself in a remote lot, meaning the restaurant's footprint could be much larger. Suddenly, restaurant locations in crowded urban locations that were not feasible because of a lack of parking are now attractive.

The fourth step is to **relate the trends to your core resources and competencies**.

Too often, people fail to appreciate the relevance of a trend or forecast because they evaluate it in terms of their organization's *current* customer needs, competencies, resources, and business model. One way to appreciate both the opportunities and threats inherent in trends is to break these components apart.

For example, the team should consider the following four questions with respect to each trend or forecast:

1. "If we look at the jobs-to-be-done that our current customers might want, how will this trend impact them?"
2. "Given our current core competencies, how might we or a new entrant to the market exploit this trend to gain competitive advantage?"
3. "Similarly, given our resources such as locations, fixed assets, and supplier relationships, how might this trend increase or decrease our competitive advantage?"

4. "If this trend plays itself out, will it strengthen or undermine our current business model?"

How does a modified Delphi group achieve results?

The Delphi Technique has been around for decades and has become even more useful in the age of virtual communities. It's named for the famous Oracle of Delphi in ancient Greece. It eliminates the tendency of opinions from outside the formal power structure to be squelched. It was invented to eliminate the tendency to argue about the familiar rather than discuss the genuinely new and different. Even more importantly, it minimizes the subtle intimidation that often occurs when groups of diverse rank and expertise are assembled.

Historically, the Delphi Technique has been most commonly used in situations requiring forecasting related to issues on which experts often disagree. It is proven to help bring about a rational, amicable consensus through the use of an iterative, thought-sharing process, where other techniques have failed.

James M. Higgins points out in his book, *101 Creative Problem Solving Techniques,* that the Delphi Technique works especially well in coming up with answers to futuristic questions like, "What are the top 10 emerging issues in new product innovation?" or "What is the correct long-term demand forecast for electric cars?"[1]

The Delphi Technique involves submitting and sharing written ideas outside of a traditional meeting. It ensures consistency with respect to both the primary ideas and the feedback provided about them. Moreover, using today's networks, it can be administered to ensure privacy while verifying participation.

To ensure consistency, rigor, and anonymity, the process requires a skilled "moderator." The moderator tees-up the trends & forecasts and presents the generated ideas in a consistent, objective, and anonymous manner.

Why is this important? In a traditional peer-to-peer online community, everyone sees the posts made by everyone else. On the contrary, a "Delphi community" has a hub-and-spokes structure: the moderator carries on dialogues with every other participant—

reformulating ideas, probing for more information, and then distributing everyone's thoughts to the group.

The Delphi Technique is especially useful for trend forecasting because it relies on expert opinion and analysis. It essentially produces imaginative insights through a process of sharing perspectives and information. Most importantly, since each participant knows that the other participants don't know who they are, and they don't know which of the other participants is making which arguments, much of the "posturing" common to expert interchanges is removed from the debate. Through the course of several iterations, groups tend to move toward the position that is best supported, rather than the one that was presented by the person with the loudest voice or most prestigious title.

The traditional Delphi approach tends to focus on iteratively reaching a "consensus" on the forecasts among group members. The Modified Delphi Technique we advocate is aimed at arriving at a set of competing "stories" about actions the company might take in response to a particular forecast, as well as documenting the concern raised about the forecasts (timing, impact, relevance, etc.). Then, the moderator presents the options to the team so it can systematically select test and select the optimal course of action.

To get a clear picture of what goes on, consider the 7 steps in the Modified Delphi Technique:

1. The moderator of the "Delphi process" solicits inputs designed to capture participants' expert opinions about how trends in the broader world are likely to impact the industry and the company (e.g., impact of new technologies on customer needs, impact of new technologies on product costs, impact of regulations on barriers to entry, etc.) Typically the moderator will create a targeted questionnaire about several preliminary forecasts and ask the participants to suggest other related trends and forecasts.
2. Using the online questionnaire as a catalyst, participants provide feedback and refinements with respect to forecasts, as well as contributing additional forecasts.
3. The moderator summarizes the responses, highlighting important areas of disagreement within the group. He or she also asks for clarification and more information.

4. The moderator sends the refined forecasts and related feedback to the participants for online responses. The moderator seeks feedback not just on the forecasts, but on the anonymous thoughts of others. As appropriate, the moderator makes sure the group considers the eight "principles" of the Digital Revolution highlighted on pages 273-275. The moderator also encourages them to modify their own original positions based on the feedback. Finally, the moderator asks each group members to rank the forecasts in terms of potential impact and potential likelihood.
5. Each participant provides feedback, ranks forecasts, and modifies his or her forecast, as appropriate.
6. Based on the results for step #5, the moderator reformulates the results by casting each of the top five forecasts in the form of two clear courses of action the company might take (assuming the forecasts are true). Here the moderator asks each participant to write out at least two "stories" (in 5 to 15 minutes each) describing how the company might respond to each of the top five forecasts. The participants write their stories, including implications for marketing, operations, and other areas of the company. This should include a list of risks and pay-offs.
7. The moderator compiles a report describing the highest impact/probability forecasts/stories and the relevant trends for use by the team and the broader organization as determined by management.

The Modified Delphi Technique works because as individuals possess more information in common—and come to understand the perspectives of others—their points of view tend to converge on an objectively correct answer. This can play a valuable role in moving the company toward a few well-supported ideas. These ideas help the leaders of the business break "out of the box" in which they find themselves.

How do you turn high-potential forecasts into bottom line results?

In the end, all of this work depends on how you translate your high-potential forecasts and stories into profits that actually show up on the bottom line. In most companies, discussions produce insights and serve to educate managers about threats and opportunities. However, these ideas seldom influence the formal strategic planning process in a meaningful way. Noting this gap between imagination and execution, former CEO A.G. Lafley and a team of world-class experts developed seven-step process to improve the strategic planning process at Procter & Gamble. This process provides a particularly pragmatic way to bridge the gap between the company-specific forecasts and stories we've been discussing and genuine bottom line results.[2]

This is where imagination gives way to a commitment of real resources. To understand how, let's examine a modified version of P&G's approach.

Step 1: Frame a choice by converting the high-potential stories/related forecasts into two mutually exclusive approaches that might capitalize on it. If they've done their jobs properly, the team has delivered a set of stories ranked by impact and probability. Now the challenge is to narrow down the multitude of potential possibilities for responding to the forecast to just two very different "what if?" scenarios. In this way, the team can begin to bring some focus to the range of possible futures. This is a task that the top management team may want to assign to the Delphi moderator, especially while the team members are getting used to the process.

Step 2: Generate possibilities by broadening your list of options. Having narrowed down the solutions to two distinctive possibilities, now it is time to expand those two ideas by considering different versions of each one. Each of these should meet Lafley's definition of a possibility: *"A possibility is a happy story that describes how a firm might succeed. Each story lays out where the company plays in its market and how it wins there. It should have internally consistent logic, but it need not be proved at this point. As long as you can imagine that it could be valid, it makes the cut."*

Characterizing possibilities as stories that do not require proof helps people discuss what might be viable, but does not yet exist. It is much easier to tell a story about why a possibility *could* make sense than to provide that data proves that it will succeed.

280

Start by asking each person on the decision-making team to spend 30 to 45 minutes sketching out three to five stories. The stories do not need to be detailed; they should truly be sketches. After this exercise, the group fleshes out the initial possibilities.

The moderator should objectively present these stories to the entire group, inviting them to ask probing questions. Lafley's team identified three kinds of probing questions which are especially useful in discovering possibilities:

1. *Inside-out questions* which start with the company's assets and capabilities, and then reason outward. For example, "What does this company do especially well that parts of the market might value and that might produce a superior wedge between buyer value and costs?"
2. *Outside-in questions* which look for openings in the market. For example, "What are the under-served needs, what are the needs that customers find hard to express, and what gaps have competitors left?"
3. *Far-outside-in questions* which use analogical reasoning. For example, "What would it take to be the Google, Apple, or Walmart of this market?"

According to the P&G team, you will know that you have a good set of possibilities if two things prove to be true:

- First, the status quo doesn't look like a brilliant idea. That is, at least one other possibility intrigues the group enough to make it really question the existing order.
- Second, at least one possibility makes most of the group uncomfortable. That is, it's sufficiently far from the status quo that the group questions whether it would be at all doable or safe.

The status quo should also be among the possibilities considered. This forces the team in later stages to specify what must be true for the status quo to be viable, thereby eliminating the common implicit assumption, "Worst case, we can just keep doing what we're already doing."

Step 3: Specify the necessary conditions for each possibility by describing what must be true for it to be strategically sound. It's worth noting that the Delphi group intentionally encourages anonymity because the free flow of ideas was more important than accountability. However, for the decision-making group, accountability becomes paramount. Therefore, while team members and other decision makers don't need to know who formulated the specific stories in step #1 or step #2, they do need to know who and why people are seeking specific validation for each possible course of action in step #3.

The purpose of this step is to specify what must be true for each possibility to be a terrific choice. Note that this step is not intended for arguing about what *is* true.

The importance of this distinction cannot be overstated. When the discussion of a possibility centers on what is true, the person most skeptical about the possibility attacks it vigorously, hoping to knock it out of contention.

If, instead, the dialogue is about *what would have to be true*, then the skeptic can say, "For me to be confident in this possibility, I would have to know that consumers will embrace this sort of offering." That is a very different sort of statement from "That will never work!" This dialog helps the proponent understand the skeptic's reservations and develop the proof to overcome them.

The objective is to answer one question about every option under consideration: "In order to pursue this option successfully, what conditions would we have to believe existed or could be created?"

In the first stage of discussion, the aim is to name all the conditions that need to hold true for everyone in the room to be able to honestly say, "I feel confident enough to make this possibility a reality." An example is, "Channel partners will support us."

When each member of the group has had a chance to add conditions to the list, the facilitator of the decision-making group should read the list aloud and ask the group, "If all these conditions were true, would you advocate for and support this choice?"

If everyone says yes, it's time to move to the next step. If any members say no, they must be asked, "What additional condition would enable you to answer yes?" This line of questioning should continue until every member replies affirmatively.

After finishing the list of conditions, review the items, asking, "If every condition but this one held true, would you eliminate the possibility or still view it as viable?" If the answer is the former, the condition is a must-have and should be maintained. If it is the latter, it is a nice-to-have and should be removed.

After arriving at a full set of possibilities and ensuring that all must-have conditions are attached to each, the group needs to bring its options to the executives whose approval will be required to ratify the final choice and to anyone else who might stand in the way. The goal is to make sure that the conditions for each possibility are well specified in the eyes of everyone with a say in the choice.

Step 4: Identify barriers by determining which conditions are least likely to hold true. Now it's time to cast a critical eye on the conditions to assess which ones you believe are least likely to hold true. Begin by asking group members to imagine that they could buy a guarantee that any particular condition will hold true. To which condition would they apply it?

The condition they choose is the biggest barrier to choosing the possibility under consideration. The next condition to which they would apply a guarantee is the next-biggest barrier, and so on. The ideal output is an ordered list of barriers to each possibility, two or three of which really worry the group.

Step 5: Design tests for each key barrier condition. Once you've identified and ordered the key barrier conditions, test each one to see whether it holds true. The test might involve surveying a thousand customers or speaking to a single supplier. It might entail crunching thousands of numbers or avoid any quantifiers at all.

The only requirement is that the entire group believes that the test is valid and can form the basis for rejecting the possibility in question or generating commitment to it.

The member who is most skeptical about a given condition should take the lead in designing and applying the test for it. This person will typically have the highest standard of proof; if he or she is satisfied that the condition has passed the test, everyone else will be satisfied.

Step 6: Conduct the tests, starting with the tests for the barrier

conditions in which you have the least confidence. It's easiest to structure this step by testing conditions in the reverse order of the group's confidence. That is, the condition the group feels is least likely to hold up is tested first.

If the group's suspicion is right, the possibility can be eliminated without any further testing. If that condition passes the test, the condition with the next-lowest likelihood of confirmation is tested, and so on. Because testing is often the most expensive and time-consuming part of the process, this approach can save enormous resources.

Step 7: Make your choice by reviewing your key conditions in light of your test results to reach a decision. In traditional strategy planning, finally choosing a strategy can be difficult and acrimonious. With the stakes high and the logic for each option never clearly articulated, such meetings often end up as negotiations between powerful executives with strong preconceptions. And once the meetings are concluded, those who are skeptical of the decision begin to undermine it.

With the possibilities-based approach, the choice-making step becomes simple, even anti-climactic. The group needs only to review the analytical test results and choose the possibility that faces the fewest serious barriers.

A final thought

Nearly seven hundred years ago, Chaucer wrote, "Time and tide wait for no man." That statement is even more true today than it was then. In fact, more now happens in a week than happened over Chaucer's entire lifetime. So it seems a particularly fitting thought with which to end a book titled, *Ride the Wave.*

Our sincere hope is that this snapshot of reality circa 2013 prepares you to seize the momentum and take command of the future. Great booms only come along once in a business career. Those of us who missed the boom that ended in the late '60s, finally have our chance to soar, but only if we are prepared.

At *Trends*, we've spent more than a decade identifying the cyclical and linear trends that give our subscribers a pathway to a profitable future. As a reader of this book, you're entitled to an invitation-only trial of a *Trends* subscription: http://www.trends-magazine.com/offer.php.

If you have questions about putting this methodology to work in your enterprise, contact us at Fred@audiotech.com or Rich@audiotech.com.

Finally, we'd love to hear how you've put these ideas to work in your business. Send us an email or, better yet, post a "review" on Amazon.com.

See you on the next wave!

Fred Rogers & Richard Lalich

END NOTES

CHAPTER 1

1. *Technological Revolutions and Financial Capital: The Dynamics of Bubbles* by Carlota Perez is published by Edward Elgar Publishing Limited, 2002.

2. *The American Interest,* July 15, 2012, "Energy Revolution 2: A Post Post-American Post," by Walter Russell Mead.
   http://blogs.the-american-interest.com/wrm/2012/07/15/energy-revolution-2-a-post-post-american-post

3. *Wall Street Pit,* June 11 2011, "Why Not Go for 5% Growth?" by John B. Taylor.
   http://wallstreetpit.com/77892-why-not-go-for-5-percent-growth

4. *The American,* August 25, 2012, "The Next Great Growth Cycle," by Mark P. Mills.
   http://www.american.com/archive/2012/august/the-next-great-growth-cycle

CHAPTER 2

1. *Physical Review Letters,* November 11, 2011, Vol. 107, Iss. 20, "Breaking the Far-Field Diffraction Limit in Optical Nanopatterning via Repeated Photochemical and Electrochemical Transitions in Photochromic Molecules," by Nicole Brimhall, et al.
   http://prl.aps.org/abstract/PRL/v107/i20/e205501

2. *MIT Technology Review,* July 13, 2012, "The Moore's Law Moon Shot," by Tom Simonite.
   http://www.technologyreview.com/news/428481/the-moores-law-moon-shot/

3. *Science,* January 27, 2012, Vol. 335, Iss. 6067, "An All-Silicon Passive Optical Diode," by Minghao Qi, et al. http://www.sciencemag.org/content/335/6067/447.abstract

4. *ACS Nano,* August 23, 2011, "Effect of Layer Stacking on the Electronic Structure of Graphene Nanoribbons," by Saroj K. Nayak, et al. http://pubs.acs.org/doi/abs/10.1021/nn200941u

5. *Small,* November 22, 2010, "Tunable Band Gap in Graphene by the Controlled Adsorption of Water Molecules," by Nikhil Koratkar, et al. http://onlinelibrary.wiley.com/doi/10.1002/smll.201001384/abstract

6. *MIT Technology Review,* January 30, 2012, "Graphene Competitor Used to Make Circuits," by Patrick Cain. http://www.technologyreview.com/computing/39561/

7. *ACS Nano,* December 27, 2011, Vol. 5, Iss. 2, "Stretching and Breaking of Ultrathin MoS2," by Andras Kis, et al. http://pubs.acs.org/doi/abs/10.1021/nn203879f

8. *Nanyang Technological University,* May 24, 2012, "Revolutionary Chipset for High-Speed Wireless Data Transfer,: from *ScienceDirect* http://www.sciencedaily.com/releases/2012/05/120524122931.htm

9. *Nature Materials,* July 8, 2012, "Ferroelectric Order in Individual Nanometre-Scale Crystals," by Mark J. Polking, et al. http://www.nature.com/nmat/journal/v11/n8/full/nmat3371.html

10. *Bloomberg,* July 10, 2012, "Intel Investing $4.1 Billion in ASML to Speed Production," by Ian King and Cornelius Rahn. http://www.bloomberg.com/news/2012-07-09/intel-agrees-to-buy-10-stake-in-asml-for-about-2-1-billion.html

CHAPTER 3

1. *Trillions: Thriving in the Emerging Information Ecology* by Peter Lucas, Joe Ballay, and Mickey McManus is published by John Wiley & Sons, Inc, 2012.

2. *Design Products & Applications,* October 18, 2012, "Internet of Things to Be the Next 'ICT Disruption,'" by Les Hunt.
http://www.dpaonthenet.net/article/53831/Internet-of-Things-to-be-the-next--ICT-disruption-.aspx

3. *McKinsey Quarterly,* August 2012, "Winning the $30 Trillion Decathlon: Going for Gold in Emerging Markets," by Yuval Astmon, et al.
http://www.mckinsey.com/insights/strategy/winning_the_30_trillion_decathlon_going_for_gold_in_emerging_markets

4. Technische Universität Darmstadt, August 28, 2011, "Beyond Smart Phones: Sensor Network to Make 'Smart Cities' Envisioned," from ScienceDaily.
http://www.sciencedaily.com/releases/2011/05/110516080130.htm

5. *Eureka,* April 12, 2011, "Low Cost Wireless Sensor Networks Open New Horizons for the Internet of Things."
http://www.eurekanetwork.org/showsuccessstory?p_r_p_564233524_articleId=868372&p_r_p_564233524_groupId=10137

6. *Internet World Stats:*
http://www.internetworldstats.com/stats.htm

CHAPTER 4

1. *IEEE Spectrum,* June 1, 2008, "Can Machines be Conscious?" by Christof Koch and Giulio Tononi.
http://spectrum.ieee.org/biomedical/imaging/can-machines-be-conscious

2. *IEEE Spectrum,* June 1, 2008, "The Consciousness Conundrum," by John Horgan.
http://spectrum.ieee.org/biomedical/imaging/the-consciousness-conundrum/1

3. Ibid.

4. *CBS News,* September 25, 2008, "What Is a Results-Only Work Environment?" by Lindsay Blakely.

http://www.cbsnews.com/8301-505125_162-51237128/what-is-a-results-only-work-environment

5. *The Guardian,* August 11, 2012, "Bartosz Grzybowski: Chematica Is an Internet for Chemistry," by Ian Tucker.
http://www.guardian.co.uk/technology/2012/aug/12/chematica-chemistry-network-bartosz-grzybowski

6. *University of Massachusetts Amherst,* "The Computational Power of Interactive Recurrent Neural Networks," by S. Jeremie Cabessa and Hava T. Siegelmann.
http://binds.cs.umass.edu/papers/CabessaSiegelmannNC12.pdf

7. *Association of American Medical Colleges:*
https://www.aamc.org/advocacy/campaigns_and_coalitions/fixdoc shortage

8. *McKinsey & Company,* May 2011, "Big Data: The Next Frontier for Innovation, Competition, and Productivity," by James Manyika, et al.
http://www.mckinsey.com/insights/business_technology/big_data _the_next_frontier_for_innovation

CHAPTER 5

1. *Robotics Online:*
http://www.robotics.org/content-detail.cfm/Industrial-Robotics-News/North-American-Robotics-Industry-Up-20-in-2012/content_id/3752

2. *International Federation of Robotics:*
http://www.ifr.org/service-robots/statistics/

3. Ibid.

4. *The Economist,* June 2, 2012, "March of the Robots."
http://www.economist.com/node/21556103

5. *The Futurist,* September/October 2011, "Thank You Very Much, Mr. Roboto," by Patrick Tucker.
http://www.wfs.org/content/futurist/september-october-2011-vol-45-no-5/thank-you-very-much-mr-roboto

6. *Cornell University:*
   http://pr.cs.cornell.edu/grasping/IJRR_saxena_etal_roboticgraspin
   gofnovelobjects.pdf

7. *IEEE Transactions on Robotics,* June 2011, "Humanoid
   Multimodal Tactile-Sensing Modules," by Philipp Mittendorfer
   and Gordon Cheng.
   http://ieeexplore.ieee.org/xpl/freeabs_all.jsp?arnumber=5711674

8. *Wired Science,* March 16, 2011, "Robot Nurses Are Less Weird
   When They Don't Talk," by Dave Mosher.
   http://www.wired.com/wiredscience/2011/03/robot-touching

9. *Information Sciences,* May 15, 2011, "RFuzzy: Syntax,
   Semantics, and Implementation Details of a Simple and
   Expressive Fuzzy Tool Over Prolog," by Susana Munoz-
   Hernandez, et al.
   http://www.sciencedirect.com/science/article/pii/S0020025510003
   610

10. *NUI Galway:*
    http://www.nuigalway.ie/about-us/news-and-events/news-
    archive/2011/july2011/researchers-mimic-nature-to-create-a-bio-
    inspired-brain-for-robots.html

11. *Eindhoven University of Technology Report,* April 22, 2010,
    "Domestic Robot Helps Sick Elderly Live Independently Longer."
    http://www.alphagalileo.org/ViewItem.aspx?ItemId=74114&Cult
    ureCode=en

12. *Bloomberg Businessweek,* December 1, 2011, "Will Driverless
    Cars Become the New Road Rage?" by Tim Higgins.
    http://www.businessweek.com/magazine/will-driverless-cars-
    become-the-new-road-rage-12012011.html

13. *U.S. Public Interest Research Group,* April 5, 2012,
    "Transportaion and the New Generation."
    http://www.uspirg.org/reports/usp/transportation-and-new-
    generation

14. *Bloomberg Businessweek,* December 1, 2011, "Will Driverless
    Cars Become the New Road Rage?" by Tim Higgins.
    http://www.businessweek.com/magazine/will-driverless-cars-

become-the-new-road-rage-12012011.html

15. *FoxNews,* December 16, 2011, "Google Granted Patent for Driverless Car Technology."
http://www.foxnews.com/leisure/2011/12/16/google-granted-patent-for-driverless-car-technology/

16. *BBC News Magazine,* May 10, 2012, "Driverless Cars and How They Would Change Motoring," by Daniel Nasaw.
http://www.bbc.co.uk/news/magazine-18012812

17. *Bloomberg Businessweek,* December 1, 2011, "Will Driverless Cars Become the New Road Rage?" by Tim Higgins.
http://www.businessweek.com/magazine/will-driverless-cars-become-the-new-road-rage-12012011.html

18. *The Wall Street Journal,* July 25, 2012, "Geico Spends Nearly $1 Billion on Ads as Car Insurers Battle," by Leslie Scism and Erik Holm.
http://blogs.wsj.com/deals/2012/06/25/geico-spends-nearly-1-billion-on-ads-as-car-insurers-battle/

19. *Silicon Valley Mercury News,* September 25, 2012, "Google's Sergey Brin Joins California Gov. Jerry Brown to Sign New Driverless Carl Law," by Mike Rosenberg.
http://www.mercurynews.com/breaking-news/ci_21627199/googles-sergey-brin-joins-jerry-brown-sign-new

20. *Computerworld,* May 31, 2012, "Privacy Group Wants Google's Driverless Cars Kept Off the Road," by Sharon Gaudin.
http://www.computerworld.com/s/article/9227585/Privacy_group_wants_Google_s_driverless_cars_kept_off_the_road

CHAPTER 6

1. *MIT Technology Review,* June 1, 2011, "Tapping Quantum Effects for Software that Learns," by Tom Simonite.
http://www.technologyreview.com/computing/37673

2. *D-Wave:*
   http://www.dwavesys.com

3. *MIT Technology Review,* June 1, 2011, "Tapping Quantum Effects for Software that Learns," by Tom Simonite.
   http://www.technologyreview.com/computing/37673

4. *USC News Release:* June 12, 2012, "Quantum Computers Could Help Search Engines Keep Up with the Internet's Growth."
   http://www.usc.edu/uscnews/newsroom/news_release.php?id=2749

5. *MIT News,* October 9, 2009, "Quantum Computing May Actually be Useful," by Larry Hardesty.
   http://web.mit.edu/newsoffice/2009/quantum-algorithm.html

6. *Forbes,* October 5, 2012, "Jeff Bezos and the CIA Invest in D-Wave's Quantum Computer," by Alex Knapp.
   http://www.forbes.com/sites/alexknapp/2012/10/05/jeff-bezos-and-the-cia-invest-in-d-waves-quantum-computer/

7. *Nature*, October 18, 2012, "Circuit Quantum Electrodynamics with a Spin Qubit," by J.R. Petta, et al.
   http://www.nature.com/nature/journal/v490/n7420/fig_tab/nature11559_ft.html

CHAPTER 7

1. *Health Affairs,* May/June 2008, "Will Generalist Physician Supply Meet Demands of Increasing and Aging Population?" by Jack M. Colwill, James M. Cultice, and Robin L. Kruse
   http://content.healthaffairs.org/content/27/3/w232.abstract

2. *Oak Ridge National Laboratory:*
   http://www.ornl.gov/sci/techresources/Human_Genome/project/info.shtml

3. *Reuters,* July 23, 2012, Ion Torrent Vies for $10 Million Genome Prize," by Sharon Begley.
   http://www.reuters.com/article/2012/07/23/us-science-genome-prize-idUSBRE86M02G20120723

4. *Co.Exist:*
http://www.fastcoexist.com/1680222/can-this-machine-sequence-
100-genomes-in-10-days-for-less-than-1000

5. *Nature,* September 6, 2012, Vol. 489, Iss. 7414, "An Expansive
Human Regulatory Lexicon Encoded in Transcription Factor
Footprints," by Shane Neph, et al.
http://www.nature.com/nature/journal/v489/n7414/full/nature1121
2.html

6. *Nature,* September 6, 2012, Vol. 489, Iss. 7414, "The Accessible
Chromatin Landscape of the Human Genome," by Robert E.
Thurman, et al.
http://www.nature.com/nature/journal/v489/n7414/full/nature1123
2.html

7. *Proceedings of the National Academy of Sciences,* June 26, 2012,
"Scaling Metagenome Sequence Assembly with Probabilistic de
Bruijn Graphs," by Jason Pell, et al.
http://www.pnas.org/content/early/2012/07/25/1121464109.abstract

8. *Michigan State University:*
http://msutoday.msu.edu/news/2012/massive-data-for-miniscule-
communities

9. *Science,* May 4, 2012, Vol. 336, Iss. 6081, "Search for Pore-
fection," by Elizabeth Pennisi.
http://www.sciencemag.org/content/336/6081/534

10. *Nanotechnology,* May 18, 2012, "Chemical Recognition and
Binding Kinetics in a Functionalized Tunnel Junction," by Shuai
Chang, et al.
http://iopscience.iop.org/0957-4484/23/23/235101/pdf/0957-
4484_23_23_235101.pdf

CHAPTER 8

1. *Harvard Business Review,* October 2007, "Realizing the Promis
of Personalized Medicine," by Mara G. Aspinall and Richard G.
Hemermesh

http://hbr.org/2007/10/realizing-the-promise-of-personalized-medicine

2. *European Organisation for Research and Treatment of Cancer:* http://www.eortc.be/services/doc/highlights/Wed_17_11_2010/PR_Matulonis_Oncomap.pdf

3. *European Society for Medical Oncology*, April 30, 2010, "Making Personalized Lung Cancer Therapy a Reality in Europe," from *ScienceDaily.* http://www.sciencedaily.com/releases/2010/04/100430131148.htm

4. *International Business Times,* April 15, 2010, "Australian Scientist to Uncover the Genes Responsible for 50 World's Most Common Cancers,." http://www.ibtimes.com/australian-scientists-uncover-genes-responsible-50-words-most-common-cancers-190769

5. *University of Texas MD Anderson Cancer Center,* June 3, 2011, "Matching Targeted Therapies to Tumor's Specific Gen Mutations Key to Personalized Cancer Treatment," from Eureka Alert. http://www.eurekalert.org/pub_releases/2011-06/uotm-mtt060311.php

6. *Biomaterials,* June 2012, "Lipid Multilayer Microarrays for *in vitro* Liposomal Drug Delivery and Screening," by Aubrey E. Kusi-Appiah, et al. http://www.ncbi.nlm.nih.gov/pubmed/22391265

7. *Knoepfler Stem Cell Blog:* https://www.ipscell.com/2012/10/top-7-challenges-facing-ips-cells-in-late-2012/

8. *Proceedings of the National Academy of Sciences,* November 18, 2012, "Conditionally Reprogrammed Cells Represent a Stem-Like State of Adult Epithelial Cells," by Frank A. Suprynowicz, et al. http://www.pnas.org/content/early/2012/11/14/1213241109

9. *McKinsey and Company,* February 2010, "The Microeconomics of Personalized Medicine," by Jerel Davis, et al. http://www.mckinsey.com/insights/health_systems_and_services/the_microeconomics_of_personalized_medicine

CHAPTER 9

1. *The iGem Foundation*:
    http://igem.org/Press_Kit

2. *Bloomberg Online,* March 7, 2009, "Harvard Scientists' Discovery Opens Door to Synthetic Life," by John Lauerman.
    http://www.bloomberg.com/apps/news?pid=newsarchive&sid=aW NwdtOMONZ8

3. *Science,* July 2, 2010, "Creation of a Bacterial Cell Controlled by a Chemically Synthesized Genome," by J. Craig Venter, et.al.
    http://www.sciencemag.org/cgi/content/full/329/5987/52

4. *Food and Agriculture Organization:*
    http://www.fao.org/news/story/en/item/35571/icode/

5. *ISAAA:*
    http://www.isaaa.org/resources/publications/briefs/44/pressrelease /default.asp

6. Ibid.

7. *Reuters,* February 20, 2013, "Record Area of Biotech Crops Used in 2012."
    http://uk.reuters.com/article/2013/02/20/crops-biotech-report-idUKL1N0BK09020130220

8. Ibid.

9. *International Journal of Biotechnology,* December 2011, "The income and production effects of biotech crops globally 1996-2009," by Graham Brookes and Peter Barfoot.
    http://www.inderscience.com/info/inarticle.php?artid=42680

10. *ISAAA:*
    http://www.isaaa.org/resources/publications/briefs/44/pressrelease /default.asp

11. *ISAAA:*
    http://www.isaaa.org/resources/publications/briefs/43/executivesu mmary/default.asp

12. Ibid.

13. *ISAAA:*
    http://www.isaaa.org/resources/publications/briefs/44/pressrelease/default.asp

14. *Reuters*, February 20, 2013, "Record Area of Biotech Crops Used in 2012"
    http://uk.reuters.com/article/2013/02/20/crops-biotech-report-idUKL1N0BK09020130220

15. *Iowa State University:*
    http://archive.news.iastate.edu/news/2011/sep/huffmangmo

16. *The Canadian Jewish News,* January 24, 2012, "Genetically Modified Plants to Resist Intense Drought," by David Allouche.
    http://www.cjnews.com/index.php?q=node/89166

17. *Environmental Science & Technology,* July 15, 2011, Vol. 45, Iss. 14, "Environmental Impacts of Cultured Meat Production," by Hanna Tuomisto, et al.
    http://pubs.acs.org/doi/abs/10.1021/es200130u

18. *Journal of Agricultural and Food Chemistry,* March 9, 2011, Vol. 59, Iss. 5, "Graft Polymerization of Native Chicken Feathers for Thermoplastic Applications," by Enqi Jin, Narendra Reddy, Zifeng Zhu, and Yiqi Yang.
    http://pubs.acs.org/doi/abs/10.1021/jf1039519

19. *The New York Times,* July 15, 2008, "Country, the City Version: Farms in the Sky Gain New Interest," by Bina Venkataraman.
    http://www.nytimes.com/2008/07/15/science/15farm.html

20. *Daily Mail,* January 7, 2011, "Wrapping That Will Tell You When Food's Going Off," by David Derbyshire.
    http://www.dailymail.co.uk/sciencetech/article-1344886/Food-wrapping-tell-contents-past-use-date.html

21. *Delft University of Technology:*
    http://www.tudelft.nl/en/current/latest-news/article/detail/getrainde-bacterie-zet-gft-om-in-bioplastics/

22. *University of Wolverhampton:*
    http://www.wlv.ac.uk/default.aspx?page=31938

23. *Human Gene Therapy*, January 2012, "It's Time for Gene Therapy to Get Disruptive!" by James M. Wilson.
http://online.liebertpub.com/doi/pdfplus/10.1089/hum.2011.2530

24. *University of Missouri-Columbia:*
http://www.biospace.com/news_story.aspx?NewsEntityId=153755

25. *Human Gene Therapy*, January 2011, "Acquisition of HIV-1 Resistance in T Lymphocytes Using an ACA-Specific E. Coli mRNA Interferase," by Hideto Chono, et al.

26. *The Endocrine Society*, June 2010, "Gene Therapy Reverses Type 1 Diabetes in Mice."
https://www.endocrine.org/news-room/press-release-archives/2010/gene-therapy-reverses-type-1-diabetes-in-mice

27. *The Telegraph*, June 19, 2011, "Pigs Could Grow Human Organs in Stem Cell Breakthrough," by Richard Gray.
http://www.telegraph.co.uk/science/science-news/8584443/Pigs-could-grow-human-organs-in-stem-cell-breakthrough.html

28. *FORA.tv:*
http://fora.tv/2012/10/16/Craig_Venter_Health_Genomics_Research_and_Power

CHAPTER 10

1. *Science*, May 20, 2010, Vol. 329, Iss. 5987, "Creation of a Bacterial Cell Controlled by a Chemically Synthesized Genome," by Daniel Gibson, et al.
http://www.sciencemag.org/content/329/5987/52.abstract

2. *Synberc:*
http://www.synberc.org/

3. *RIKEN:*
https://database.riken.jp/sw/en/General_Review/cria303s3ria303s6i/

4. GenoCon:
http://genocon.org/

5. *Financial Times,* July 27, 2012, "Synthetic Life: The Revolution Begins," by Clive Cookson.
    http://www.ft.com/intl/cms/s/2/918ef6ae-d5f4-11e1-a5f3-00144feabdc0.html#axzz2XR6zxSIa

6. *iGem:*
    http://2010.igem.org/Main_Page

7. *New York Times,* February 10, 2010, "Do-It-Yourself Genetic Engineering," by John Mooallem.
    http://www.nytimes.com/2010/02/14/magazine/14Biology-t.html?pagewanted=all&_r=0

CHAPTER 11

1. *Nature Neuroscience,* February 2011, Vol. 14, No. 2, "How Advances in Neural Recording Affect Data Analysis," by Ian H. Stevenson and Konrad P. Kording.
    http://www.nature.com/neuro/journal/v14/n2/abs/nn.2731.html

2. *ABC News:*
    http://abcnews.go.com/blogs/health/2011/09/27/roborat-israelis-create-rodent-with-robot-brain/

3. *PLoS Biology,* January 2012, "Reconstructing Speech from Human Auditory Cortex," by Brian N. Pasley, et al.
    http://www.plosbiology.org/article/info%3Adoi%2F10.1371%2Fjournal.pbio.1001251

4. *Daily Mail,* February 22, 2011, "Look, No Hands (or Feet): Scientists Develop Car That Can Be Driven Just by THINKING," by Daniel Bates.
    http://www.dailymail.co.uk/sciencetech/article-1359512/Computer-scientists-Germany-invented-car-steered-power-thought.html

5. *Journal of Neural Engineering,* June 2011, Vol. 8, No. 3, "Using the Electrocorticographic Speech Network to Control a Brain-Computer Interface in Humans," by Eric C. Leuthardt, et al.
    http://iopscience.iop.org/1741-2552/8/3/036004

6. *Nature,* November 10, 2011, Vol. 479, No. 7372, "Active Tactile Exploration Using a Brain-Machine-Brain Interface," by Miguel A.L. Nicolelis, et al.
http://www.nature.com/nature/journal/v479/n7372/full/nature1048 9.html

7. *The Journal of Neuroscience,* December 15, 2010, Vol. 30, No. 50, "Incorporating Feedback from Multiple Sensory Modalities Enhances Brain-Machine Interface Control," by Nicholas G. Hatsopoulos, et al.
http://www.jneurosci.org/content/30/50/16777.full

8. *Journal of Neurophysiology,* October 2011, "Neural Decoding of Treadmill Walking from Noninvasive Electroencephalographic Signals," by José Luis Contreras-Vidal, et al.
http://jn.physiology.org/content/106/4/1875.abstract?sid=7be5e14f -040e-48f0-9c91-eeac5b34cdd3

9. *University of Michigan:*
http://ns.umich.edu/new/releases/8445

10. *Nature Reviews Neuroscience,* April 2010, Vol. 11, No. 4, "Neuromarketing: The Hope and Hype of Neuroimaging in Business," by Dan Ariely and Gregory S. Berns.
http://www.nature.com/nrn/journal/v11/n4/abs/nrn2795.html

11. *Brandchannel:*
http://www.brandchannel.com

12. *Journal of Consumer Research,* August 2010, "Language Abstraction in Word of Mouth," by Gaby A.C., et al.
http://www.journals.uchicago.edu/doi/abs/10.1086/651240?journa lCode=jcr

13. *Tel Aviv University:*
http://aftau.org/site/News2?page=NewsArticle&id=11563

14. *New York Times,* September 9, 2007, "Sense and Sensibility," by James Vlahos.
http://www.nytimes.com/2007/09/09/realestate/keymagazine/909S CENT-txt.html?pagewanted=print&_r=0

15. *Sense of Smell Institute:*
http://www.senseofsmell.org/smell101-

detail.php?id=1&lesson=How%20Does%20the%20Sense%20of%20Smell%20Work?

16. *Brandessence:*
http://www.brandessence.com.tr/en/koku_bilimi.html

17. *The New York Times,* September 9, 2007, "Scent and Sensibility,'"
by James Vlahos.
http://www.nytimes.com/2007/09/09/realestate/keymagazine/909S
CENT-txt.html?pagewanted=all&_r=0

18. Ibid.

19. *Science,* February 27, 2009, Vol. 323, Iss. 5918, "Blue or Red?
Exploring the Effect of Color on Cognitive Task Performances,"
by Ravi Mehta and Rui (Juliet) Zhu.
http://www.sciencemag.org/cgi/content/abstract/323/5918/1226

20. *The New York Times,* February 6, 2009, "Reinvent Wheel? Blue
Room. Defusing a Bomb? Red Room," by Pam Belluck.
http://www.nytimes.com/2009/02/06/science/06color.html

21. Ibid.

22. *Scandinavian Journal of Work, Environment & Health,* 2008, Vol.
34, No. 4, "Blue-Enriched White Light in the Workplace Improves
Self-Reported Alertness, Performance and Sleep Quality," by A.U.
Viola, et al.
http://www.sjweh.fi/show_abstract.php?abstract_id=1268

23. *The Journal of Clinical Endocrinology & Metabolism,* September
2003, Vol. 88, Iss. 9, "High Sensitivity of the Human Circadian
Melatonin Rhythm to Resetting by Short Wavelength Light," by
Steven W. Lockley, et al.
http://jcem.endojournals.org/cgi/content/abstract/88/9/4502

24. *The Overflowing Brain* by Torkel Klingberg, is published by
Oxford University Press, 2008.

25. *New Straits Times,* April 22, 2012, "The Impact of Violent Video
Games on Children," by Wan A. Hulaimi.
http://www.nst.com.my/opinion/columnist/the-impact-of-violent-
video-games-on-children-1.76360

26. *The Independent*, November 24, 2009, "What the Web is Teaching

Our Brains," by Anastasia Stephens.
http://www.independent.co.uk/life-style/health-and-families/features/what-the-web-is-teaching-our-brains-1826419.html

27. *Bright Focus:*
http://www.brightfocus.org/alzheimers/about/understanding/facts.html

28. *Science Daily,* January 15, 2013, "Major Step Toward an Alzheimer's Vaccine.
http://www.sciencedaily.com/releases/2013/01/130115143852.htm

29. *NAMI Policy Research Institute*:
http://www.nami.org/Content/NavigationMenu/Inform_Yourself/About_Public_Policy/Policy_Research_Institute/Policymakers_Toolkit/Impact_and_Cost_of_Mental_Illness_the_Case_of_Depression.pdf

30. *University of New South Wales,* March 6, 2013, "New Depression Treatment "Safe and Effective."
http://newsroom.unsw.edu.au/news/health/new-depression-treatment-%E2%80%9Csafe-and-effective%E2%80%9D

31. *National Institute for Neurological Disorders and Stroke:*
http://www.ninds.nih.gov/disorders/parkinsons_disease/detail_parkinsons_disease.htm

32. *Science Daily,* "April 4, 3012, "Eating Flavonoids Protects Men Against Parkinson's Disease, Study Finds.
http://www.sciencedaily.com/releases/2012/04/120404161939.htm

33. *Journal of Clinical Investigation,* January 2, 2013, "Autologous Mesenchymal Stem Cell–Derived Dopaminergic Neurons Function in Parkinsonian Macaques," by Takuya Hayashi, et al.
http://www.jci.org/articles/view/62516

34. *Los Angeles Times*, December 20, 2007 "The Nation—They're Bulking Up Mentally," by Karen Kaplan and Denise Gellene.
http://articles.latimes.com/2007/dec/20/science/sci-braindoping20

35. *The FASEB Journal,* September, 2012, "Acute and Chronic Elevation of Erythropoietin in the Brain Improves Exercise Performance in Mice Without Inducing Erythropoiesis," by Max

Gassmann, et al.
http://www.sciencedaily.com/releases/2012/06/120611105307.htm

36. *Journal of Neuroscience,* January 26, 2011, "Theta-Burst Transcranial Magnetic Stimulation Alters Cortical Inhibition," by Klaus Funke.
http://www.jneurosci.org/content/31/4/1193.full

37. *The Conference Board Review,* Summer 200, "A 'Better' Workforce?" by Michael Schrage.
https://hcexchange.conference-board.org/attachment/a-better-workforce1.pdf

38. *BMC Biology,* September 8, 2008, "Erythropoietin Enhances Hippocampal Long-Term Potentiation and Memory," by Bartosz Adamcio, et al.
http://www.biomedcentral.com/1741-7007/6/37

39. *The New York Times,* June 8, 2008, "Moving Mountains with the Brain not a Joystick," by Anne Eisenberg.
http://www.nytimes.com/2008/06/08/technology/08novel.html

CHAPTER 12

1. *McKinsey Quarterly,* June 2012, "Manufacturing Resource Productivity," by Stephen Mohr, Ken Somers, Steven Swartz, and Helga Vanthournout.
http://www.mckinseyquarterly.com/Manufacturing_resource__pro ductivity_2982

2. *Chatham House,* "A Global Redesign? Shaping the Economy."
http://www.chathamhouse.org/publications/papers/view/182376

3. *An Essay on the Principle of Population* by Thomas Malthus is published by Oxford University Press, Inc. First published in 1798.

4. *Peak Everything* by Richard Heinberg is published by New Society Publishers, 2007.

5. *Limits to Growth* by Donella H. Meadows is published Signet,

1972.

6. *Science,* August 25, 1967, Vol. 157, No. 3791, "Famine—1975!" by James Bonner.
   http://www.sciencemag.org/content/157/3791/914.2.extract

7. *The Population Bomb* by Paul R. Ehrlich is published by Buccaneer Books, Inc.

8. *Famine—1975! America's Decision: Who Will Survive?* by William and Paul Paddock is published by Little, Brown and Company.

9. *National Post,* October 13, 2010, "Dan Gardner: The Nation-Killing Famine that Never Was," by Dan Gardner.
   http://fullcomment.nationalpost.com/2010/10/13/dan-gardner-the-nation-killing-famine-that-never-was/

10. *The Futurist,* March-April 2013, "How Innovation Could Save the Planet," by Ramez Naam.
    http://www.wfs.org/futurist/2013-issues-futurist/march-april-2013-vol-47-no-2/how-innovation-could-save-planet

11. Ibid.

12 Ibid.

13. *MIT Technology Review,* February 28, 2011, "A Pacemaker the Size of a Tic Tac," by Emily Singer.
    http://www.technologyreview.com

14. *University of California San Francisco:*
    http://www.ucsf.edu/news/2010/09/4450/ucsf-unveils-model-implantable-artificial-kidney-replace-dialysis

15. *MIT Technology Review,* February 10, 2011, "The Smallest Computing Systems Yet," by Kate Greene.
    http://www.technologyreview.com/computing/32302/?p1=A1&a=f

16. *Science Daily,* April 14, 2009, "Researchers Develop World's First Flying Microrobot for Microscale Applications."
    http://www.sciencedaily.com/releases/2009/04/090413205339.htm

17. *Angewandte Chemie International Edition,* May 13, 2008, "Clockwork PCR Including Sample Preparation," by Juergen Pipper, Yi Zhang, Pavel Neuzil, and Tseng-Ming Hsieh.

18. *Chemical & Engineering News,* September 10, 2007, "Mimicking Biological Systems," by Celia Henry Arnaud.

19. *IEEE Sensors Journal,* August 2010, "Toward Sensitivity Enhancement of MEMS Accelerometers Using Mechanical Amplification Mechanism," by A. Ya'akobovitz and S. Krylov. http://ieeexplore.ieee.org/xpl/freeabs_all.jsp?arnumber=5471792

20. *International Journal of Materials and Structural Integrity,* April 2010, "Wireless and Embedded Nanotechnology-Based Systems for Structural Integrity Monitoring of Civil Structures: A Feasibility Study," by Mohamed Saafi, et al. http://www.inderscience.com/search/index.php?action=record&rec_id=32494&prevQuery=&ps=108m=or

21. *Science Daily,* November 5, 2008, "Low Cost Vehicle Stability Chip Reduced Rollover Chip." http://www.sciencedaily.com/releases/2008/11/081103145111.htm

22. *Science,* May 13, 2011, Vol. 332, Iss. 6031, "Beating Crystallization in Glass-Forming Metals by Millisecond Heating and Processing," by W.L. Johnson, et al. http://www.sciencemag.org/content/332/6031/828.abstract

23. *Nature Materials,* February 2011, "A Damage-Tolerant Glass," by M.D. Demetriou, et al. http://www.nature.com/nmat/journal/v10/n2/abs/nmat2930.html

24. *Nature Materials,* November 2009, Vol. 8, No. 11, "MgZnCa Glasses Without Clinically Observable Hydrogen Evolution for Biodegradable Implants," by Bruno Zberg, et al. http://www.nature.com/nmat/journal/v8/n11/full/nmat2542.html

25. *Architerials.com,* January 10, 2011, "10 Awesome Materials from 2010 and Reasons They Are Awesome." http://www.architerials.com/2011/01/10-awesome-materials-from-2010-and-reasons-they-are-awesome/

26. *Architerials.com,* April 21, 2011, "Stronger than Kevlar: Plastic Reinforced with Nanocellulose Fibers from Pineapples!"

27. *University of Amsterdam*
http://english.uva.nl/news/archive.cfm/5860E32D-18B3-4615-982FA6B7AF8BEDE1

28. *Angewandte Chemie International Edition,* April 4, 2011, "Salalen Titanium Complexes in the Highly Isospecific Polymerization of 1-Hexene and Propylene," by Moshe Kol, et al.
http://onlinelibrary.wiley.com/doi/10.1002/anie.201007678/abstract

29. *Architerials.com,* February 22, 2011, "Alert! New Plastics Capable of Conducting Electricity."
http://www.architerials.com/2011/02/alert-new-plastics-capable-of-conducting-electricity/

30. *Nature Chemistry,* June 2012, "Light Triggered Self-Construction of Supramolecular Organic Nanowires as Metallic Interconnects," by Vina Faramarzi, et al.
http://www.nature.com/nchem/journal/v4/n6/abs/nchem.1332.html

31. *Fraunhofer-Gesellschaft*:
http://www.archiv.fraunhofer.de/archiv/pi-en-2004-2008/EN/press/pi/2008/12/ResearchNews122008Topic7.html

32. *American Chemical Society:*
http://portal.acs.org/portal/acs/corg/content?_nfpb=true&_pageLabel=PP_ARTICLEMAIN&node_id=222&content_id=CNBP_029646&use_sec=true&sec_url_var=region1&__uuid=63bec567-9382-4b93-81cb-457a6baee6fc

33. *University of Boras:*
http://www.hb.se/wps/portal/pressreleases/pressrelease?name=hb_2007-11-07_newbone

34. *National Aeronautics and Space Administration:*
http://www.nasa.gov/offices/c3po/home/spacexfeature.html

35. *Virgin Galactic:*
http://www.virgingalactic.com/news/item/virgin-galactic/

36. *CNet News,* February 1, 2010, "Obama Ends Moon Program, Endorses Private Spaceflight," by William Harwood. http://news.cnet.com/8301-19514_3-10445227-239.html

37. *Discover Magazine*, July 2004, "Going Up," by Brad Lemley. http://discovermagazine.com/2004/jul/cover#.UkJCQn8kJSo

38. *The Jerusalem Post,* June 26, 2007, "Scientists Develop 'Fantastic Voyage'-Like Robot Sub," by Judy Siegel-Itzkovich. http://www.jpost.com/servlet/Satellite?cid=1182409639914&page name=JPost%2FJPArticle%2FShowFull

39. *The Future of Things:* http://thefutureofthings.com/news/1042/microrobots-to-travel-in-our-blood-vessels.html

40. *The Boston Globe,* May 7, 2007, "He Develops Robotics to Assist Surgery," by Andrew Rimas. http://www.boston.com/news/globe/health_science/articles/2007/0 5/07/he_develops_robotics_to_assist_surgery

41. *New Scientist,* April 21, 2007, Iss. 2600, "Creepy-Crawly Robot to Mend a Broken Heart," by Tom Simonite. http://www.newscientist.com/article/mg19426006.900-creepycrawly-robot-to-mend-a-broken-heart.html

42. *Technology Review,* April 13, 2007, "Propellers for Microrobots," by Duncan Graham-Rowe. http://www.technologyreview.com/nanotech/18532

43. *The Economist,* September 4, 2008, "Swallow the Surgeon." http://www.economist.com/node/11999269

44. *Carnegie Mellon University NanoRobotics Lab:* http://nanolab.me.cmu.edu/projects/swimming/

45. *The Economist,* September 4, 2008, "Swallow the Surgeon." http://www.economist.com/node/11999269

46. *Yale News,* December 7, 2011, "Novel Nanoparticle Mimicking Virus Offers New Route to Gene Therapy," by Eric Gershon. http://news.yale.edu/2011/12/07/novel-nanoparticle-mimicking-virus-offers-new-route-gene-therapy

47. *Nature Materials,* January 2012. Vol. 11, No. 1, "Biodegradable

Poly(amine-co-ester) Terpolymers for Targeted Gene Delivery," by W. Mark Saltzman, et al.
http://www.nature.com/nmat/journal/v11/n1/full/nmat3187.html

48. *Nano Letters,* March 9, 2011, Vol. 11, Iss. 3, "Laser-Induced Damage and Recovery of Plasmonically Targeted Human Endothelial Cells," by Antonios G. Kanaras, et al.
http://pubs.acs.org/doi/abs/10.1021/nl104528s

49. *Cornell University:*
http://www.news.cornell.edu/stories/March10/GoldNanoparticles.html

50. *Nanotechnology,* March 2010, Vol. 21, No. 10, "Gold Hybrid Nanoparticles for Targeted Phototherapy and Cancer Imaging," by Dickson K. Kirui, et al.
http://iopscience.iop.org/0957-4484/21/10/105105?fromSearchPage=true

51. *Journal of the American Chemical Society,* February 10, 2010, Vol. 132, Iss. 5, "Nuclear Targeting of Gold Nanoparticles in Cancer Cells Induces DNA Damage, Causing Cytokinesis Arrest and Apoptosis," by B. Kang, M.S. Mackey, and M.A. El-Sayed.
http://pubs.acs.org/doi/abs/10.1021/ja9102698

52. *Theranostics*, 2012, Iss. 2(1), "Magnetic Nanoparticle-Based Hyperthermia for Head & Neck Cancer in Mouse Models," by Qun Zhao, et al.
http://www.thno.org/v02p0113.htm

53. *Virginia Tech:*
http://www.vtnews.vt.edu/articles/2010/11/112310-engineering-puri.html

54. *The Ellen MacArthur Foundation:*
at:http://www.ellenmacarthurfoundation.org/circular-economy/circular-economy/towards-the-circular-economy

55. Ibid.

56. *Makers: The New Industrial Revolution* by Chris Anderson is published by Crown Business, an imprint of the Crown Publishing Group, a division of Random House, Inc.

57. *Knowledge@Wharton,* December 17, 2012, "'Makers' Chris Anderson on DIY Manufacturing."
http://knowledge.wharton.upenn.edu/article.cfm?articleid=3134

58. *Thaindian News,* June 8, 2010, "New Method to Detect Tumours Faster."
http://www.thaindian.com/newsportal/health/new-method-to-detect-tumours-faster_100376829.html

CHAPTER 13

1. American Enterprise Institute:
http://www.aei-ideas.org/2013/03/us-was-worlds-largest-petroleum-producer-in-november-surpassing-saudi-arabia-for-first-time-in-ten-years

2. *ABC News:*
http://abcnews.go.com/Business/american-oil-find-holds-oil-opec/story?id=17536852

3. *Financial Times,* July 15, 2012, "Welcome to the New World of American Energy," by Edward Luce.
http://www.ft.com/intl/cms/s/0/3f86b2fc-cce4-11e1-9960-00144feabdc0.html#axzz2XR6zxSIa

4. *The American Interest,* July 15, 2012, "Energy Revolution 2," by Walter Russell Mead.
http://blogs.the-american-interest.com/wrm/2012/07/15/energy-revolution-2-a-post-post-american-post/

5. *Financial Times,* July 15, 2012, "Welcome to the New World of American Energy," by Edward Luce.
http://www.ft.com/intl/cms/s/0/3f86b2fc-cce4-11e1-9960-00144feabdc0.html#axzz2XR6zxSIa

6. *Wood MacKenzie Energy Consulting,* September 11, 2011, "U.S. Supply Forecast and Potential Jobs and Economic Impacts (2012-2013)".
http://www.api.org/newsroom/upload/api-us_supply_economic_forecast.pdf

7. *American Petroleum Institute/PricewaterhouseCoopers,* July 2013 "Economic Impacts of the Oil and Natural Gas Industries on the US Economy in 2011."
http://www.api.org/~/media/Files/Policy/Jobs/Economic_Impacts_ONG_2011.pdf

8. *The Boston Consulting Group:*
http://www.bcg.com/documents/file84471.pdf

9. *International Business Times,* June 2, 2012, "U.S. Manufacturing Jobs Begin the Long March Back from China (and Elsewhere)," by Moran Zhang.
http://www.ibtimes.com/articles/348058/20120602/manufacturing-renaissance-shale-gas-cat-f.htm

10. *Ohio Energy Resource Alliance,*
http://www.ohioenergyresource.org/topics/job-and-economic-impact?print=true

11. *Bloomberg,* October 29, 2009, "NCR Opens New ATM Manufacturing Facility in Columbus, GA."
http://www.bloomberg.com/apps/news?pid=newsarchive&sid=ahKWMFjV.fxE

12. *The Boston Consulting Group:*
http://www.bcg.com/documents/file84471.pdf

13. *Wall Street Journal,* February 1, 2013, "Cheap Natural Gas Lets Nucor Factory Rise Again on Bayou," by John W. Miller.
http://online.wsj.com/article/SB10001424127887323854904578264080157966810.html

14. *Dow.com:*
http://www.dow.com/news/press-releases/article/?id=5646

15. *International Business Times,* June 2, 2012, "U.S. Manufacturing Jobs Begin the Long March Back from China (and Elsewhere)," by Moran Zhang.
http://www.ibtimes.com/articles/348058/20120602/manufacturing-renaissance-shale-gas-cat-f.htm

16. Ibid.

17. *The American Interest,* July 15, 2012, "Energy Revolution 2," by

Walter Russell Mead.
http://blogs.the-american-interest.com/wrm/2012/07/15/energy-revolution-2-a-post-post-american-post/

18. *Pacific Standard,* March 4, 2013, "The Deluge," by Vince Beiser.
http://www.psmag.com/environment/oil-production-peak-oil-fracking-kern-river-north-dakota-brazil-energy-53395

19. Ibid.

20. *The Australian* February 22, 2013, "'Nothing Off Limits' in Climate Debate,'" by Graham Lloyd.
http://www.theaustralian.com.au/news/nothing-off-limits-in-climate-debate/story-e6frg6n6-1226583112134#

21. *Nature,* November 15, 2012, "Little Change in Global Drought over the Past 60 Years," by Justin Sheffield, et al.
http://www.nature.com/nature/journal/v491/n7424/full/nature1157
5.html?WT.ec_id=NATURE-20121115

22. *Forbes,* August 22, 2012, "Is Global Warming Causing a Record Breaking Lack of Tornado Activity?" by James Taylor.
http://www.forbes.com/sites/jamestaylor/2012/08/22/is-global-warming-causing-a-record-breaking-lack-of-tornado-activity/

23. *EurActiv.com:*
http://www.euractiv.com/climate-environment/energy-poverty-takes-toll-balkan-news-513402

24. The Blaze, March 10, 2012, "Wind Turbines Kill 70 Golden Eagles Each Year at California's Altamont Pass," by Erica Ritz.
http://www.theblaze.com/stories/2012/03/10/wind-energy-under-attack-for-thousands-of-wildlife-deaths

25. *Eco-Imperialism: Green Power Black Death* by Paul Driessen is published by Free Enterprise Press. 2003.

CHAPTER 14

1. *101 Creative Problem Solving Techniques* by James M. Higgins is published by New Management Pub. Co.

2. *Harvard Business Review,* September 2012, "Bringing Science to
    the Art of Strategy," by A.G. Lafley, et al.
    http://hbr.org/2012/09/bringing-science-to-the-art-of-strategy/ar/1

ABOUT THE AUTHORS

Fred Rogers is publisher and founder of *Trends Magazine*. He is also the author of *Innovation@Work,* the world's most popular educational program for corporate innovators. Fred earned a reputation for extraordinary foresight as a leading innovation and strategy consultant to the Fortune 500, working with firms including Booz & Company, Accenture, and Bluestone Management Corporation. His clients included S. C. Johnson Wax, General Electric, GlaxoSmith-Kline, Sears Holdings, J.C. Penney, Medtronic, Bombardier, and many others. He also worked as an executive with IBM and Time-Warner. He holds an MBA in Strategy & Operations from Harvard Business School.

Richard Lalich is an author, journalist, editor, and strategist. He is the Executive Editor of *Trends Magazine, Business Briefings,* and *Innovation@Work.* He has written extensively about business, management, demographics, psychology, and technology for those publications and others, and has published hundreds of articles and interviews on a variety of subjects in such publications as *Success, Chicago Tribune, Solutions, Playboy, Spy, Rolling Stone, Us, Chicago Business, Graphis,* and *Outside.* He is also co-author of *Zero Proof* (St. Martin's Press).

How Can You Stay on Top of the Wave?

Ride the Wave has introduced you to the 12 technologies that will change the world. But technologies are relentlessly advancing, and every day new breakthroughs are shattering the boundaries of what is possible.

How can you make sure you are always alert to what will happen, why it will happen, and how you can profit from it?

You could hire a team of analysts to monitor and interpret a broad set of geo-demographic, technological, and psychological trends on a real-time basis. Or you could go right to the #1 source for the latest intelligence on the crucial trends that matter to you, your career, and your investments.

Only *Trends* consistently delivers the powerful insights that drive bottom-line results. Consider how business owners, consultants, and top executives use the insights they receive each month from *Trends* to help them stay on top of the wave:

- *"I use it to get my head out of the specific industry I am in and to get a better view of a global picture; i.e., what are the global trends several years away that may affect our specific business?"* —**John Foster, President of Skytech, Inc.**
- *"It keeps me in front of the curve, and I can plan for when your information hits the general press/media - I can position in front of it."* —**Timothy J. O'Brien, Former Director of The Institute for Stress Management & Performance Improvement**
- *"I utilize Trends to position my company for the future. Trends forecasts both general trends and specific trends that*

will affect my business so we anticipate rather than react." — **Scott Webster, President, Pono Group**

- *"**Trends** keeps me informed about what is over the horizon... I keep the information handy for making decisions in all aspects of life."* —**Stephen (Stever) Rousseau, Automation Project Lead Manager, Applied Medical**
- *"**Trends** gets right to the point and cuts through many assumptions that the media creates."* —**Paul Gutman, Co-Owner of Bennett Contracting**
- *"I have found **Trends** to be cutting-edge and very practical in how things are shaping up for the future, and the new ideas and technology information is invaluable. **Trends** is tomorrow's information now!"* —**Dr. Louis Sportelli, Board of Directors, NCMIC Group Inc.**

Since 2002, *Trends* subscribers have been the <u>first</u> to find out about emerging consumer needs, game-changing technologies, and disruptive business models in hundreds of disciplines. As a result, they've been able to seize hidden opportunities, and avoid subtle, but deadly, threats.

Keep reading to learn how you can stay on top of the wave when you try *Trends* at no risk. If it doesn't prove indispensable, simply discontinue it and pay nothing. In any case, we wish you continuing success,

Fred Rogers
Richard Lalich

Invitation for readers of *Ride the Wave*

Take the 60-Day Challenge and be the first to learn about breakthrough technologies and the forecasts you need to profit from trends in demographics, the economy, and consumer preferences.

It's concise.
It's timely.
It's convenient.
It's indispensable.
It's Trends Magazine.
It's yours to review for 60-days for FREE.

As a read er of ***Ride the Wave*** you are entitled to a 100% risk-free trial of ***Trends*** Magazine. We are confident that once you've started reading – and listening – to ***Trends***, you will not want it to end. And if we can't convince you that ***Trends*** is indispensable, you'll pay nothing.

Simply visit us at www.crucialtrends.com/challenge or call us at 1-800-776-1910 and let us know that you're ready to take the 60-Day challenge.